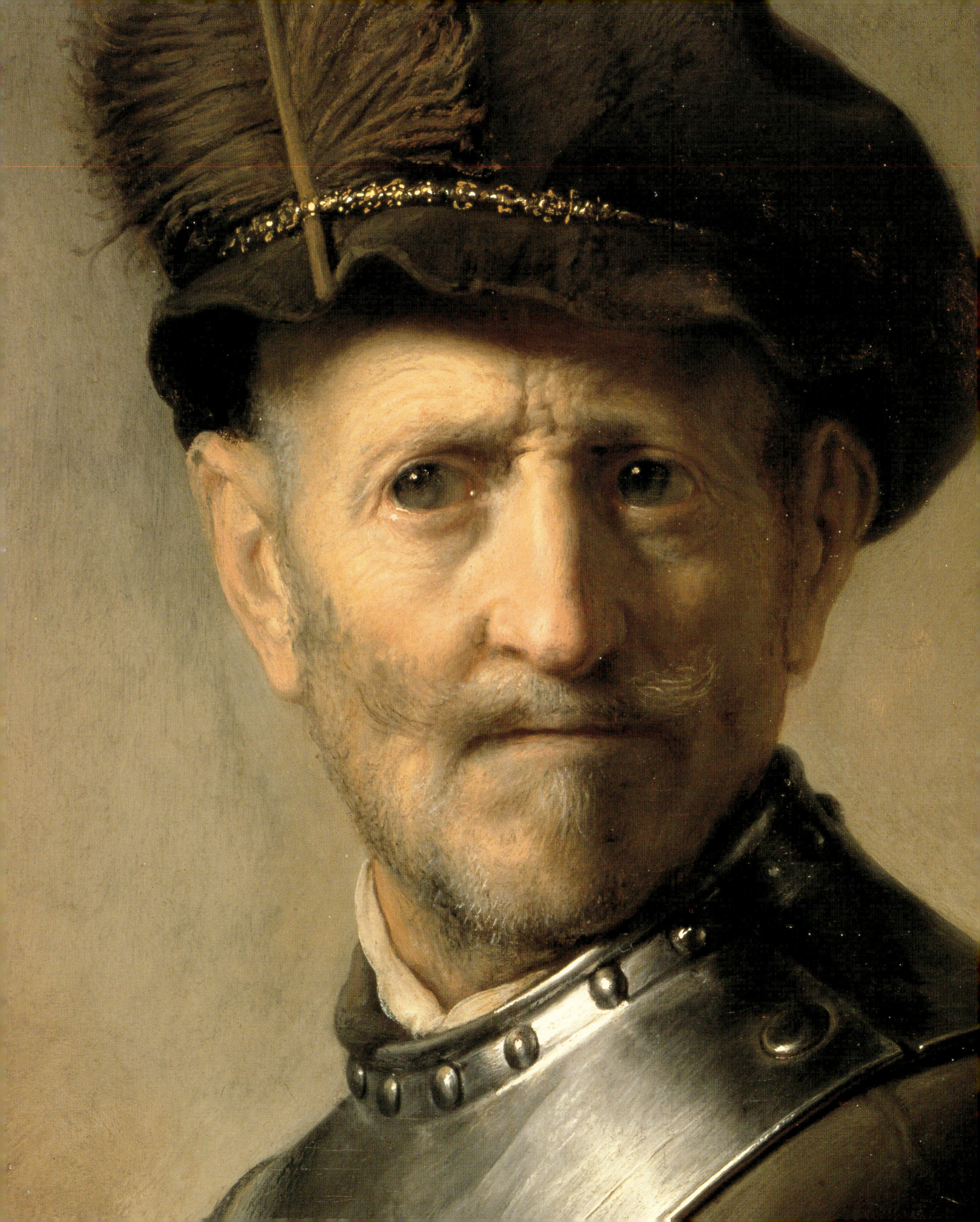

Rembrandt Creates *Rembrandt*

Art and Ambition in Leiden, 1629–1631

ESSAYS
Arthur K. Wheelock Jr.
Mariët Westermann
Chistopher White
Alan Chong

CATALOGUE
Hilliard Goldfarb
Michael Zell
Alan Chong

EDITED BY
Alan Chong

CURATED BY
Hilliard Goldfarb

Isabella Stewart Gardner Museum, Boston
Waanders Publishers, Zwolle

This book is published to accompany the exhibition, *Rembrandt Creates Rembrandt: Art and Ambition in Leiden, 1629–1631*, held at the Isabella Stewart Gardner Museum, Boston, from September 21, 2000 to January 7, 2001.

EDITOR
George Cruger

DESIGNER
Roelof Koebrugge bNO, Heerde

EDITORIAL COORDINATOR
Richard Lingner

PRINTED BY
Waanders Printers, Zwolle

ISBN 90 400 9468 3

The exhibition and catalogue, *Rembrandt Creates Rembrandt: Art and Ambition in Leiden, 1629–1631*, are made possible by a generous grant from The Andrew W. Mellon Foundation.

The exhibition is supported by an indemnity from the Federal Council on the Arts and Humanities.

Scholarly exhibitions at the Isabella Stewart Gardner Museum are supported by endowment funds from The Ford Foundation and the National Endowment for the Humanities.

THIS PROJECT IS FUNDED IN PART BY
MASSACHUSETTS CULTURAL COUNCIL
A state agency that funds your community's local cultural council

In addition, a portion of the Museum's general operating funds for this fiscal year has been provided through grants form the Institue of Museum and Library Services, a Federal agency, and the Massachusetts Cultural Council, a state agency that receives support from the National Endowment for the Arts.

Contents

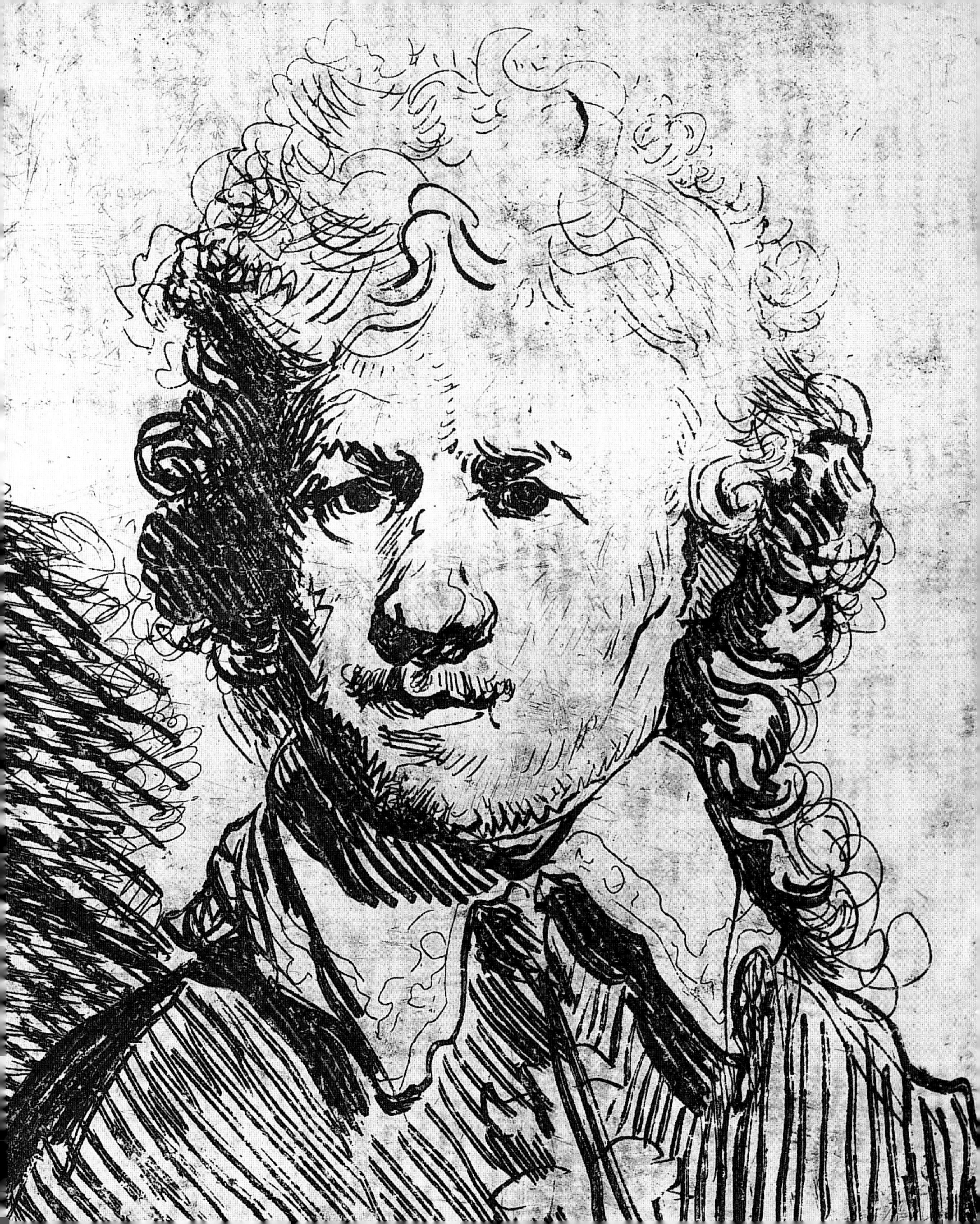

Foreword

The emergence of an artistic genius always stirs the imagination. In 1631, Constantijn Huygens, secretary to the Prince of Orange and a devoted connoisseur of all forms of art and learning, reported almost breathlessly of his encounter with the twenty-five-year-old Rembrandt. While recognizing the skillful compositions and emotional power of Rembrandt's paintings, he also communicated the visceral thrill of coming into contact with a personality that he believed would rival the best artists of Italy, Flanders, and even the ancient world. This exhibition explores the full range of Rembrandt's work at exactly the period when he began to achieve true greatness. In the years from 1629 to 1631, Rembrandt's rising ambition matched his maturing artistic prowess—a volatile combination that led him to leave his home town of Leiden to seek greater fortune and fame in Amsterdam.

Rembrandt's self-portrait of 1629, shown in this exhibition, was among Isabella Stewart Gardner's very first serious acquisitions. Indeed, the importance of the purchase crystallized her resolve to create an art museum in Boston dedicated to the education and enjoyment of the public. It opened in 1903. And like Rembrandt, Mrs. Gardner used her collection and her social circle to fashion a new image for herself. Both surrounded themselves with thinkers, performers, and artists.

The development of the young Rembrandt also relates to Mrs. Gardner's dedicated support of young creators—painters, writers, musicians, and scholars. In the past decade, the Isabella Stewart Gardner Museum has sought to contribute to contemporary culture by supporting emerging performers and artists. *Rembrandt Creates Rembrandt* is therefore a perfect introduction to our centennial initiatives which will culminate in 2003.

In recent years, the Gardner Museum has mounted a series of intimate, focused exhibitions highlighting aspects of the permanent collection. Scholars and institutions from around the world have supported exhibitions such as *Titian and Rubens: Power, Politics and Style* and *Sargent: The Late Landscapes*. Generous financial support for these projects, as well as for the current exhibition, has come from The Andrew W. Mellon Foundation. This exhibition is also supported by indemnity from the Federal Council on the Arts and the Humanities.

Above all, we are deeply indebted to the lenders who have made this exhibition possible. Warm thanks go to Hilliard Goldfarb, who conceived the exhibition while he was curator at the Isabella Stewart Gardner Museum. He arranged the loans, wrote the entries, and commissioned the catalogue's authors, who have written insightful contributions. I am grateful to Alan Chong and Richard Lingner who finalized the catalogue and exhibition. They collaborated closely with the publisher, Waanders, to prepare an admirable book to commemorate the exhibition. Many thanks also to all the trustees and staff at the Gardner for their hard work on this project.

It is indeed a great honor to host the magnificent works of art presented in this exhibition.

Anne Hawley
Director, Isabella Stewart Gardner Museum

Acknowledgments

First and foremost, we appreciate the generosity of the lenders and the assistance furnished by their staffs:

Rijksmuseum, Amsterdam
Museum of Fine Arts, Boston
Harvard University Art Museums, Cambridge
Mauritshuis, The Hague
British Museum, London
J. Paul Getty Museum, Los Angeles
Isabel and Alfred Bader, Milwaukee
Pierpont Morgan Library, New York
National Gallery of Canada, Ottawa
Bibliothèque nationale de France, Paris
Cevat Collection
Private collection, courtesy of Richard Feigen

In addition to their written contributions, the authors of the catalogue have provided valuable advice and support: Arthur Wheelock, Mariët Westermann, Christopher White, and Michael Zell. Special thanks are due Kenneth Bohač, Frits Duparc, Richard Feigen, Mark Henderson, Roman Herzig, Wouter Kloek, Gerbrand Kotting, Ger Luijten, Patrick McMahon, Otto Naumann, Nadine Orenstein, and Martin Royalton-Kisch.

Roelof Koebrugge designed a beautiful book; George Cruger was a superb editor. At Waanders, Marjoleine van Nielen and Anne-Marie van Ommen carefully guided the production of the catalogue, while Richard Lingner at the Gardner Museum provided critical editing and support. Thanks also to Andrew Barlow, Stephen Campbell, Quint Gregory, Kristina Herntrich, Kate Harper, Kate Lapine, Claire Lauf, Lynn Orr, Kristin Parker, Thomas Rassieur, Konrad Renger, and Brian Waldron.

Note to the Reader

The essays are followed by entries on the exhibited paintings (labelled "cat. 1" and so forth). Detailed information on the provenance and literature of the exhibited entries can be found in the Catalogue Documentation section. Dimensions for works of art are normally height followed by width; prints are measured to the platemark unless otherwise noted.

The illustrations are numbered in three sequences: "fig. 1" refers to a reproduction in the essays; "cat. 1" refers to an entry in the Catalogue; "fig. 1a" refers to a comparative illustration in the Catalogue. Abbreviated references are listed in the Bibliography. The index lists the life and death dates for most artists and writers mentioned in the texts.

Common references

Bartsch
Adam Bartsch. *Catalogue raisonné de toutes les estampes qui forment l'oeuvre de Rembrandt, et ceux de ses principaux imitateurs.* 2 vols. Vienna, 1797. The basic catalogue employing Bartsch's numbering is: Christopher White, Karel G. Boon, *Hollstein's Dutch and Flemish Etchings, Engravings and Woodcuts,* vols. 18, 19 (Amsterdam, 1969).

Benesch
Otto Benesch. *The Drawings of Rembrandt.* 6 vols. 2nd edition. London, 1973. Revised by E. Benesch.

Corpus
A Corpus of Rembrandt Paintings. 3 vols. The Hague, 1982–89. By Josua Bruyn et al.

Introduction

In the autumn of 1631, Rembrandt moved from Leiden, his birthplace, to Amsterdam, the largest city in the Dutch Republic. By that time, he had attracted the attention of Constantijn Huygens, one of the most important connoisseurs in Holland, who was secretary to the stadhouder and facilitator of artistic patronage at the court in The Hague. It is almost certain that Rembrandt already had clients in Amsterdam. But what would have happened if Rembrandt somehow had failed to reach Amsterdam in late 1631? If Rembrandt's artistic activities had ended with his Leiden period, how would history remember him? Would we remember him at all?

Between 1629 and 1631, his period of training and youthful experimentation complete, Rembrandt embarked on a remarkable variety of subjects and formats, in several different media. By the end of his Leiden period, he was producing images full of intense emotion and drama. His religious and mythological paintings, which demonstrated increasing complexity and psychological range, entered the collection of the stadhouder Frederik Hendrik. He made numerous drawings and etchings of similar arrangements and subjects. Rembrandt also loved to portray characterful old people: men and women who have often been identified as his father and mother. And most famously, Rembrandt painted himself. A vast number of early self-portraits survive, whether drawn, etched, or painted. Some of these appear to be character studies or explorations of expression; a few were later employed as motifs in religious paintings. Other self-portraits seem to be experiments in format and presentation that would equip the young artist for fancy society commissions. However, many of the self-portraits are entirely independent of any practical, external function, and evince the artist's delight in painting his own face in various guises, as though he were continually creating new personalities. And since Charles I acquired one of Rembrandt's very early self-portraits, it appears that contemporary connoisseurs of the greatest sophistication were equally enthralled by this audacious young artist, whose works were so full of drama and character. The emergence of Rembrandt's mature artistic personality—his genius, in other words—seems to have occurred at the end of his stay in Leiden.

Rembrandt was born in Leiden in 1606. The second largest Dutch town and the site of a burgeoning textile industry, Leiden was also Holland's center of religion and scholarship. In 1575, the new Dutch Republic founded the University of Leiden to ensure the training of Reformed Protestant theologians and preachers, as well as other scholars. In a sense, the university also recognized the tremendous sacrifice Leiden had suffered during the horrific siege of 1573–74, a key event in the revolt of the Netherlands against Spain. Rembrandt himself attended the Latin school in Leiden, which allowed him to matriculate at the university, although he did not graduate.

Amsterdam could not have been more different from Leiden. It was by far the largest and wealthiest city in the Dutch Republic, and it also possessed the most active art market in Europe. As a trading and commercial center, Amsterdam prospered in times of peace; therefore its civic politics firmly opposed renewal of the war with Spain. A diverse array of religious groups further encouraged liberalism. Rembrandt would revel in this atmosphere, competing enthusiastically in the local art market, as both artist and collector, and coming into contact with a richly varied circle. Rembrandt worked for Mennonites, Catholics, Remonstrants, and Jews, as well as for Calvinists of the official Reformed Church. Hendrick Uylenburgh provided him with accommodation, studio space, and a steady stream of commissions. And in 1633, Rembrandt married Uylenburgh's cousin Saskia. Rembrandt's immediate success in Amsterdam, although accompanied by important changes in his style, suggests that his preparation in Leiden had been thorough and effective.

Constantijn Huygens' perceptions of Rembrandt, recorded in early 1631 (see Appendix), resound throughout this catalogue, not only because he met the artist during the very period under discussion, but also because his observations are erudite and fresh. Huygens also made a simple plea that resonates with all art historians. He requested that Rembrandt and Lievens (having asked the same of Rubens) keep a catalogue of their works, "making short notes about the reasons and the process by which individual works were conceived, arranged, and worked out. This would prove to be a wonderful book for the ages." Rembrandt did not heed this request, at least as far as we know, causing centuries of confusion not only as to which of his pictures are authentic, but also as to what the artist intended to achieve in his works. This exhibition is dedicated to exploring these and other questions.

AC

Chronology

1606
Rembrandt Hermansz van Rijn is born in Leiden on July 15.

1613
Attends the Latin school in Leiden, the normal preparation for admission to the university.

1620
Enrolls at the University of Leiden, but may not have attended.

1622–1625
Trains as an artist, first with Jacob van Swanenburg in Leiden (1620–1623), then for a short time in Amsterdam with Pieter Lastman.

1625
Rembrandt returns to Leiden and sets up a studio as an independent master. Date of earliest painting (fig. 37).

1626
Rembrandt's first dated paintings and earliest etchings are made in this year. Begins a friendship and collaboration with Jan Lievens.

1628
Gerrit Dou becomes a pupil of Rembrandt. Arnold Buchelius mentions Rembrandt.

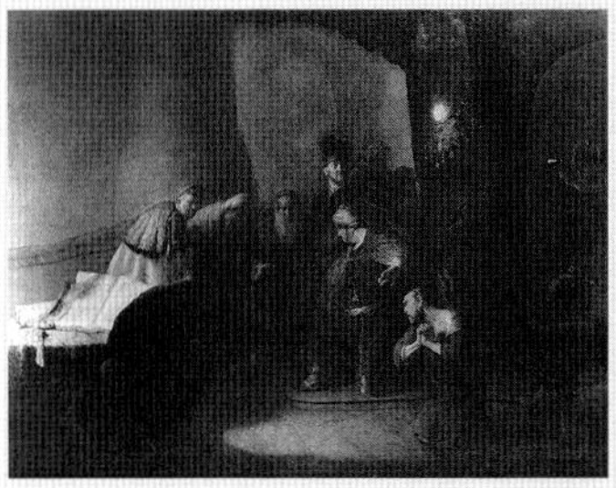

1629
Paints *Judas Returning the Thirty Pieces of Silver* (fig. 24), which is seen by Constantijn Huygens, secretary of the stadhouder, who describes the works of Rembrandt and Lievens. Rembrandt begins to sign his works "RHL" (Rembrandt Harmensz of Leiden).

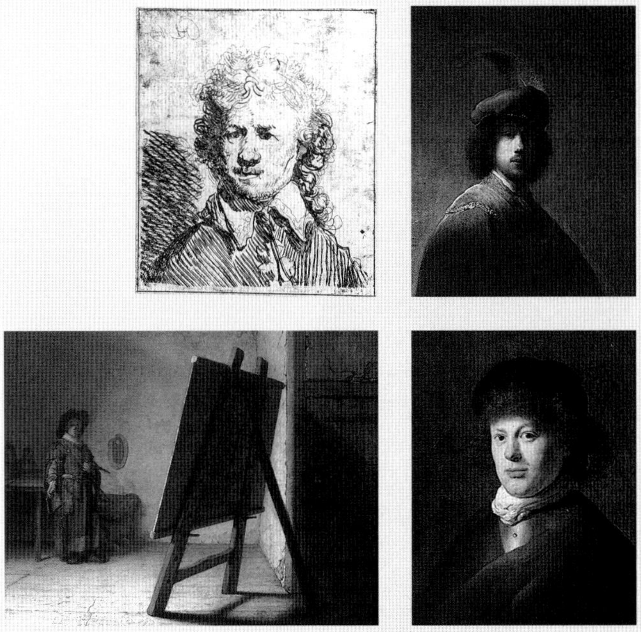

Rembrandt's self-portraits (cats. 1, 4, 5) and of Lievens' portrait of him (cat. 7).

1630
Begins collaboration with the etcher Johannes Gillsz van Vliet who reproduces several works by Rembrandt (see figs. 25, 16d). Isack Jouderville becomes a pupil. Rembrandt's father dies.

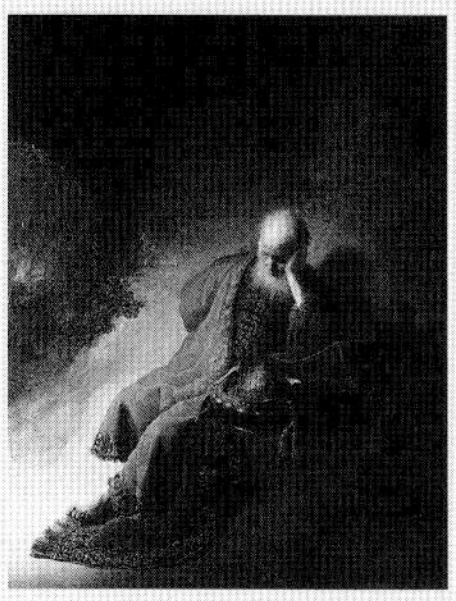
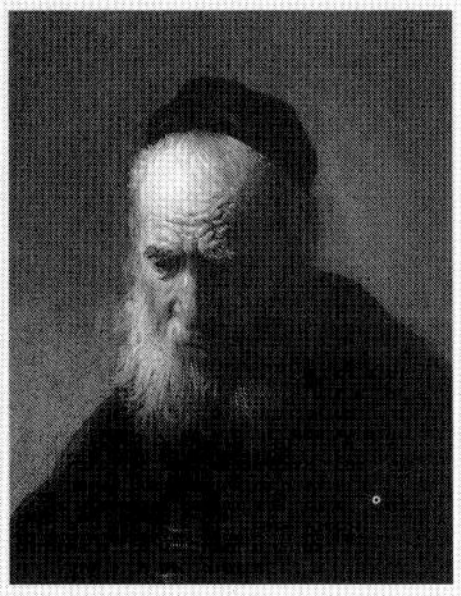
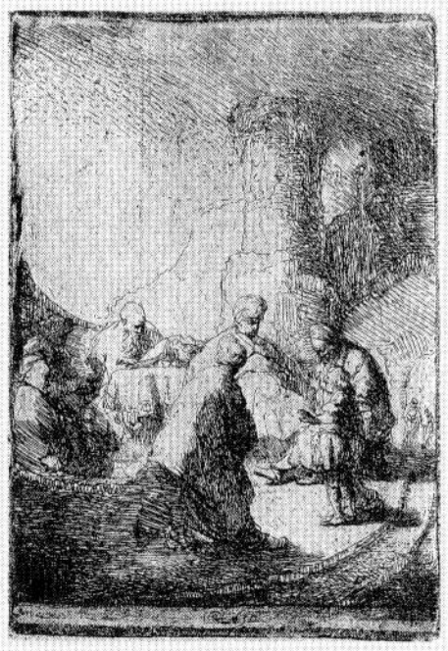
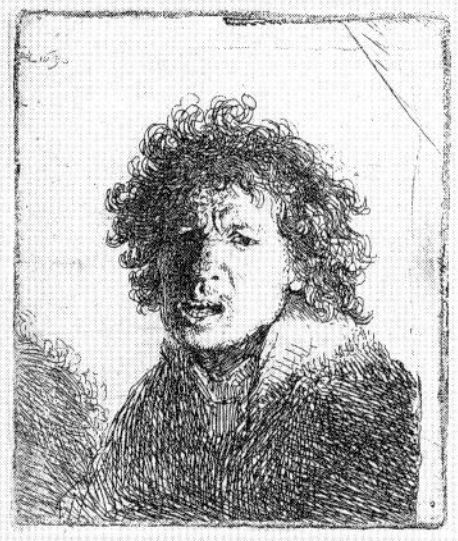
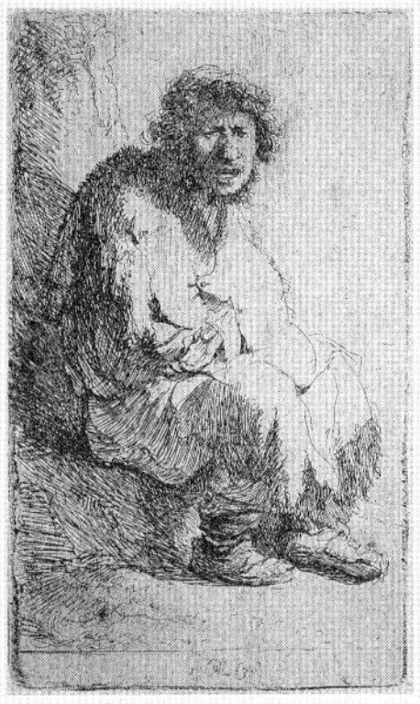

Jeremiah Lamenting the Destruction of Jerusalem (cat. 14), *Old Man Wearing a Cap* (cat. 16), the etching *Christ Disputing with the Doctors* (cat. 9), self-portraits (cats. 12, 13).

1631
Hendrick van Uylenburgh, an art dealer in Amsterdam, borrows 1,000 guilders from Rembrandt, van Uylenburgh is the uncle of Rembrandt's future wife Saskia. At the end of the year, Rembrandt moves to Amsterdam to work in van Uylenburgh's studio. Rembrandt's first commissioned portrait is of Nicolaes Ruts (fig. 68).

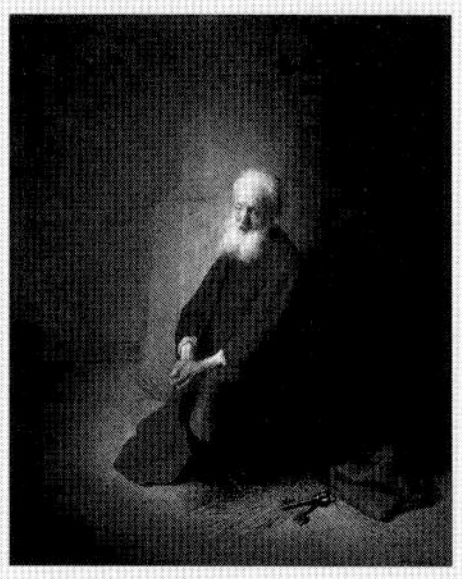
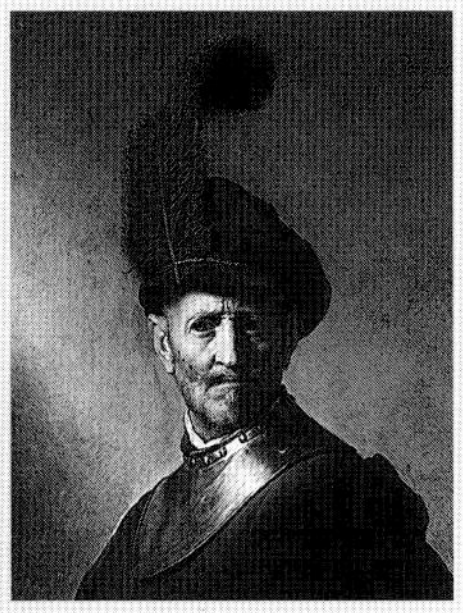
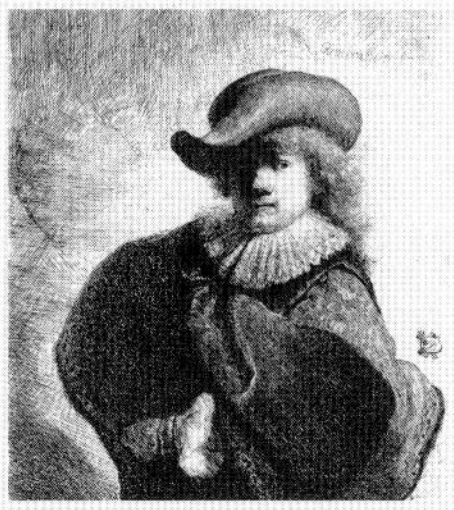

Apostle Peter Kneeling (cat. 18), *Old Man in Military Costume* (cat. 17); began etching *Self-Portrait in a Soft Hat and Cloak* (cat. 19).

1632
Several paintings by Rembrandt are recorded in the stadhouder's inventory.

1633
Rembrandt paints prolifically; signs his name "Rembrandt".

1634
Becomes a citizen of Amsterdam, joins the Saint Luke's guild, and marries Saskia van Uylenburgh.

1639
Buys a house (today the Museum het Rembrandthuis).

1640
Paints the *Nightwatch* (Rijksmuseum, Amsterdam).

1641
A son, Titus (1641–1668), is born.

1642
Saskia dies.

1649
Rembrandt begins a long relationship with Hendrickje Stoffels (1626–1663).

1656
Rembrandt declares bankruptcy and an extensive inventory of his possessions is drawn up.

1667
Cosimo III, grandduke of Tuscany, visits Rembrandt.

1669
Rembrandt dies on October 4.

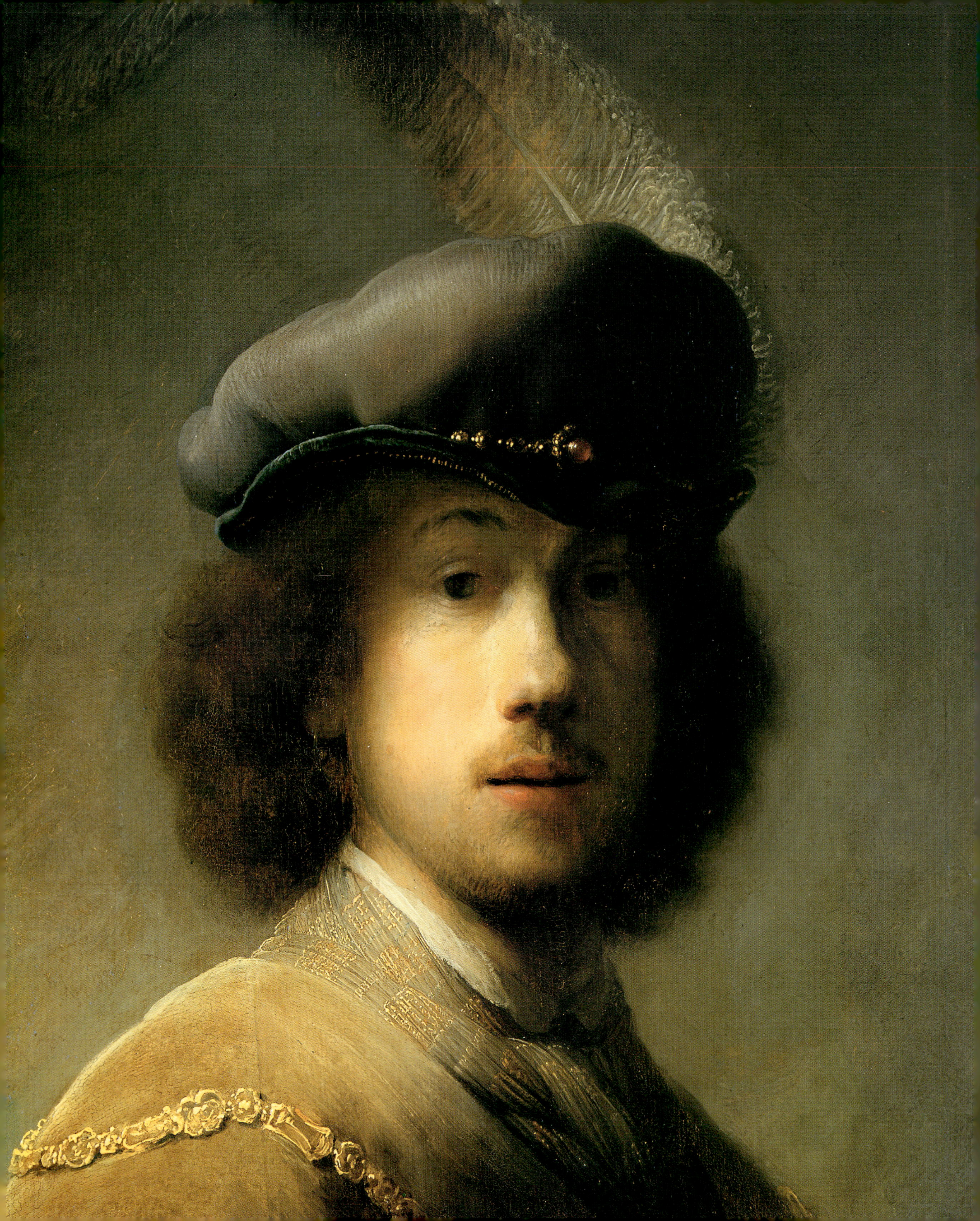

Arthur K. Wheelock Jr.

Rembrandt Inventing Himself

The image of the young Rembrandt, proud in bearing as he sports his exotic feather-plumed, gold-trimmed, bejeweled beret, is well-known to Boston art lovers (fig. 1; cat. 5). Rembrandt's portrait was one of the first old master paintings acquired by Isabella Stewart Gardner, and it has graced this remarkable collection for more than one hundred years. The painting is not easily overlooked or forgotten. With eyes gently shaded by the beret's soft brim, Rembrandt's gaze is compelling in its directness. One cannot help but stare back, and thus become engaged in silent communication with the artist. It is a strange phenomenon: suddenly, but without recognizing the moment in which it occurs, the physical reality of the painted image blurs, and the psychological rapport between the viewer and Rembrandt begins.

Rembrandt's expression, while open and searching, is also assertive and somewhat haughty. Strong contrasts of light and dark illuminate his face and body, reinforcing the impression that he was a self-assured young man, uncompromising in his approach to the world. At the same time, the exotic dress, complete with gold-striped scarf and gold chain, emphasizes the artist's individuality as one who stands apart from the lawyers, merchants, soldiers, university professors, and ministers who were at the core of the cultural and social fabric of the Dutch Republic during the 1620s.

The painting seems so characteristic of Rembrandt's work that it is easy to overlook how striking and unusual it must have appeared to his contemporaries. Of course, twentieth-century viewers have come to judge Rembrandt's character and artistic personality through the sum total of his life and work. Numerous paintings, drawings, and etchings, as well as documents, stories, and myths, have left an indelible impression of his extraordinary artistic achievements throughout a long, memorable career. Therefore, it is difficult to place oneself in Leiden in 1629, to imagine how such an image—with its unusual costume, expressively direct gaze, broad brushwork, and stark contrasts of light and dark—would have been received by contemporaries familiar with a far more precisely rendered portrait tradition.

fig. 1 Rembrandt, *Self-Portrait,* 1629 (cat. 5, detail).

At that point, Rembrandt had not yet become a famous artist, much less a legend in his own time.[1] Although he appears to have been "highly esteemed" in Leiden circles, the Utrecht jurist, Arnold Buchelius, considered that the judgment had been levied "prematurely."[2] Rembrandt's reputation, indeed, did not yet extend far beyond Leiden. He had not yet begun to work for the court of the Prince of Orange in The Hague, nor had he yet sought to broaden his contacts and further his career by moving to Amsterdam to work for the art dealer Hendrik van Uylenburgh.

When Rembrandt painted the Gardner portrait he was not wealthy, and although he had students, among them Gerrit Dou, he was not yet the head of a large workshop. He had not met Saskia, had not acquired a large home, nor had he begun building a collector's cabinet to demonstrate his broad humanist interests and enhance his social status. He had also not seen his personal life fall into disarray after Saskia's death in 1641, nor had he experienced the financial woes that led to his bankruptcy in the mid-1650s. Finally, he had not yet executed the powerful self-portraits of the 1650s and 1660s that convey both his worldly cares and his inner dignity—those haunting and moving evocations of the human soul that so profoundly colored later appreciations of his character and artistic genius (fig. 2).

And so we must ask, what led Rembrandt to paint the bold Gardner Museum portrait at this early stage of his career, and how accurate is the projection of his personality that this self-representation conveys? Was there an inner urge to project himself as someone different from ordinary Dutch burghers? Was an image like this a marketing ploy, a way to distinguish his artistic personality from those of his contemporaries? What was, in fact, the market for his self-portraits? Although these questions are perhaps unanswerable, they do suggest that self-portraits are a more complicated phenomenon than one might initially expect.[3]

In 1629 no one—least of all the artist himself—knew what Rembrandt would become. He was caught in a vortex of conflicting artistic ideals and styles of painting that he had yet to reconcile into a consistent whole. Although he had studied to become a his-

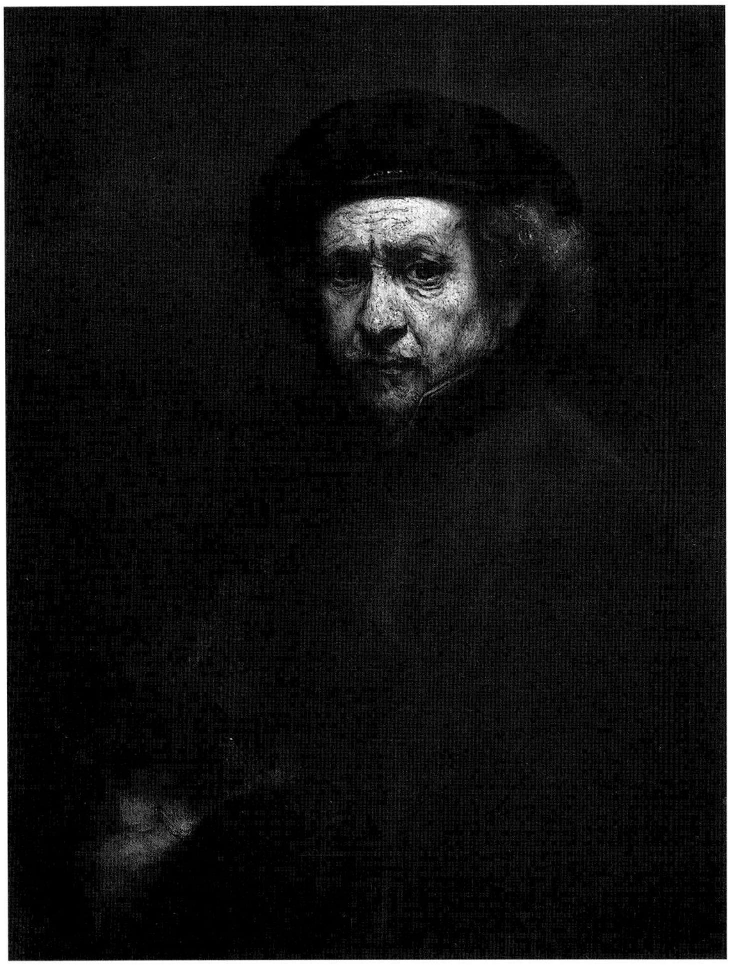

fig. 2 Rembrandt, *Self-Portrait,* 1659. Oil on canvas, 84.4 × 66 cm. National Gallery of Art, Washington.

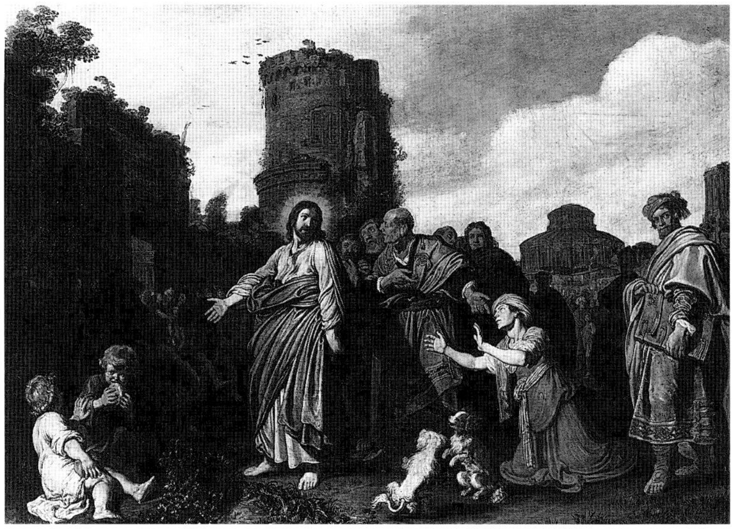

fig. 3 Pieter Lastman, *Christ and the Woman of Canaan,* 1617. Oil on wood, 78 × 108 cm. Rijksmuseum, Amsterdam.

fig. 4 Rembrandt, *History Painting (Palamedes Protesting His Innocence),* 1626. Oil on wood, 90.1 × 121.3 cm. Stedelijk Museum De Lakenhal, Leiden.

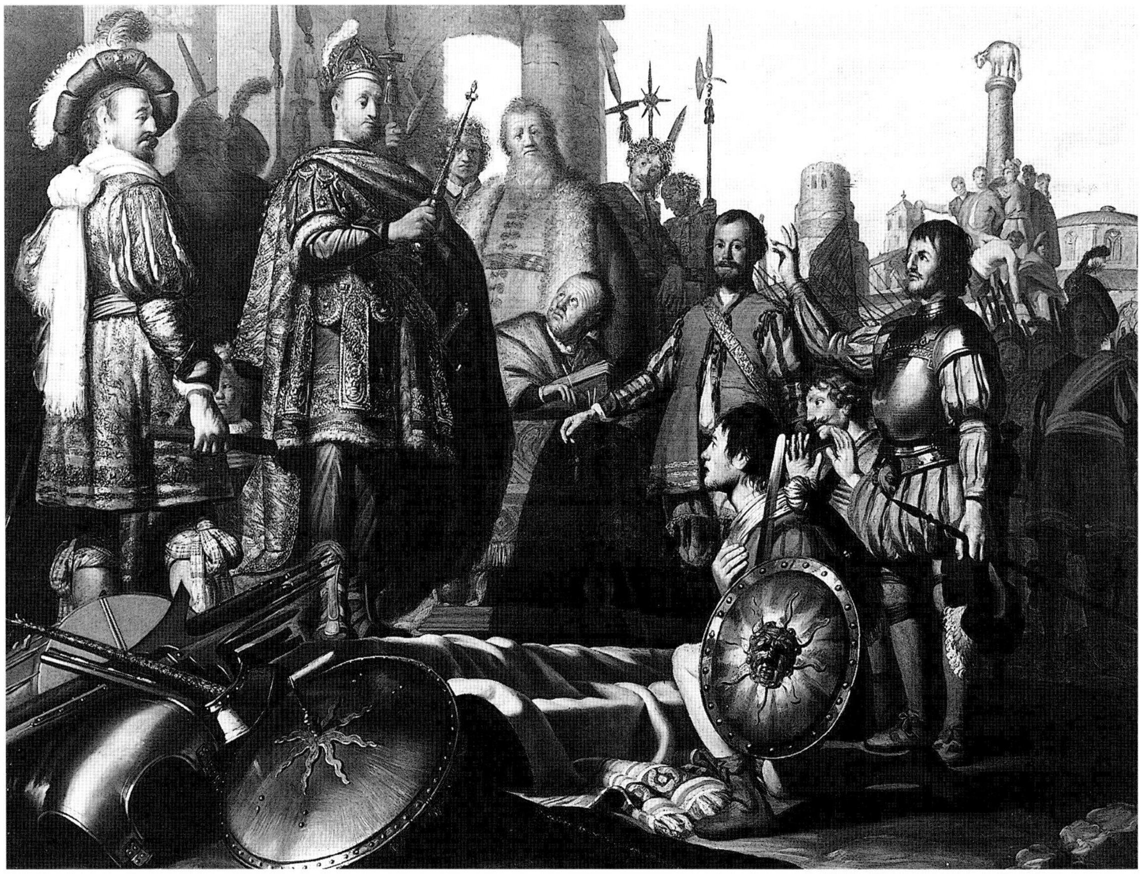

tory painter with Pieter Lastman in Amsterdam (fig. 3), his early efforts to create multi-figured biblical and mythological scenes in Lastman's manner were inevitably awkward and staged (fig. 4). These works had none of his master's compositional assurance or ease of manner. Indeed, Rembrandt's contemporary in Leiden, Jan Lievens, who began his career somewhat earlier than Rembrandt, was the more successful of the two in assimilating Lastman's teachings.

Lievens, even more than Rembrandt, also understood how to combine in one painting a broad manner of execution with more delicate, refined strokes (fig. 5). Rembrandt experimented with both manners of painting, often changing his style to suit his subject matter, but initially he seemed unable to integrate the two into a consistent whole. Lievens was also the first of the two artists to embrace the use of dramatic chiaroscuro contrasts, a style that was currently being introduced to the Netherlands by Gerard van Honthorst and artists of the Utrecht school. Nevertheless, by 1629 Rembrandt had also fully embraced this radical stylistic approach and had begun adapting it to suit his own ends. He understood not only the power of contrasts of light and dark to focus compositional energy, but also to enhance the emotional intensity of individual expressions.

Constantijn Huygens, the renowned poet, musician, art lover, and secretary to the Prince of Orange, was one of those impressed with the expressive character of Rembrandt's work. He praised in particular the artist's "sure touch and liveliness of emotions." Huygens made his comments in an unpublished autobiography, which he wrote between May 1629 and April 1631, a text that included discussions of a number of artists he knew and admired (see Appendix). His assessment of Rembrandt's achievement was probably based on a visit he made to Leiden in 1629, for he praised at length *Judas Returning the Thirty Pieces of Silver*, which is signed and dated to that year (fig. 24). Huygens concluded his comments with this acclamation:

> All this [the expressiveness of Rembrandt's "despairing Judas"] I compare with all the beauty that has been produced throughout the ages. This is what I would have those naïve beings know, who claim (and I have rebuked them for it before) that nothing created or expressed in words today has not been expressed or created in the past. I maintain that it did not occur to Protogenes, Apelles, or Parrhasios, nor could it occur to them, were they to return to earth, that a youth, a Dutchman, a beardless miller, could put so much into one human figure and depict it all.

Because art historians have placed so much emphasis on Huygens' comments about Rembrandt, it might come as a surprise to learn that this connoisseur apparently came into contact with Rembrandt only after he had had his portrait painted by Jan Lievens. Huygens' vivid description of his initial encounter with Lievens has allowed scholars to date that meeting to October or November of 1628.[4]

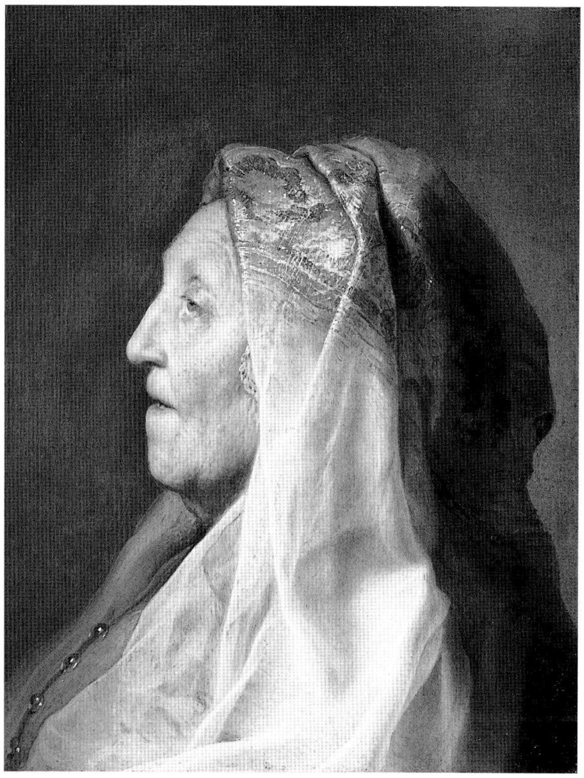

fig. 5 Jan Lievens, *An Old Woman (called Rembrandt's Mother)*, ca. 1629 (cat. 8).

By this time, Lievens was already a successful artist whose reputation extended beyond the city limits of Leiden. Indeed, Huygens writes admiringly about paintings by Lievens in collections of courtiers in The Hague. Even the Prince of Orange owned one of Lievens' paintings, an imposing half-length image of an *Oriental* (Stiftung Schlösser und Gärten Potsdam-Sansouci). Thus, in 1629–30, Rembrandt's self-conscious efforts to define himself artistically were probably also motivated by competition with Lievens, to which Huygens implicitly alludes with his comparative assessments of the strengths and weaknesses of the two artists.

Although Rembrandt was not yet acclaimed as an artistic genius in 1629, he was not without self-confidence. He was also a canny self-promoter. He understood how self-portraits such as the one in the Isabella Stewart Gardner Museum could aid his efforts to become recognized as a bold artist, one not afraid to forge new avenues of artistic expression and to mark them with his own distinctive personality. In this respect, Rembrandt was well aware of the enormous civic pride felt for artists. The extensive biographies of illustrious Netherlandish and German painters in Karel van Mander's *Het Schilder-boeck*, first published in Haarlem in 1604, had significantly raised the profile of artists within Dutch society. Van Mander's accounts, which stressed the fame Dutch artists had brought to their country and native cities, were echoed by authors who published compilations of engraved artist portraits, and by historians who began to incorporate artists' biographies in their city histories.[5] Moreover, it would not have escaped Rembrandt's notice that portraits of artists were highly esteemed in princely collections. In 1623, for example, the Prince of Wales had commissioned a self-portrait from the great Flemish master Peter Paul Rubens.

The most significant figure for understanding Rembrandt's aspirations during his Leiden period was the sixteenth-century artist Lucas van Leyden, who was particularly revered in the early seventeenth century.[6] Not only were his prints and paintings highly valued, but copies of his works, including self-portraits, were also avidly acquired by discriminating collectors.[7] Van Mander's celebration of Lucas van Leyden in *Het Schilder-boeck* was reprinted by Jan Orlers in his history of Leiden published in 1614.[8] Like the sixteenth-century poet Dominicus Lampsonius, van Mander, and hence Orlers, stressed Lucas' close associations with his native Leiden. Lampsonius' ode to Lucas van Leyden's fame appeared beneath Hieronymus Cock's engraved portrait of Lucas in *Pictorum aliquot celebrium Germaniae Inferioris effigies* of 1572 (fig. 7), a publication of portraits of famous Netherlanders. It concluded with the couplet: "And let our poem lead forward the fame / Of your name with that of your birthplace, Leiden."[9] The poem, which Van Mander quoted, also appeared in Hendrick Hondius' 1610 expanded edition of the Lampsonius / Cock publication.[10]

Van Mander's biographical account placed great emphasis on Lucas' natural ability, his studiousness, and his wide-ranging artistic interests:

> Amongst the many spirits, subtle and versatile in our art of painting, who have excelled since the springtime of their lives ... I do not know one who can compare with the naturally gifted Lucas van Leijden ... who seems to have been born with the art of painting and drawing and with brush and burin in hand. ... Lucas, who was a master by nature ... used his time well with constant application, to which end he often extended day into night by means of candle-light. His knucklebones and toys consisted of all manner of artists' tools — such as charcoal, chalk, pen, brush, burin, and the like. ... He never stopped drawing everything from life: faces, hands, feet, houses, landscapes and all manner of fabrics, in which he took a particular pleasure. He was in fact universal, or familiar with ... all that the art of painting comprehends; for he painted histories, portraits, landscapes and figures in oil and watercolor and practiced glass-painting and engraving from an early age.[11]

Rembrandt took to heart Lucas' reputation as a naturally gifted child prodigy who extended his mastery of the arts through dedication and long hours of study, drawing constantly from life, even by candlelight.[12] Lucas was a model he could emulate, an artist who excelled in both the graphic arts and painting, and who depicted a wide range of subjects, including portraiture and history scenes. Rembrandt similarly drew from life and made etchings during the earliest years of his career. Significantly, he based one of his earliest etchings, *The Rest on the Flight into Egypt* of around 1626 (Bartsch 59), on a Lucas van Leyden prototype.[13] Rembrandt's admiration for Lucas van Leyden's work is also evident in the passion with which he collected his prints, eventually acquiring in 1637 a book of Lucas' engravings for the enormous sum of 637 guilders.[14]

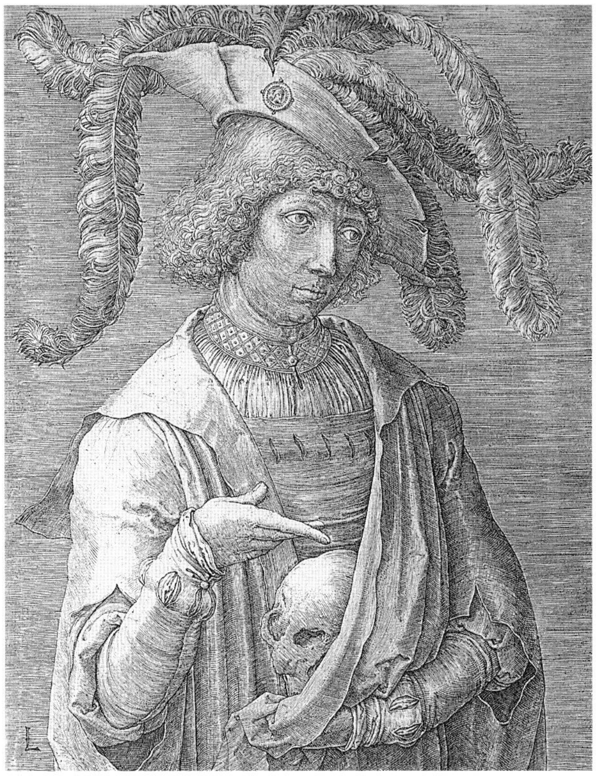

fig. 6 Lucas van Leyden, *Portrait of a Young Man with a Skull*, ca. 1519. Engraving, 18.4 × 14.4 cm. National Gallery of Art, Washington.

Rembrandt undoubtedly recognized that Lucas' self-portraits, or the copies thereof that were circulating at the time, helped ensure the Leiden artist's lasting reputation. Thus, it seems probable that during the late 1620s Rembrandt was conscious of the role self-portraits played in strengthening an artist's reputation, and that he created images such as the Gardner *Self-Portrait* to associate himself with Leiden's artistic heritage. A print after Lucas' *Young Man with a Skull* of about 1519 (fig. 6), which was identified as a self-portrait in the 1600 edition of *Pictorum aliquot celebrium Germaniae Inferioris effigies* and in Hendrick Hondius' expanded volume of 1610, may even have inspired Rembrandt to portray himself wearing outmoded fashions, including a plumed beret.[15]

If Rembrandt's early painted self-portraits announced both his artistic lineage and his independence from tradition, his etched self-portraits from 1630 were even more radically innovative. Traditionally, portraits of artists — for example, those in Cock's publication — depict dignified, well-dressed individuals, posed with attributes of their professions (fig. 7).[16] Rembrandt's quickly rendered self-portrait etchings were the opposite in the extreme (fig. 8; cat. 12). He gave himself no attributes. Moreover, the rough-hewn, unrefined figures in these small-scale etchings could hardly be seen as paragons of social virtue. His features are coarse, his curly hair is unkempt, and his ill-defined clothes are simple. Most dramatically, strong contrasts of light and dark emphasize momentary expressions, often rather unpleasant ones, an approach entirely different from the solemn and reflective gazes in earlier portrayals of artists. None of those depicted in the Lampsonius / Cock publication laughed, frowned, shouted, or snarled.

Why did Rembrandt portray himself in this manner? (His contemporaries would surely have recognized that these small images were depictions of himself.) Was he searching to understand how to depict feelings and emotions that would reveal the deep recesses of the human psyche?[17] Was he using himself, a convenient model, to study expressions in preparation for history paintings, particularly those where he included himself as one of the protagonists?[18] Was he using these images to demonstrate his mastery of chiaroscuro to emphasize momentary expressions? As has often been noted, Rembrandt's later pupil, Samuel van Hoogstraten, may have been citing Rembrandt's advice when he wrote, in his chapter on history painting, that an artist would benefit from depicting his passions as he sees them in a mirror, where he is simultaneously the performer and the beholder.[19]

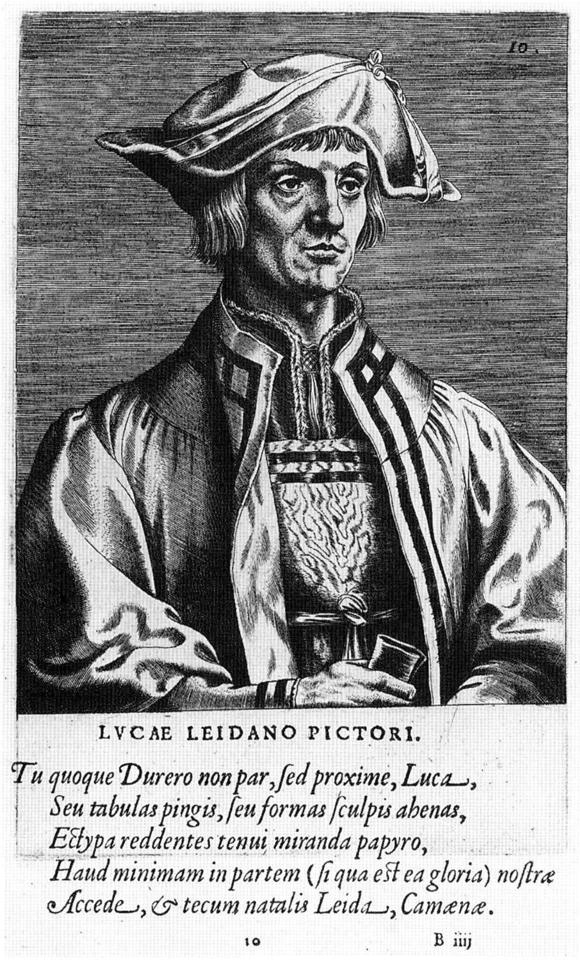

fig. 7 Hieronymus Cock, *Lucas van Leyden, Painter,* 1572. Engraving from *Pictorum aliquot celebrium Germaniae Inferioris effigies.* Rijksmuseum, Amsterdam.

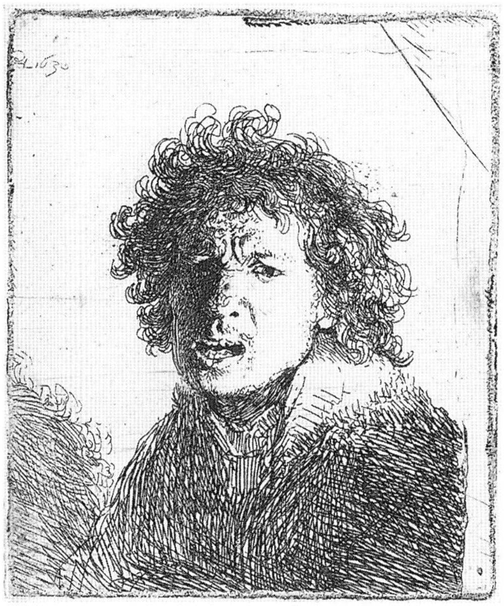

fig. 8 Rembrandt, *Self-Portrait, Open-Mouthed,* 1630 (cat. 12).

While such explanations are entirely valid, they overlook the fact that Rembrandt's self-portrait etchings were public images rather than private studies. While he probably did not print a large number of these images, he nevertheless created them as independent works of art intended for sale and distribution. What were contemporary viewers to think when encountering such an image for the first time? Perhaps they would have greeted these works with the same shock viewers experience today—astonishment at Rembrandt's conceit of portraying himself with outrageous expressions that lack decorum, wonder at the truthfulness of the emotions depicted, and amazement at the roughness and spontaneity of the etching technique.[20] Whatever the reaction, contemporary viewers would have been forced to acknowledge that, as with Rembrandt's self-portrait paintings, this young prodigy had chosen unconventional means to boldly assert his place in the proud artistic traditions of his native city.

Another explanation for the dramatic expressiveness of Rembrandt's self-portrait etchings may be found in Huygens' autobiography. Huygens begins his account of Rembrandt and Lievens by describing their background and training. In the broader context of that text, the implications of his description of Rembrandt as "a beardless miller" becomes clear.[21] In his introductory paragraphs, Huygens asserts: "One of our two youths [Lievens] was the son of a commoner, an embroiderer, the other [Rembrandt] a miller's son, but assuredly not of the same grain. Who could help but marvel that two such prodigies of talent and skill should ripen from such humble seeds. Inquiring as to their childhood teachers, I discover men whose reputation was scarcely known outside the common classes. Due to their parents' straitened circumstances, the youths were compelled to take teachers whose fees were modest." He concludes that "these two owe nothing to their teachers but everything to their aptitude."

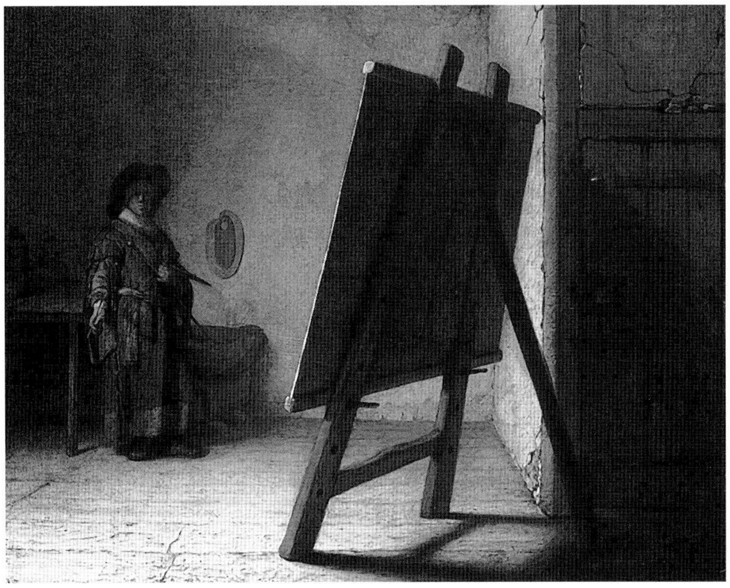

fig. 9 Rembrandt, *The Artist in His Studio,* ca. 1629 (cat. 4).

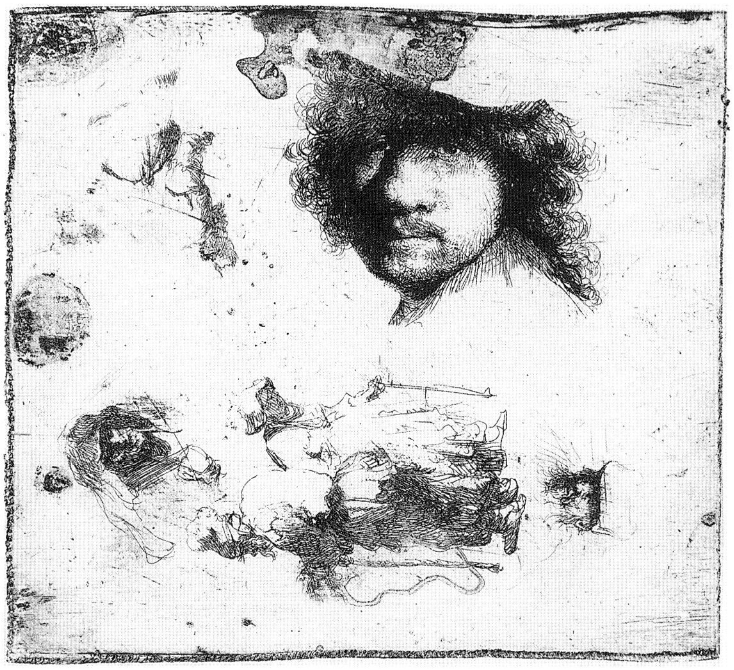

fig. 11 Rembrandt, *Sheet of Sketches with a Self-Portrait,* ca. 1631. Etching, 10.1 × 11.4 cm. British Museum, London. Bartsch 363 (1st state).

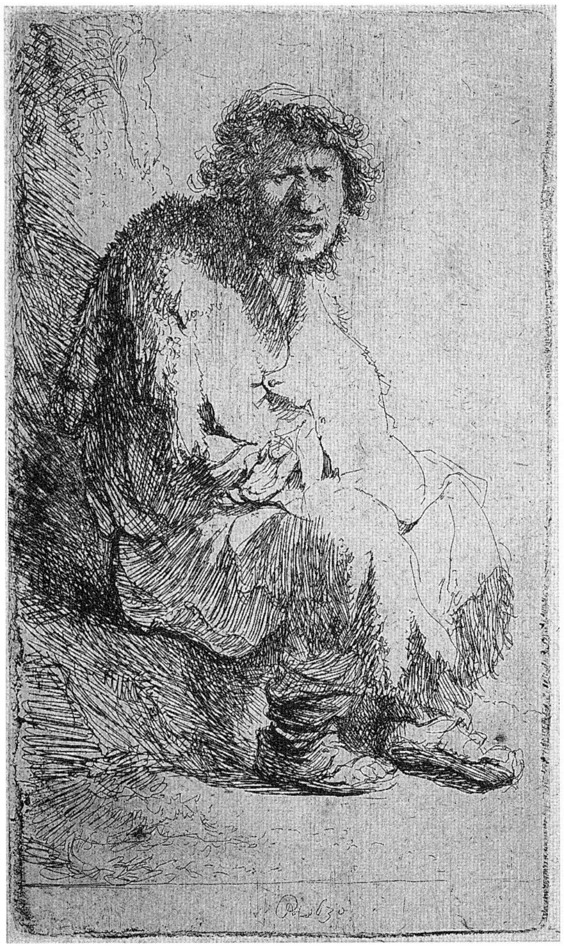

fig. 10 Rembrandt, *Beggar Seated on a Bank,* 1630 (cat. 13).

The very fact that Rembrandt and Lievens had achieved what they did from such common roots and without the benefit of great teaching was, according to Huygens, testimony to their genius. In fact, Huygens' view followed well-established literary conventions, already seen in van Mander's account of Lucas van Leyden's life, and only roughly reflected reality. In regards to Rembrandt, not only was his family financially better off than Huygens implied, but his parents had also enrolled him in the prestigious Latin school. Rembrandt had also studied with Lastman, one of the preeminent history painters in the Netherlands, who taught him tremendous amounts about composition, expression, and drama.

Rembrandt must have been aware of the myth that Huygens, in his hyperbole, was helping to foster. In fact, it seems quite likely that in 1629 and 1630 he consciously portrayed himself as a rough, beardless figure, untutored and unrefined, to reinforce this very mythology — that his genius was inborn and not dependent upon his family's economic status, his training, or his social and political connections. The striking self-portrait of the artist in his studio from the Museum of Fine Arts, Boston, is not unrelated (fig. 9; cat. 4). Here, a diminutive Rembrandt, more child than not, stands prepared to paint in a bare, simple room. With no drawings in sight to guide him, the artist gazes intently at a large panel on an imposing easel in the foreground as he considers the image he is about to create.

Nevertheless, around 1630 a curious dialectic occurs in Rembrandt's self-portraits. In addition to portraying himself in his etchings and paintings as an outsider—one whose character, and hence genius, cannot be identified with the Dutch middle class—he also poses as an accepted member of society, elegantly dressed and honored with gold chains. In one remarkable print, dated 1630, he appears as a forlorn beggar, dressed in the poorest of rags while seated on an earthen mound (fig. 10; cat. 13). Perhaps he created this image to convey his empathy with the poor and homeless, whom he represented so poignantly in his drawings and etchings during these years. Indeed, in one other instance, he included his self-portrait in an etched study sheet of beggars (fig. 11). In total contrast, in an etching begun in the spring of the following year, he portrayed himself as a fashionable middle-class burgher, jauntily wearing a wide-brimmed hat and an expensive cloak (fig. 12).

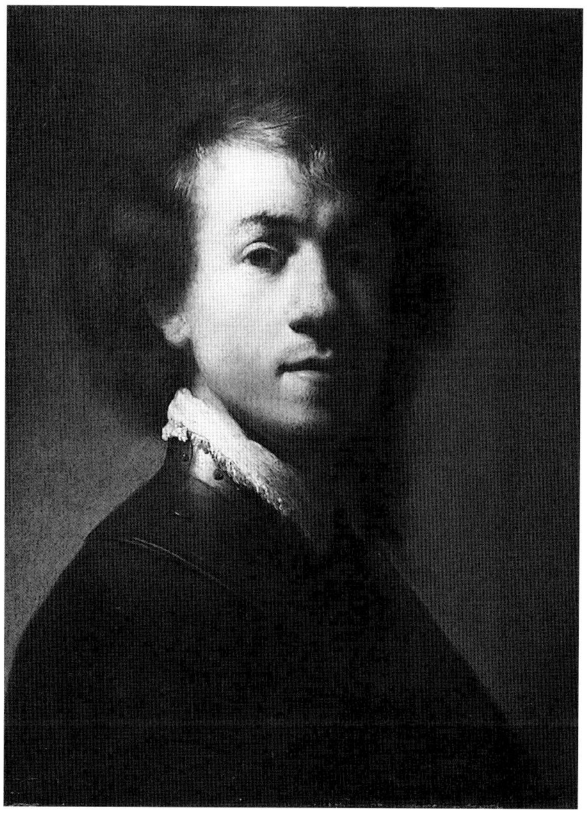

fig. 13 Rembrandt?, *Portrait of Rembrandt*, ca. 1630 (cat. 6).

The schizophrenic character of Rembrandt's self-images in the paintings and etchings of the late 1620s and early 1630s raises many fascinating questions about his sense of self. Is it possible that the image of himself as a beggar also expresses his feelings of alienation from society? Did he intend this shocking image to bring attention to his disdain for social and artistic conventions?[22] Do images that represent him in a respectable manner indicate the ambitious side of his personality, one that yearned for social acceptance and economic advancement? It is perhaps significant that Rembrandt worked inordinately hard on the *Self-Portrait in a Soft Hat and Cloak* (fig. 12; cat. 19), making many small adjustments before being satisfied with the image in its eleventh state.

The etching techniques Rembrandt employed in these two works reinforce the different concepts of self that the artist wished to convey. When depicting himself as a beggar, he used boldly aggressive, quickly rendered strokes to emphasize strong contrasts of light and dark. On the other hand, he executed the *Self-Portrait in a Soft Hat and Cloak* with finer, more detailed hatching to allow for a more modulated image appropriate for the refined status he wished to portray.

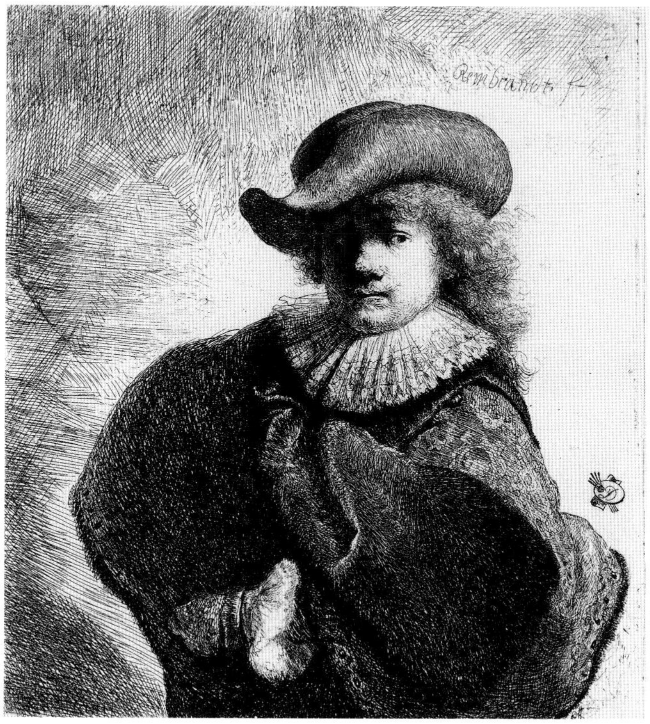

fig. 12 Rembrandt, *Self-Portrait in a Soft Hat and Cloak*, 1631-33 (cat. 19).

By the late 1620s, Rembrandt had developed a clear sense of the relationship between technique and artistic purpose, and had begun to adjust his techniques to accommodate differences in intent. He demonstrated this ability not only in etching, but also in painting. Thus, despite recent claims to the contrary, it is entirely possible, indeed probable, that the elegant *Portrait of Rembrandt* from the Mauritshuis (fig. 13; cat. 6) is by Rembrandt himself rather than an unknown follower.[23] Although the Mauritshuis painting is demonstrably a second version of the self-portrait in Nuremberg (fig. 6a), the greater refinement of the brushwork and the aristocratic appearance of the image is more likely the result of different artistic intent than a different hand.[24] Rembrandt may have painted a second version of this portrait because he wanted to project himself in a more fashionable manner than he had done in the Nuremberg example, perhaps to curry favor, and procure a commission from the court. Indeed, the most apt comparison of the refined manner of execution in the Mauritshuis portrait is not to the Nuremberg *Self-Portrait*, but to one of Rembrandt's first formal, commissioned portraits, the imposing portrait of a militiaman from The Hague, Joris de Caullerij, dated 1632 (fig. 14).[25]

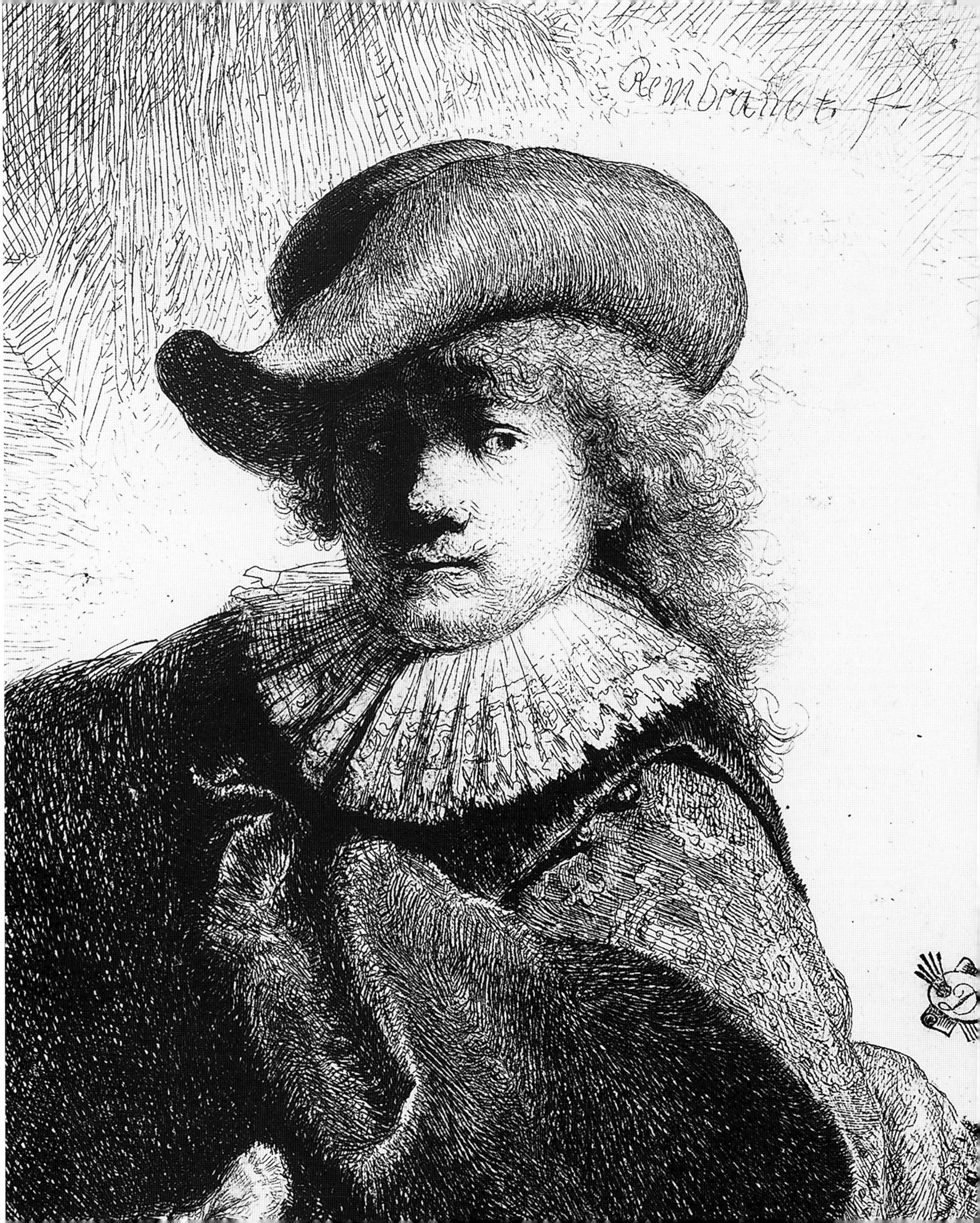
Rembrandt f

Mariët Westermann

Making a Mark in Rembrandt's Leiden

There is something haphazard about Rembrandt's choice of career, by seventeenth-century standards, though once he had decided on it he deployed a combination of creative ability, savvy, and ambition well-suited to success in the competitive artistic culture and market of the Dutch Republic. Famously a miller's son, Rembrandt had no artists in his immediate family or among relatives further afield. His father, Harmen Gerritsz van Rijn, was of good middle-class stock, having inherited the family malt mill, De Rijn, which was located on one of the city walls overlooking the Oude Rijn, or Old Rhine River. As the daughter of a baker, Rembrandt's mother, Neeltgen Willemsdr van Zuytbrouck, was of comparable parentage, although she was also related to an old regent family of Leiden. With ten children the family was large (even after three infants had died), but it supported itself without difficulty. As children of an artisanal family, Harmen and Neeltgen's sons would have been expected to enter traditional trades, and Rembrandt's older brothers indeed went into milling, baking, and shoemaking. The ninth child and youngest son, Rembrandt stood no chance of inheriting the mill. More significantly for his prospects, he must have been quite bright, for according to Jan Jansz Orlers (Rembrandt's first biographer, writing in 1641), his parents sent him to the local Latin school in hopes of preparing him for a university education. In an age when few children—especially ninth children—went to a Latin school, Rembrandt's enrollment is a sign of his educational promise as well as the family's prosperity.

Orlers states that Rembrandt's parents sent him to school so that he "might serve the town and the common good with his learning," a phrasing that suggests their interest in having Rembrandt become a lawyer or city administrator.[1] Since Leiden had become officially Reformed in 1566, allegiance to that church would have been a prerequisite for a political or bureaucratic career. Baptismal records indicate that the van Rijn family indeed belonged to the Reformed Church, although Neeltgen's relatives had remained Catholic. Her family members could no longer hold government office, but they would have been able to guide Rembrandt in the ways of political advancement.

fig. 19 Rembrandt, *Self-Portrait in a Soft Hat and Cloak,* 1631–33 (cat. 19).

Rembrandt entered Latin school about 1616, when he was ten years old. His progress must have been satisfactory, for in 1620 the University of Leiden—at that time the only institution of higher learning in the Dutch Republic—listed him on its rolls as a student of letters, a course of study we might today call "liberal arts." This designation would have been consistent with his Latin school preparation in classical languages, religion, and math, and appropriate to a future career in law or government. But his name never again appears on the university register, for, as Orlers makes clear, Rembrandt resisted his parents' hopes:

> He had no desire or inclination whatsoever in this direction because by nature he was moved toward the art of painting and drawing. Therefore his parents were compelled to take him out of school, and according to his wish they brought and apprenticed him to a painter from whom he would learn the basic and principal rules of art.[2]

Rembrandt's deviation from the educational plans of his parents is a familiar motif of artists' biographies in the Renaissance, introduced for numerous Italian artists by Giorgio Vasari in his extensive series of *Lives of the Most Excellent Painters, Sculptors, and Architects*, published in 1550. Thus the young Filippo Brunelleschi was "always investigating ingenious problems of art and mechanics," thwarting his father's efforts to make him a lawyer or physician; the child Michelangelo spent his time in grammar school drawing, thereby incurring his father's wrathful blows. Karel van Mander told the same anecdote for Netherlandish artists in his *Schilder-Boeck* of 1604, which copied many of Vasari's biographies and offered new ones for northern European painters. And so the prodigiously talented Maerten van Heemskerck, a farmer's son, willfully spilled a bucket of milk and hid in a haystack to escape the agricultural track; the "wealthy parents" of "the gifted Joris Hoefnagel… urged him towards becoming a merchant, in contradiction to his nature: for although his entire or utmost inclination was turned towards the art of painting they would not permit the boy, at home or at school, to do what Mother Nature continually insisted…."[3] Yet for all its hackneyed phrasing, Orlers' account of Rembrandt's nature rings true. It has often been said that

Rembrandt's university registration in 1620 was a ploy to escape civic guard duty and to receive the standard student waiver of duties on beer and wine, but the chronological evidence suggests that he did not seek a painter's career until 1621.[4] He may indeed have had a change of heart during his first year of university studies, prompted by a sudden recognition of his artistic potential.

Accepting the inevitable, the worried fathers of Vasari's and van Mander's subjects usually apprenticed their talented sons to artists they knew through family connections and acquaintances, and Rembrandt's parents fit this mold. They are not even on record as having protested his change of direction. There would have been little reason for concern, for painting was a respectable trade, certainly no less, and possibly more, than that of the miller, baker, or cobbler. Moreover, Dutch painting had for three decades been a rapidly expanding and diversifying industry. Although the Reformed Church in its many Dutch variants objected to the use of paintings in worship, causing the previous flow of religious commissions to slow to a trickle, economic and social conditions in Holland simultaneously promoted the growth of a market for domestic luxury products, including paintings. The Dutch Republic's secession from Spain had brought spectacular economic advantages to Amsterdam and, eventually, most of the Dutch provinces. The state of war allowed Dutch naval ships to block the mouth of the broad Scheldt River, which provided entry into the harbor of Antwerp. In the sixteenth century Antwerp had been the leading port of northern Europe and therefore the most powerful economic and artistic center of the Netherlands, but the decades-long Dutch blockade allowed the port of Amsterdam to take over both roles. The city became the hub of a Dutch maritime empire that stretched north to the Baltic, east to India, Indonesia, and Japan, south to the Cape of Good Hope, and west to Brazil and Surinam. Like other Dutch cities, Amsterdam served not only as a clearinghouse for international bulk and luxury trade but also as a center of refined manufacturing, one of the most profitable types of industry in seventeenth-century Europe. The cities of Holland, including Leiden, were the main beneficiaries of these developments, not least because in the last two decades of the sixteenth century they had absorbed tens of thousands of highly skilled Protestant refugees from Antwerp and other southern Netherlandish cities. While the many visual artists among these immigrants stimulated the production of art, an increasingly wealthy urban population of homeowners provided brisk demand for it.

Under these conditions, painting was a reasonable economic prospect for an adolescent with an aptitude for it, not least because, after Amsterdam, Leiden was the second largest and most prosperous town in Holland, which was itself the leading province of the Dutch Republic. With the influx of thousands of immigrants in the textile trades, the city had in previous years revitalized and diversified its textile industry from basic wool weaving to the manufacturing and refinement of different types of cloth. In the first quarter of the century, the city's university, still a rarity in its Protestant denomination, attracted more than six thousand students from the Netherlands and abroad, and the city was thus a magnet for intellectuals who might foster collecting. Soon after the university's founding in 1575, its governors began to acquire and donate a rather eclectic mix of painted and printed portraits of leading Renaissance and contemporary scholars.[5] Several of Rembrandt's and Lievens' earliest paintings represent the evangelists and Peter and Paul as great biblical exegetes, rather than martyrs, and it is possible that these pictures were aimed at Leiden's lively community of Protestant intellectuals (fig. 20).[6]

Despite such favorable conditions for aspiring artists, Leiden's artistic culture around 1620 was one of promise rather than strong accomplishment. The Guild of Saint Luke had been abolished in 1572 and would not be resurrected until 1648. While Leiden had drawn many textile workers from the southern Netherlands, it had not attracted leading, innovative Protestant painters from Antwerp. Unlike Amsterdam and Haarlem, where many of these southern Netherlandish artists had settled, the city had not yet replaced the loss of church patronage for the arts with a flourishing market for private pictures. Of the approximately fifty painters documented in Leiden in the 1620s, almost a quarter were active as glass painters. Their fragile works are mostly lost, but even for most painters on panel and canvas, little survives besides their names. There were no painters of the caliber of Lucas van Leyden, the city's most famous artist of the past, whose prints were to exert considerable influence on Rembrandt. Jan van Goyen, who eventually became Leiden's most accomplished landscape painter, had taken early apprenticeships with the best local painters, including Isaac van Swanenburg, but for his specialization he wisely moved to Haarlem, where the innovative landscapist Esaias vanden Velde steered his earliest efforts in the genre.

The social structure of Leiden goes some way towards explaining why, around 1620, the city lacked both a strong collecting tradition and a vigorous art market catering to a broad middle class. Like Rembrandt's parents, the majority of the city's 45,000 inhabitants belonged to the artisanal class or to the solid merchant class, neither of which was especially wealthy. An annual family income of several thousand guilders would allow most people to own a few portraits of loved ones and perhaps some landscape pictures or scenes from the Bible, but it did not encourage lavish expenditure on home decoration. While Leiden's expansion and economic success in the 1640s and 1650s provided favorable conditions for the city to become a great center of collecting and patronage, in the 1620s the city experienced some economic recession (like most Dutch cities), and income was limited.[7]

Commissions and holdings of art in Leiden were invariably modest compared with collections in Amsterdam or Haarlem, where collectors had begun to amass substantial groups of paintings before the end of the sixteenth century. The inventory of the Leiden couple Frans Ghijsbrechtsz van Zuytwijck and Marijtgen Willemsdr de Roos, taken in 1626, included fine furnishings, valuable silver, and lots of clothes, but rather few paintings.

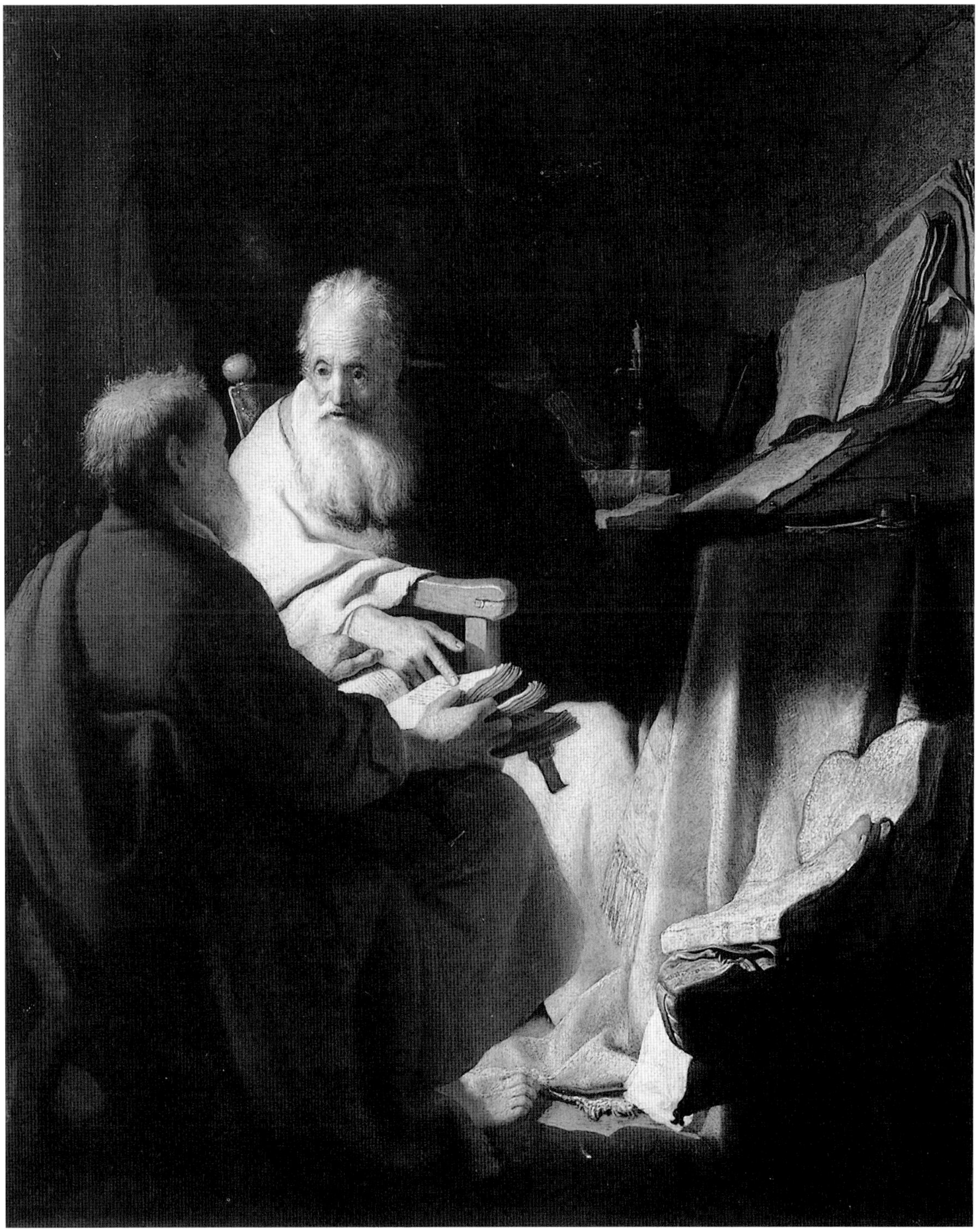

fig. 20 Rembrandt, *Two Scholars in Conversation (Saint Peter and Saint Paul)*, 1628. Oil on wood, 72.3 × 59.5 cm. National Gallery of Victoria, Melbourne.

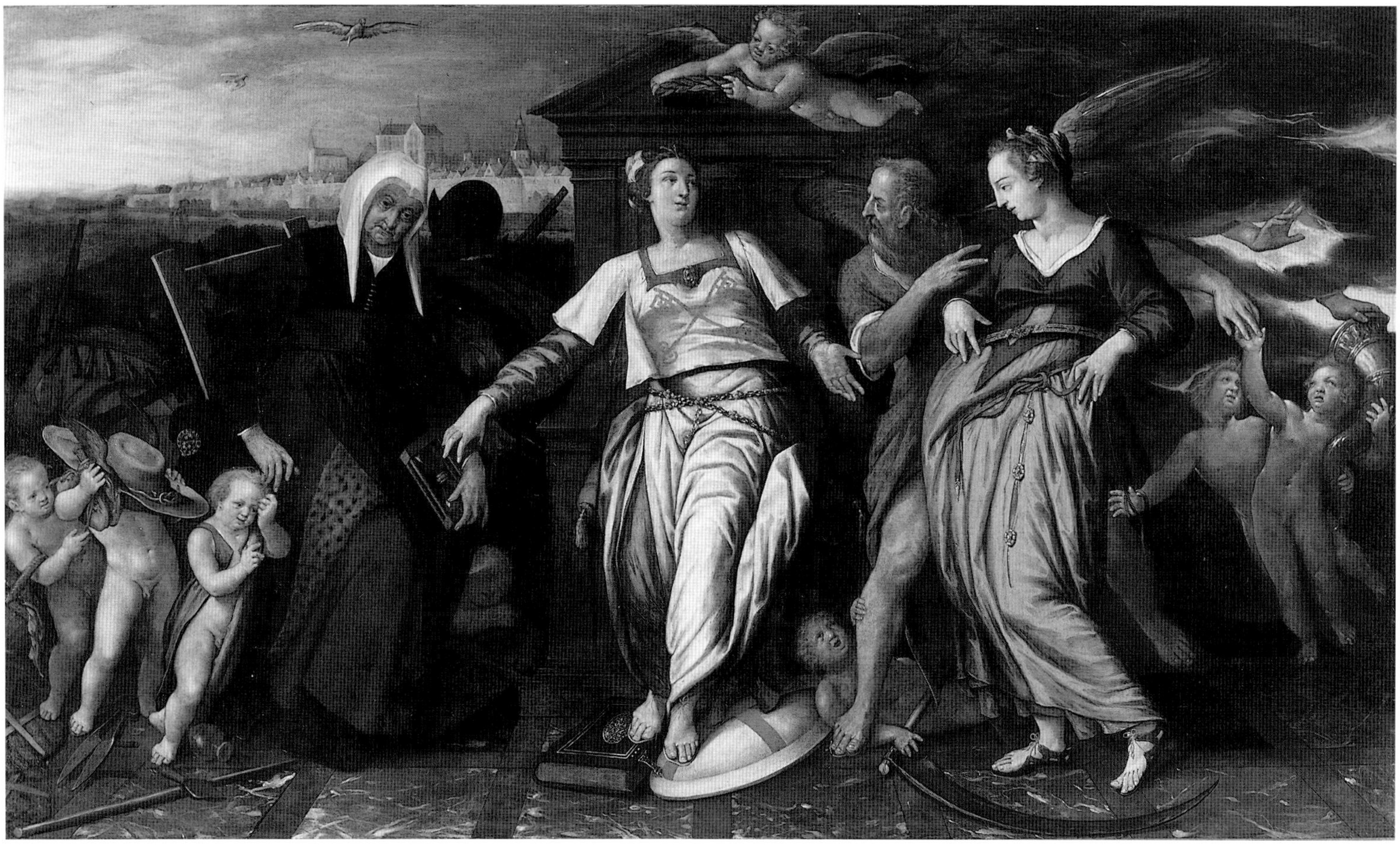

fig. 21 Isaac van Swanenburg, *Allegory of the Restoration of the Leiden Cloth Industry in the Presence of the City Maid of Leiden*, ca. 1600–10. Oil on wood, 136 × 240.5 cm. Stedelijk Museum De Lakenhal, Leiden.

The pictures were listed amongst all the other items in a given room. They were rarely identified by subject and never by artist, and their valuations were low, ranging from one to two guilders, equivalent in the same inventory to the value of a fine undershirt.[8] On the other hand, Jan Orlers, the city *burgemeester* and town historian who wrote Rembrandt's early biography, had an obvious interest in the visual arts and built a dedicated collection. His inventory of 1640 included a separate list of his paintings (about ninety, valued together at 643 guilders) and those of his daughter (more than fifty, estimated at 439 guilders). Orlers described the subjects of these pictures with care, and he attributed most of them, and even individual parts or figures, to specific masters. Copies after named artists were listed as such, occasionally with the name of the copyist. Identified painters ranged from Leiden contemporaries such as Jan van Goyen, Jan Lievens, and David Bailly to fashionable landscape painters of Haarlem, including Esaias vanden Velde, Jan Porcellis, and Pieter Molijn. Orlers also attributed some paintings to earlier masters: Abel Grimmer, Karel van Mander, and Hieronymus Bosch (these last two surely represented by copies). Valuations were respectable; while the average estimate per picture was about 7.5 guilders, the majority were valued at five to fifteen guilders, and a few were estimated at twenty to twenty-five guilders. Nevertheless, at a combined total of 1,082 guilders, the collection of Orlers and his daughter was no match for the finest collections of paintings in Amsterdam.[9] In 1622 Arnoldus Buchelius, a lawyer from Utrecht who described distinguished collections in the major Netherlandish cities, visited Leiden to meet Cornelis Boissens, a calligrapher who owned a fine group of drawings, and the lawyer Jeronimus de Backere, who collected paintings, primarily landscapes and portraits. Both collectors owned mostly sixteenth and early seventeenth-century works by deceased artists, although de Backere had acquired landscapes by Esaias vanden Velde. Almost all artists mentioned by Buchelius had lived and worked outside Leiden.[10]

In this unassuming artistic environment, Jacob Isaacsz van Swanenburg, Rembrandt's first teacher, was one of the few prominent painters. He was the son of Isaac, van Goyen's early teacher, who had enjoyed significant patronage from the Leiden textile guild (fig. 21). Rembrandt's mother may well have known Jacob van Swanenburg because he was a member of a prominent Catholic family. As a reasonably well-connected painter who had worked in Italy for more than a decade, he was as good a choice as any to teach Rembrandt, who at fifteen or sixteen was a relatively

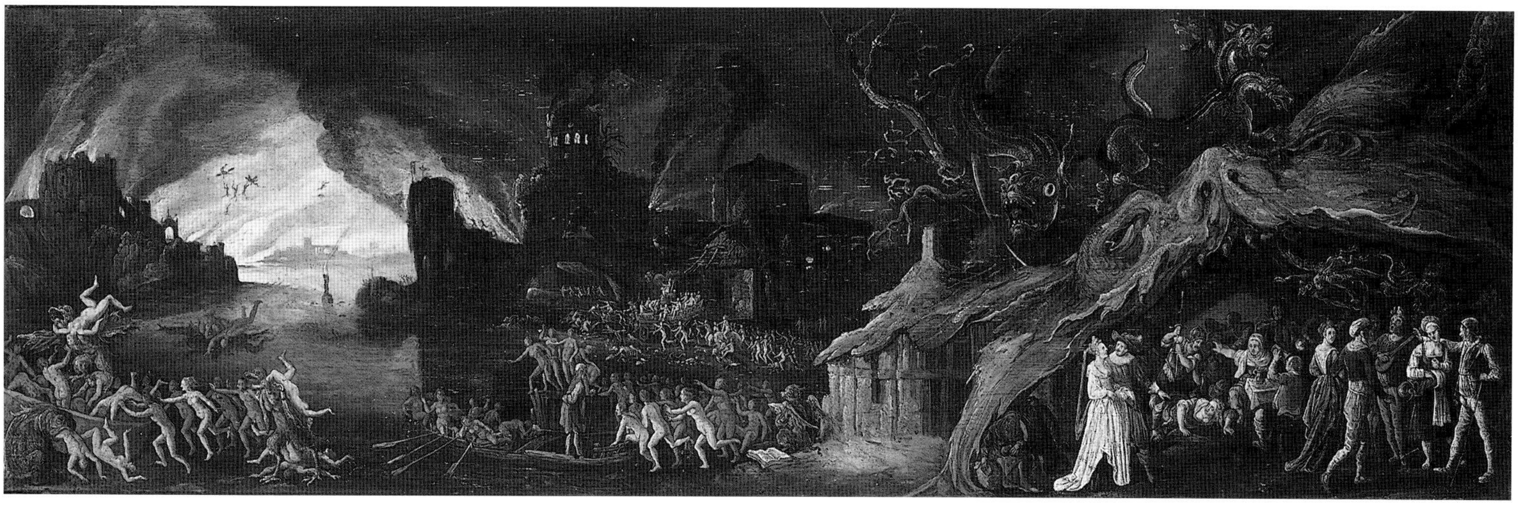

fig. 22 Jacob van Swanenburg, *Last Judgment and Seven Deadly Sins.* Oil on wood, 28 × 88 cm. Rijksmuseum, Amsterdam.

old apprentice. Van Swanenburg's paintings of infernal subjects (fig. 22) are usually dismissed as old-fashioned and derivative, and the lack of visual evidence of Rembrandt's interest in his art has occasionally been interpreted as the young painter's recognition of its outmoded character.[11] The master's small panels of countless tiny figures swirling through fiery landscapes indeed capitalized on the long-lasting, though surely declining fashion for pictures in the manner of Hieronymus Bosch, but the absence of paintings by Rembrandt in this vein is no mark of his opinion of them. It is more readily explained by the seventeenth-century system of artistic education, under which masters taught apprentices the basic materials, tools, and processes of painting. For this reason, many pre-modern artists show no trace of their masters' influence in their works, even when their teachers were more original and gifted than van Swanenburg. Pieter de Hooch and Jacob Ochtervelt, for example, were both apprenticed to Claes Berchem, a distinguished specialist in Italianate landscape and pastoral painting, but their refined pictures of life in and around the home have nothing to do with their master's art. Berchem himself was the son of the still-life painter Pieter Claesz, who surely trained him, yet Berchem's sunny landscapes and lusciously painted staffage betray nothing of that training.

As for all these artists, the primary purpose of Rembrandt's learning period would have been to acquire the artisanal fundaments of painting, and under the normal terms of the apprenticeship Rembrandt would have done little independent painting.[12] Van Swanenburg would have taught him how to prepare painting materials; some tools and materials were available commercially, but many had to be made or finished in the workshop. In 1643 Leendert Hendricx Volmarijn applied to the Leiden town government for permission to open an art supply store; this is the earliest documentary evidence that painting materials were supplied commercially in Leiden.[13] Rembrandt would have learned about the standard sizes and constructions of oak panels, and about the different ways of stretching canvases on wooden frames. Van Swanenburg would have demonstrated various recipes for mixing grounds, in case the panel or canvas did not come already prepared. During his apprenticeship Rembrandt would also have learned to prepare paints by grinding pigments into fine particles and mixing them into oils with varying consistencies and drying times. Another essential skill was the arrangement of the paints onto a palette. Van Swanenburg must have shown Rembrandt how to manipulate brushes and palette knives to obtain different pictorial effects. While acquiring the material science of painting, Rembrandt would have observed the stages of inventing and producing a finished painting, from preliminary drawing and dead-coloring to final finish and varnish. Only after he had mastered the elements of drawing would he have begun to paint in oil, copying pictures or helping van Swanenburg fill in details of his paintings on the master's explicit instructions and in his manner.

Rembrandt may well have been involved in the painting of van Swanenburg's works, but it is highly unlikely that he would have been permitted to sign or sell his own pictures or even to paint independently. Although Leiden no longer had a painters' guild, artistic tradition probably caused its workshops to observe the sorts of guild regulations enforced in other Dutch cities. Any guild, and that of Saint Luke was no exception, served to protect practitioners of a trade from the lower prices that might be offered by tradesmen from out of town or by less fully trained competitors, and the guild thus set and upheld standards of training and product quality, and forbade all non-members from selling their products. Under this regimen, painters were not allowed to sell paintings in their own name unless they had established themselves as independent masters who paid guild dues. Assistants could work within a master's studio without such obligations, but they could not sign works with their own names, as a regulation of the Utrecht guild, recorded in 1641, states explicitly. In order to ensure that each Utrecht workshop produced a recognizable "trademark" product, this same regulation required that apprentices and journeymen paint only in the manner of the workshop's master.[14] It is plausible that, in the absence of a guild, painters in Leiden still tried to uphold traditions designed to prevent destructive competition; indeed, in the first decades of the century, the city's painters requested the town government to institute the sorts of protection from non-resident artists that guilds provided elsewhere.[15] While in van Swanenburg's studio, therefore, Rembrandt may not even have painted in a manner that was noticeably distinct from that of his master.

Whatever Rembrandt learned in van Swanenburg's studio, he was no child prodigy. Longstanding efforts to find paintings that he could have made before 1625, the year of his first signed and dated work, have been unsuccessful. And even if certain awkward, heavily painted pictures are accepted as works of his hand, rather than efforts by early followers, they would confirm that Rembrandt in his late teens was an inexperienced novice who might have been pleased to paint as well as his first teacher.[16] These works would not bear out Orlers' claim, which again echoes familiar *topoi* of artistic biography, that during his three years with van Swanenburg, "his progress was so great that art lovers were most amazed, for it was clearly evident that he would one day become an exceptional painter."[17]

What is extraordinary about Rembrandt's independent career in Leiden from 1625 to 1631 is the astonishing rapidity with which he became a versatile, original, and justly celebrated artist, having come to painting relatively late by the standards of his time. Gerard ter Borch was an accomplished draftsman by the time he was fifteen. He was the son of a painter, but other great Netherlandish artists were early starters as well. Anthony van Dyck was amazing Antwerp connoisseurs, including his teacher Rubens, when he was in his mid to late teens. Jan van Goyen, a young independent master in Leiden when Rembrandt entered his first apprenticeship, had begun to study painting when he was ten; Gerrit Dou entered Rembrandt's studio in Leiden when he was fifteen and painted refined pictures in his master's most meticulous manner within two years.

Rembrandt's sudden development as an original artist in the second half of the 1620s had its germ, as Orlers recognized, in an additional apprenticeship, which he appears to have sought of his own accord: "His father then agreed to bring and board him at the renowned painter P. Lastman, who lived in Amsterdam, for further and better instruction."[18] At eighteen, Rembrandt apparently realized that he needed additional training with a leading painter of the previous generation, even though it meant asking his parents for an additional investment in his already lengthy education. If the tuition fees Rembrandt later charged are a good indication of the expense, his stint in Pieter Lastman's studio would have cost his family at least fifty guilders, in addition to travel, lodging, and perhaps six months of lost income. Rembrandt's gamble was an intelligent one, for Lastman was an established innovator of history painting in Amsterdam, the most flourishing art market in Holland. Although it is unclear whether Lastman trained any of the slightly younger history painters who worked in his manner, by 1621 he certainly stood at the center of their circle. Working with Lastman, Rembrandt would have encountered most of these successful painters, including Jan Tengnagel, the brothers Jan and Jacob Pynas, Adriaen van Nieulandt, Claes Cornelisz Moeyaert, and François Venant. The group had international cachet. Most of its members spent significant time in Italy in the first decades of the century, and around 1619 Lastman, Jan Pynas, and van Nieulandt were commissioned to paint works for the private chapel of Christian IV, king of Denmark. The artistic benefits of Rembrandt's half-year stay in this environment are abundantly evident in the first paintings he made as a newly independent artist in Leiden, and they are rightly seen as the fruits of his youthful ambition to become a painter of historical subjects, the highest challenge for the artist in the canon developed in Italian and Netherlandish art theory.

Rembrandt probably sought out Lastman on van Swanenburg's recommendation. Between 1601 and 1606 Lastman, too, had lived and worked in Italy, where, like van Swanenburg, he had specialized in historical subjects. Lastman appears to have fostered the notion that Italian credentials were central to his lively historical pictures, which were full of emotionally direct narrative and archaeological flavor. Even after his return to Amsterdam he kept signing his works "Pietro Lastman," thus giving them an Italian stamp. By going to Lastman, Rembrandt also followed the example of Jan Lievens, his younger contemporary and fellow townsman, who had studied with Joris van Schooten in Leiden and gone to Lastman about 1618 or 1619. Seeking a second or even third apprenticeship for highly specific reasons was not uncommon in the seventeenth century. Having taken several basic apprenticeships in Leiden, van Goyen had specialized in landscape painting with Esaias vanden Velde. The erudite writer and painter Adriaen van de Venne was first trained in draughtsmanship, manuscript illumination, and painting, all in the studio of Simon de Valck in Leiden. But then, the biographer Cornelis de Bie claimed, van de Venne apprenticed himself to the unknown Jeronimus van Diest, a specialist in grisaille painting, because he was interested in "seeing the fruits and hidden secrets of this art." In his subsequent career van de Venne produced masterpieces in all of his areas of training: illumination, polychrome painting, and grisaille.[19] Frans van Mieris of Leiden switched masters four times, each time to improve his career prospects, it seems. Having begun his training with a goldsmith in the late 1640s, he soon turned to Abraham Toorenvliet, a successful glass painter and draughtsman of Leiden. In the early 1650s he wisely apprenticed himself to Gerrit Dou, who had become the preeminent "fine" painter of Leiden. He then studied with Abraham van den Tempel, one of the most successful painters of large history paintings and portraits in the city, but perhaps recognizing the particularities of his own talent and the profitability of Dou's manner, he returned to Dou to finish his artistic education and to become, in the master's words, "the prince of his pupils."

In Amsterdam, Rembrandt eventually emulated Lastman in becoming a magnet for young but fully trained artists such as Jacob Backer, Govaert Flinck, and Ferdinand Bol. These painters were attracted by the special accomplishments of his portraiture and history painting, and presumably by the economic power of his sizeable workshop, which in the 1630s gained a huge share of the market for portraiture. During the 1640s Rembrandt also appears to have gained renown as a teacher of life drawing, bringing in talented young artists such as Samuel van Hoogstraten and Nicolaes Maes. In his biography of Maes, Arnold Houbraken was quite explicit about the painter's efforts to improve on his training throughout his career. Having learned to draw from "a plain Master" in his native Dordrecht, the young Maes went to Amsterdam in the late 1640s to study painting with Rembrandt. In 1653 he returned to his hometown to become an independent master, but according to Houbraken he later undertook a research trip to Antwerp to study the works of Rubens and van Dyck, and to visit the ageing Jacob Jordaens, Rubens' most prominent heir in the city.[20]

Orlers wrote that after six months in Lastman's workshop, Rembrandt "decided to practice the art of painting entirely on his own." Instead of setting up shop in Amsterdam, with its lively patronage and flourishing art market, he returned to Leiden, undoubtedly for sound economic and artistic reasons. In Amsterdam, Rembrandt could have become an independent master only if he were a member of the Guild of Saint Luke, and to gain that membership he needed first to become a resident of the city. Residency in turn would have required him to live in Amsterdam for at least a year, working as a journeyman or assistant to Lastman or another artist and forgoing direct income from his paintings.[21] In his hometown, where there was no guild, Rembrandt could avoid residency requirements and guild dues, become an independent painter right away, live at home, and receive continued support from his parents. Sharply aware of the pronounced discrepancies at this time between the artistic cultures of Amsterdam and his native city, Rembrandt perhaps realized that, with his new expertise in Lastman's mode of history painting, he could become the proverbial big fish in Leiden's small pond. He also could expect to benefit straight away from his family's network of acquaintances.[22] Although it is difficult to trace these relationships directly, one may assume that in a town of Leiden's size Rembrandt's long-resident family would have known, or been able to bring him in contact with, some of the prominent people who can be associated with his early career. It was not uncommon for members of the political and educational elite to have close contacts with the artisanal middle class. Between 1606 and 1608, for example, Caspar Barlaeus, a university professor and Remonstrant preacher, lodged in the house of the grain trader Gilles van Vliet. Van Vliet was the father of Jan van Vliet, the printmaker who was to reproduce some of Rembrandt's early works, and in 1634 Barlaeus was still sufficiently familiar with the van Vliets to write to the stadhouder on Jan's behalf.[23]

In his first years as an independent artist, Rembrandt gained access to people of Barlaeus' educational and social standing. His early introduction to leading citizens in and around Leiden had profitable consequences later in his career, when he was establishing himself as one of the leading history painters and portraitists of Amsterdam. Several of these people owned pictures by Rembrandt; others commented on his art. Systematic consideration of these figures and of the paintings by Rembrandt they owned or knew confirms that he did well to set up shop in Leiden. It also suggests how, in the competitive art market of the 1620s, artistic careers were built on the right mix of promising contacts, artistic daring, financial wherewithal, and effective self-promotion. Rembrandt had what it took to become, within about four years, a leading painter in Leiden and a young artist with a reasonable shot at replicating and multiplying his success in Amsterdam. Not all of this was a matter of chance.

Rembrandt's most significant early contact, of course, was Constantijn Huygens, whose well-known admiration of Rembrandt and Lievens brought the young painters to the attention of Frederik Hendrik and Amalia van Solms. The stadhouder and his wife are among the earliest recorded owners of Rembrandt's works. In 1632 the inventory of Frederik Hendrik's cabinet—a private space often used for the display of works of art—included "a painting in which Simeon, being in the Temple, holds Christ in his arms, done by Rembrandt or Lievens" that is most likely identical with Rembrandt's meticulous, coloristically refined painting of 1631, now in the Mauritshuis (fig. 74).[24] The scribe's indecisiveness in matters of attribution is typical of references to works by Rembrandt and Lievens from their Leiden period, in their time as in our own. A 1639 inventory of the collection of Charles I attributed three paintings to Rembrandt, one of which was correctly identified ten years later as from the hand of Lievens.[25] Two other pictures in the 1632 inventory of Frederik Hendrik's gallery were listed as by Lievens, but their subject description and attributions in subsequent inventories establish beyond doubt that they were the early paintings of *Minerva* and *The Abduction of Proserpina* by Rembrandt (figs. 64, 63).[26] It has even been proposed that another reference in Frederik Hendrik's inventory to "A piece of painting in which Samson's hair is cut off, made by Jan Lievensz" may refer to Rembrandt's painting now in Berlin (fig. 62), although Rembrandt's rendition of a moment preceding the cutting of Samson's hair renders this possibility implausible.[27]

The early references to Rembrandt and Lievens in these distinguished collections may not settle all matters of attribution, but they establish how effectively contact with Huygens advanced their careers. In 1629, at least some of the three pictures attributed to Rembrandt in the English royal inventory of 1639 may have been acquired by Sir Robert Kerr, an envoy of Charles I to the court in The Hague. Since Orlers claimed that the Prince of Orange had bought a work—now lost—by Lievens and given it to Kerr, it is possible that Huygens or Frederik Hendrik also gave these three works to the envoy, who then gave them to his king.[28] Alterna-

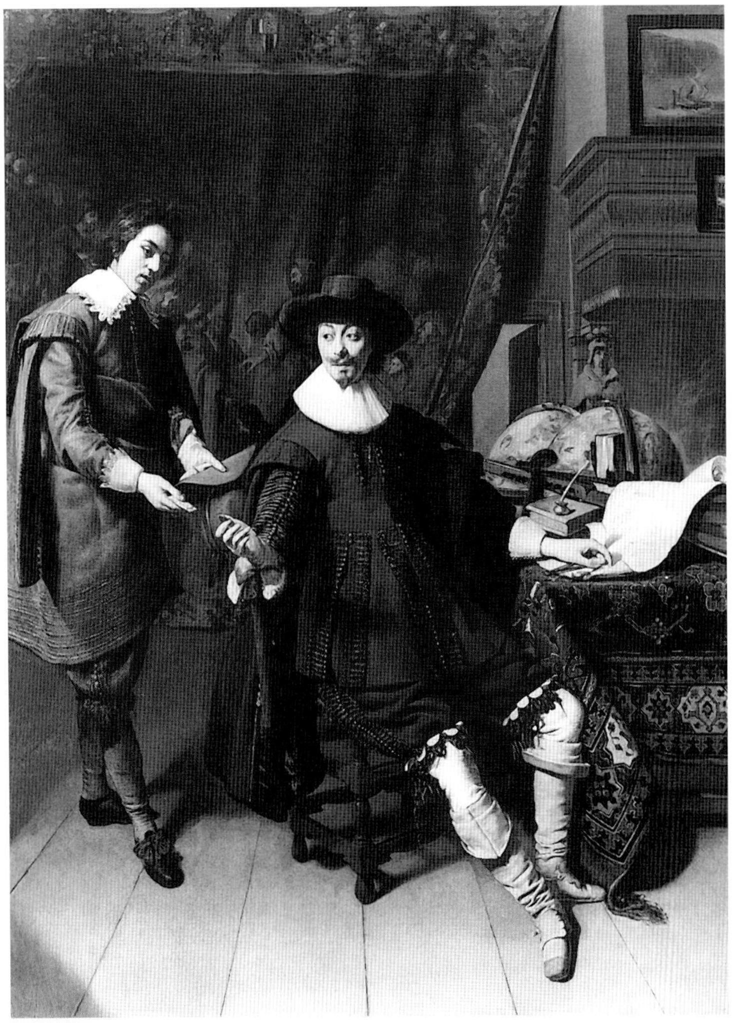

fig. 23 Thomas de Keyser, *Constantijn Huygens and His Clerk,* 1627. Oil on wood, 92.4 × 69.3 cm. National Gallery, London.

tively, Huygens or one of his associates may well have pointed Kerr to the young painters so that he might buy paintings from them.[29] On the strength of Huygens' word and of Rembrandt's early pictures, Rembrandt was commissioned to paint a profile portrait of Amalia van Solms, completed in 1632 as an intended pendant to the portrait of Frederik Hendrik by Gerard van Honthorst. About the same time, Rembrandt received the order for the first two, and possibly all, of the five paintings in the Passion series for the stadhouder. After consideration of the reasons for Huygens' support of Rembrandt, we will return to the possible genesis of this crucial commission.

Huygens' salutary intervention in Rembrandt's early career is often considered a lucky break, but the stadhouder's adviser had not happened upon the young painter by accident. After Frederik Hendrik was appointed stadhouder in 1625, he initiated a concerted campaign to build an internationally cultured court in The Hague.[30] In emulation of Charles I, who bought the cream of the collection of the Duke of Mantua in 1625, and Philip IV of Spain, who in this period rapidly expanded the already impressive Spanish holdings in Italian and Flemish painting, Frederik Hendrik dedicated special efforts to the patronage and collecting of art.[31] His principal agent for this program was Huygens, a connoisseur and amateur draftsman who had himself been portrayed by Thomas de Keyser, the leading portraitist of Amsterdam (fig. 23), and who wrote perceptively about the Netherlandish artists of his time. He undoubtedly undertook his visit to Rembrandt and Lievens about 1629 as an effort to scout the latest native talent, and he presumably prepared for it by prior reference checking, as he notes at the outset of his account: "when I say that [Rembrandt and Lievens] will soon trump the [aforementioned absolute] geniuses, I am merely representing the expectations the best connoisseurs harbor of them on the basis of their astonishing debut." The polymathic secretary would have had no time to scour the studios of all the young artists in Leiden, in a period when the stadhouder's military and diplomatic efforts against the Spanish Netherlands required his consummate attention. Huygens evidently knew Leiden collections, including that of the German merchant Matthijs van Overbeke, who had settled in the city in 1621. Perhaps Huygens also knew the opinion of Buchelius, who in 1628 had claimed that "the son of a Leiden miller is highly, if prematurely, esteemed." But even if Huygens had never heard of Buchelius, the record of his opinion makes clear that Rembrandt's promise was a well-known fact in and around Leiden.

Huygens' account of his encounter with Rembrandt identifies what contemporaries found so exciting and novel about his art and why these qualities might have appealed to Frederik Hendrik. Quite rightly, Huygens noted that, unlike Lievens, Rembrandt preferred to test himself in small, lively, and inventive paintings of historical subjects. These were the types of themes that were most prestigious at the courts of the international princes to whose standing Frederik Hendrik and Amalia aspired, but Rembrandt painted them on a scale more suited to the competitive Dutch art market of the 1620s, in which limited public patronage and a broader economic recession forced painters to find profitable niches. In this climate, painting large works without a specific buyer in mind would have exposed an untried painter to serious economic risk. Although the stadhouder and his wife favored the grander historical paintings of van Honthorst and of Rubens, whom Huygens considered "one of the seven wonders of the world, the king, the Apelles among painters," Rembrandt's youthful historical experiments offered local innovation in the great genre. Huygens' description of Rembrandt's *Judas Returning the Thirty Pieces of Silver* (fig. 24) outdoes Rembrandt's emotionally incisive mode of representation; to understand the purposes to Huygens' extravagance, it is worth reading once more his puzzling lines:

> Compare this with all Italy and whatever marvels remain from deepest antiquity. The gesture of that one despairing Judas (to remain silent about all the other impressive figures in this one painting), that one maddened Judas, screaming, begging for forgiveness, but devoid of all hope, all traces of hope erased from his face; his gaze wild, his hair torn out by the roots, his

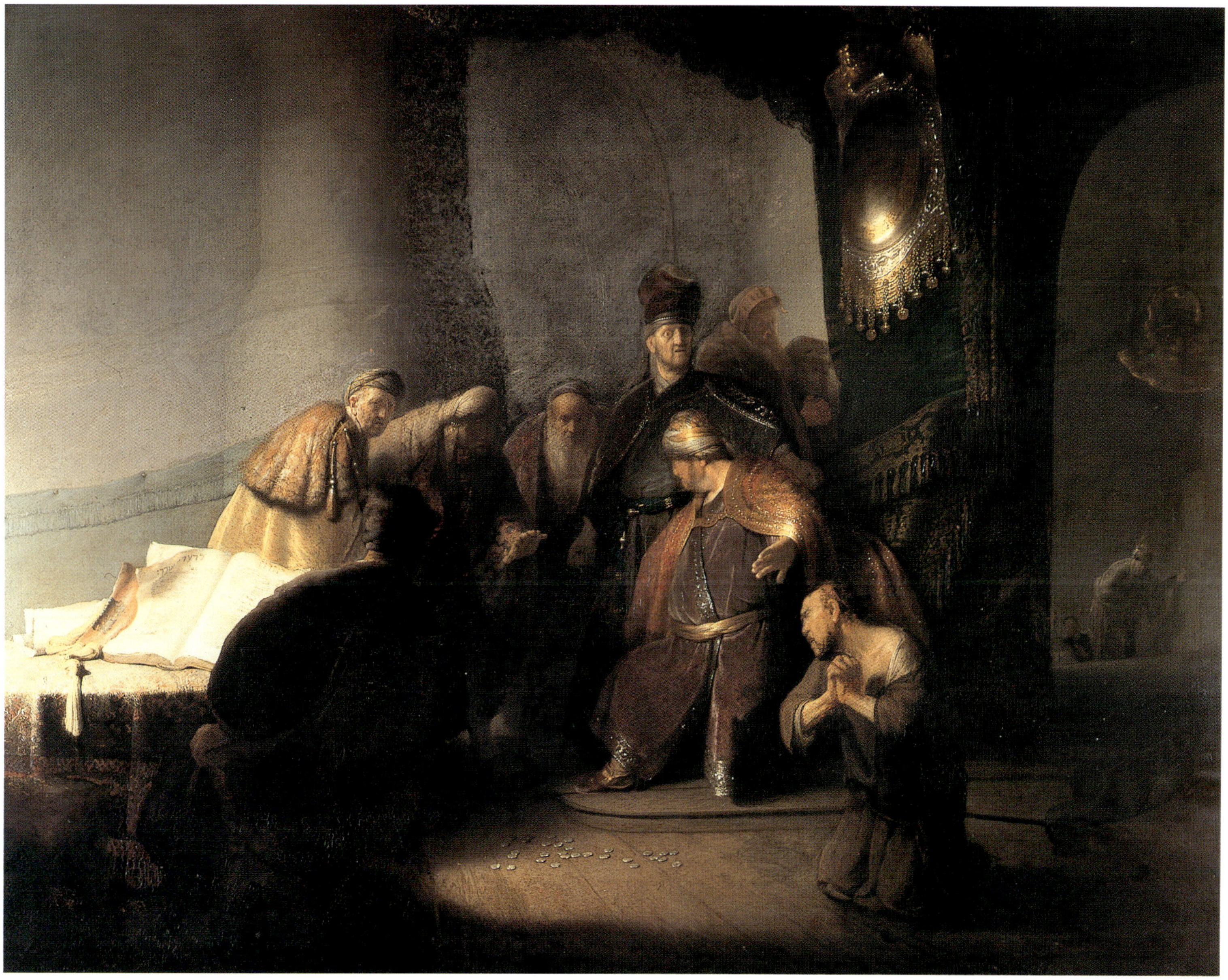

fig. 24 Rembrandt, *Judas Returning the Thirty Pieces of Silver*, 1629. Oil on wood, 79 × 102.3 cm. Private collection.

garments rent, his arms contorted, his hands clenched until they bleed; a blind impulse has brought him to his knees, his whole body is writhing in pitiful hideousness. All this I compare with all the beauty that has been produced throughout the ages. This I wish to put before those naives ... who wish to claim that nothing is now made or expressed in words that had not previously been made or expressed in Antiquity. I maintain that it would never occur to Protogenes, Apelles, or Parrhasios, should they return today, that a youth, a Dutchman, a beardless miller, could put so much, and so completely, into one figure. Praise to Rembrandt! Bringing Troy, yes all of Asia to Italy is a smaller accomplishment than transferring the highest mark of honor from Greece and Italy to the Hollanders—and that by a Hollander who barely set foot outside the walls of his native city.

Huygens' peaked enthusiasm for, and misstatements about, Rembrandt's unusual painting can be explained only in part as lapses of visual memory. An accomplished Latinist—his memoir is written in a dense, difficult Latin—Huygens was familiar with the classical rhetorical tradition of writing *ekphraseis*, vivid descriptions of things, scenes, persons, and, most crucially here, paintings that would bring the matter at hand "before the mind's eye" of the listener or reader. By his energetic rhetoric, building up descriptions by finely differentiated levels of emotional representation and staggered increases in praise, Huygens may have sought to evoke in his readers the visual experience of seeing Rembrandt's painting, and by extension the feelings that it had generated in him. Rembrandt's own opinion of the Judas figure—clearly the focal point of his composition—apparently stroked with that of Huygens, for while the Judas may seem to us a straightforward development of the despairing Tobit from 1626 (fig. 48), Rembrandt in 1634 engaged the printmaker Jan van Vliet to make an etching after his top part (fig. 25), presumably to circulate his fine invention. In the painting, Judas' emotional eloquence is shared by the Pharisees, whose various responses of interest, surprise, disgust, and rejection Rembrandt described with care.

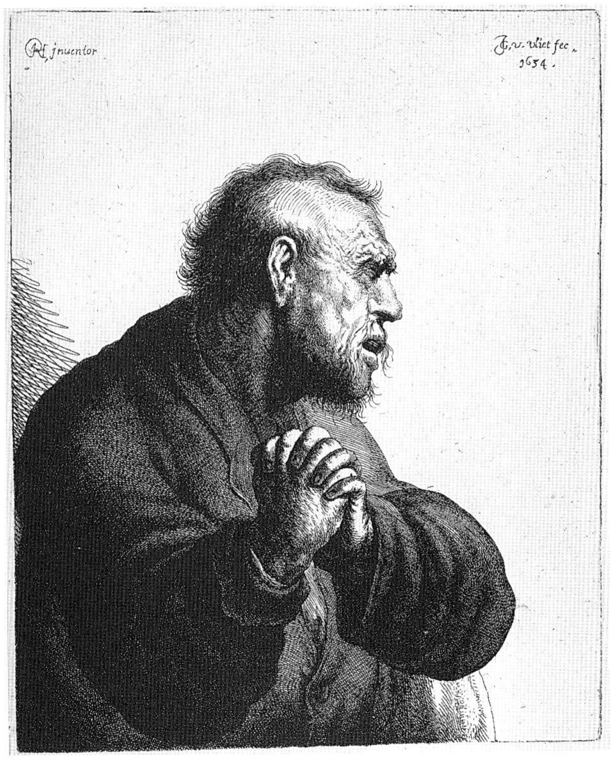

fig. 25 Jan Gillisz van Vliet, after Rembrandt, *Grieving Man, from Judas Returning the Thirty Pieces of Silver,* 1634. Etching, 22.5 × 18.9 cm. Rijksmuseum, Amsterdam. Bartsch 22.

Huygens was fascinated by paintings that evoked forceful passions in the viewer, no matter how abject the theme. Of the many paintings he could have eulogized to demonstrate Rubens' inventive powers, he chose the uncharacteristic painting of Medusa's decapitated head,

> wreathed with snakes sprouting from her hair. The face of this wondrously beautiful woman has retained its grace, but simultaneously evokes repulsion by its recent death and by the circle of horrid snakes. The combination is executed with such refinement that the viewer is not only shocked by the sudden confrontation (the painting is normally covered), but simultaneously moved by the life-likeness and beauty with which the cruel subject has been represented.[32]

Something of this contradiction, between forceful artistic beauty and debased subject, must have spurred Huygens' love of Rembrandt's *Judas*, and incisive and varied emotional content is, indeed, one of the characteristics that sets Rembrandt's art apart from that of his contemporaries in Amsterdam and Leiden. Other distinguishing traits, to a contemporary eye, can be teased out of Huygens' narrative.

The secretary's treatment of Rembrandt and Lievens together, as "a notable pair of youths," in a memoir that otherwise discusses artists individually, confirms what their closely connected art in these years suggests: that the young painters were sharing a studio.[33] It was unusual, and forbidden according to guild regulations from other cities, for independent painters to keep a common workspace. Presumably, the guilds wanted to prevent painters from gaining the unfair economic advantages of shared rent, hired hands, models, tools, and materials, but in Leiden the absence of a guild would have allowed the young painters to enjoy just these competitive benefits. More significantly for the history of art, the joint efforts of Rembrandt and Lievens spurred remarkable creativity, in the best tradition of artistic rivalry, and Huygens was onto this. Not only by the narrative structure of his account, which moves back and forth between the strengths and foibles of the individual painters, but also by its specific language, Huygens indicated that he saw the competition between the two painters as an enabling condition of their early success. His sustained praise of the duo is suffused with agonistic description, and it presents the rivals as burning with competitive spirit.

In his opening lines Huygens claims that "they are the only ones among all mortals who have equalled" earlier Netherlandish paragons; in his conclusion he expresses amazement that in their hunger for success they "dismiss even the most innocent pleasures of youth as a waste of time." While they are thus seen to compete with their Netherlandish peers and with time itself, Huygens also has the young men competing with each other, their fathers, and their teachers; with antiquity, with Italy, and, in the description of the Judas, with Huygens' own powers of *ekphrasis*. The two youths, one the son of "a common citizen, an embroiderer," the other that of a miller, "but not baked of the same flour," first transcend the plain status of their fathers, having been ennobled by their talent alone: as Huygens puts it, "they offer the strongest evidence against the existence of a nobility of the blood." Next they outdo their teachers, "who enjoyed hardly any fame outside the lower circles," and "if one would now confront these teachers with their pupils, they would feel the same shame that must have been experienced by the first people who taught poetry to Virgil, rhetoric to Cicero, and mathematics to Archimedes." Then Huygens sets up the painters as rivaling each other in different aspects of art: "in sureness of touch and liveliness of emotions Rembrandt is better than Lievens. Conversely, [Lievens] wins the prize by a grandness of invention and boldness of subjects and forms." After detailing Lievens' ambitions to paint on a larger-than-life scale and his success in portraiture, and after adducing the *Judas* as proof that Rembrandt achieves "results in a small format that one would seek in vain in the largest pieces of others," Huygens complains that in their ambition the two youths have become so cocksure that they refuse to travel to Italy and "feast their eyes on the creations of so many gigantic geniuses." The well-traveled Huygens could have been expected to make this wistful comment, but for him it had rhetorical purpose beyond the obligatory stamp of approval on Italian Renaissance art, for "how quickly would they be able to outdo all of that and give the Italians reasons to come to their own Holland."

Huygens' comparison of Rembrandt's *Judas* to "all the beauty that has been produced throughout the ages" and especially to the achievements of Protogenes, Apelles, and Parrhasios, is no standard flourish either. Rather, the idea that Rembrandt and Lievens were competing with the great artists of antiquity may have been suggested to him by the artists themselves, and certainly by the specific preoccupations of their art in the 1620s. Rembrandt and Lievens surely knew of the famous competitions between their Greek predecessors. Van Mander and others loved to recount the feats of Zeuxis and Parrhasios, who outdid each other in making paintings that fooled the beholder's eyes, or of Protogenes and Apelles, who contested each other's talents for the finest line drawing. The well-known instances, on at least five occasions, where Rembrandt and Lievens tried their hands, with slight and subtle variations, at the same subjects and similar artistic challenges can be seen as deliberate exercises in such creative competition.

Several striking pictorial interests of Rembrandt and Lievens in the second half of the 1620s confirm their conscious efforts to emulate

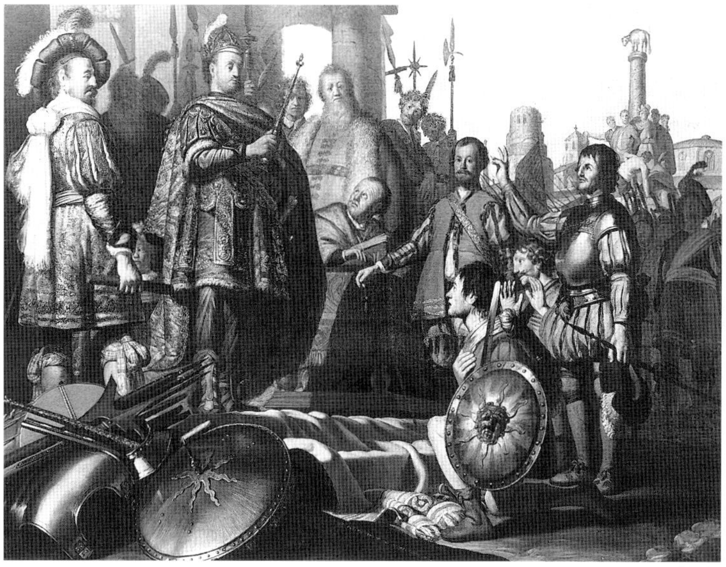

fig. 26 Rembrandt, *History Painting (Palamedes Protesting His Innocence)*, 1626. Oil on wood, 90.1 × 121.3 cm. Stedelijk Museum De Lakenhal, Leiden.

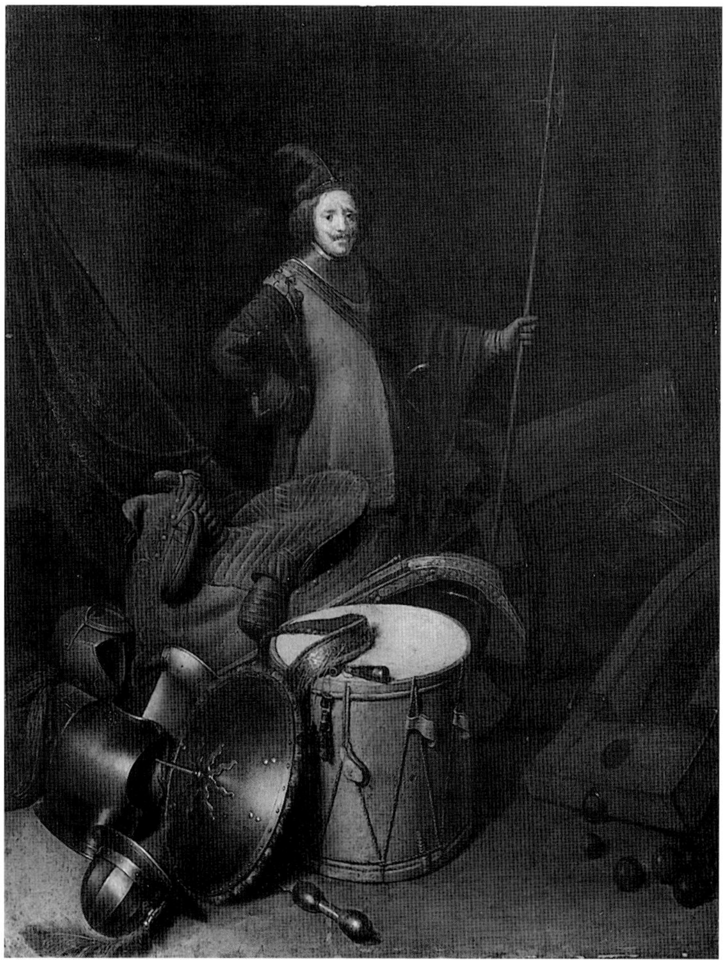

fig. 27 Gerrit Dou, *Standing Soldier with Weapons*, ca. 1635. Oil on wood, 66 × 51 cm. Szépművészeti Múzeum, Budapest.

the legendary artists of the Greek past. As Ernst van de Wetering has demonstrated in telling detail, the two artists in their first independent works set out to better the efforts of Lastman and his associates in the lifelike representation of surface texture.[34] The gleaming pile of armor that serves as conspicuous repoussoir in *History Painting (Palamedes Protesting His Innocence?)* is a fine exercise in capturing the reflections of light off different types of metal (fig. 26); the ageing skin of Anna and Tobit is given its mottled and wrinkled character with minute touches of finely variegated color (fig. 48). These displays of textural representation evoke the achievement of Zeuxis, whose grapes fooled birds, and especially of Parrhasios, whose illusionistically painted drape over a painting deceived even Zeuxis. The prominent shield in the *History Painting* became a standard bit of virtuosity in the works of Dou (fig. 27), who took his master's early efforts in textural veracity to such heights of refinement that he became known as "the Dutch Parrhasios."[35]

Rembrandt's early interest in strong emotional expression, so evident in his *Judas* and *Anna and Tobit*, and matched by Lievens' extroverted *Wrath of Ahasuerus* (fig. 28), recalls another feat of the antique painters, exemplified best by Zeuxis and Timanthes. Following Pliny and modern Italian writers, van Mander celebrated the capacity of both painters for representing in the most lifelike fashion the diverse passions that rouse the human soul. In a feat that may have served as a model for Rubens' *Medusa* or Rembrandt's *Judas*, Zeuxis turned the horrific into truly moving art:

> In old times one could see a fearful panic in a painting of King Amphitrion and Alcmene, the mother of Hercules, who appeared terrified because they saw the young Hercules prove his power on two vicious snakes, which he squeezed forcefully to strangle them. The maternal heart appeared captive to fear and anxiety by this horrific scene. One should not hide who made this work: it was the painter Zeuxis of Heraclea; none outdid him in painting the emotions.[36]

While Zeuxis excelled at suffusing an entire work with a single intense emotion, Timanthes was praised for his ability to differentiate emotions within a painting. Van Mander exemplified this ability by recounting Timanthes' famous differentiation of states of grief in his depiction of the many witnesses at the sacrifice of Iphigenia by her father, Agamemnon. Following Pliny, van Mander evoked the diverse expressions Timanthes must have invented for

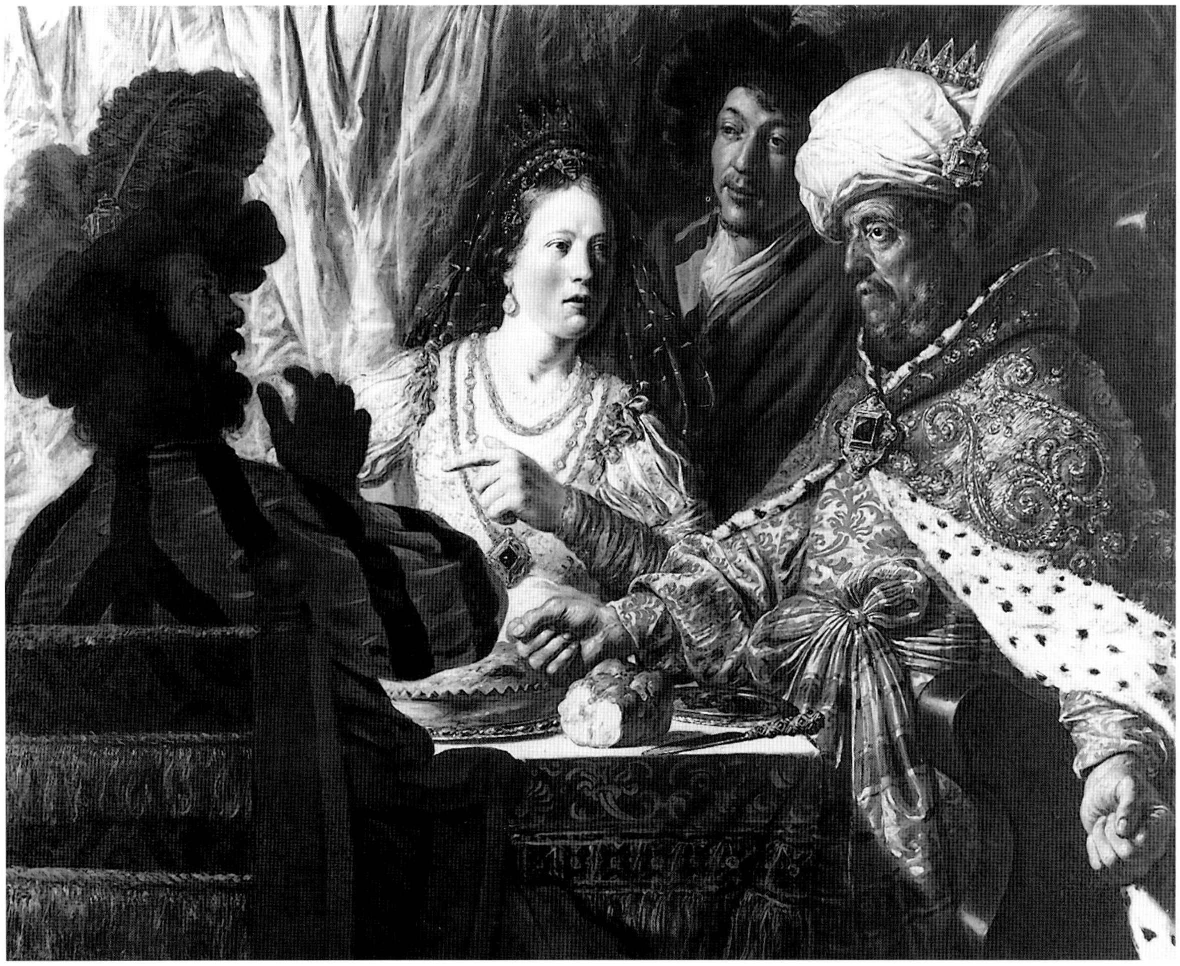

fig. 28 Jan Lievens, *The Banquet of Esther and Ahasuerus*, ca. 1625. Oil on canvas, 134.6 x 165 cm. North Carolina Museum of Art, Raleigh.

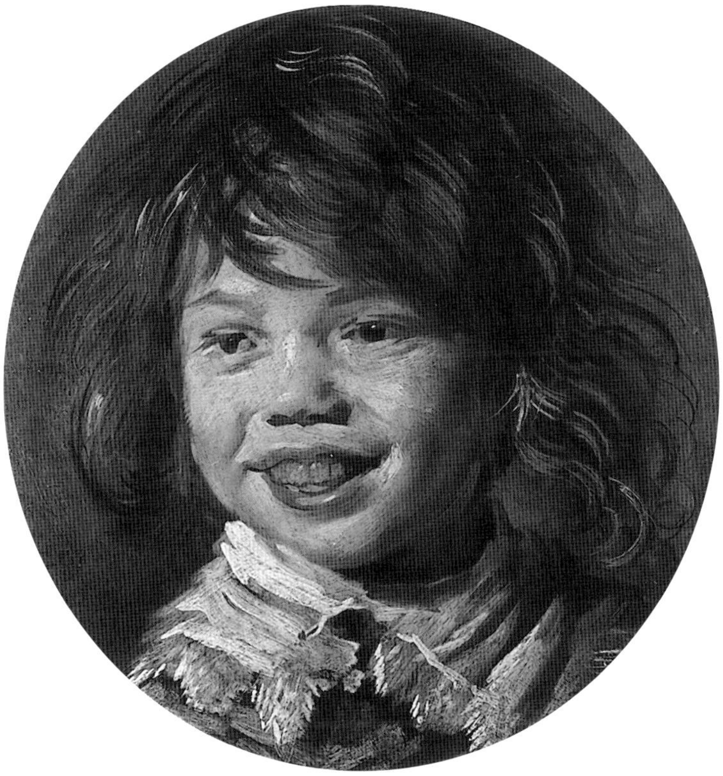

fig. 29 Frans Hals, *Laughing Boy*, ca. 1620–25. Oil on panel, diam. 29.5 cm. Mauritshuis, The Hague.

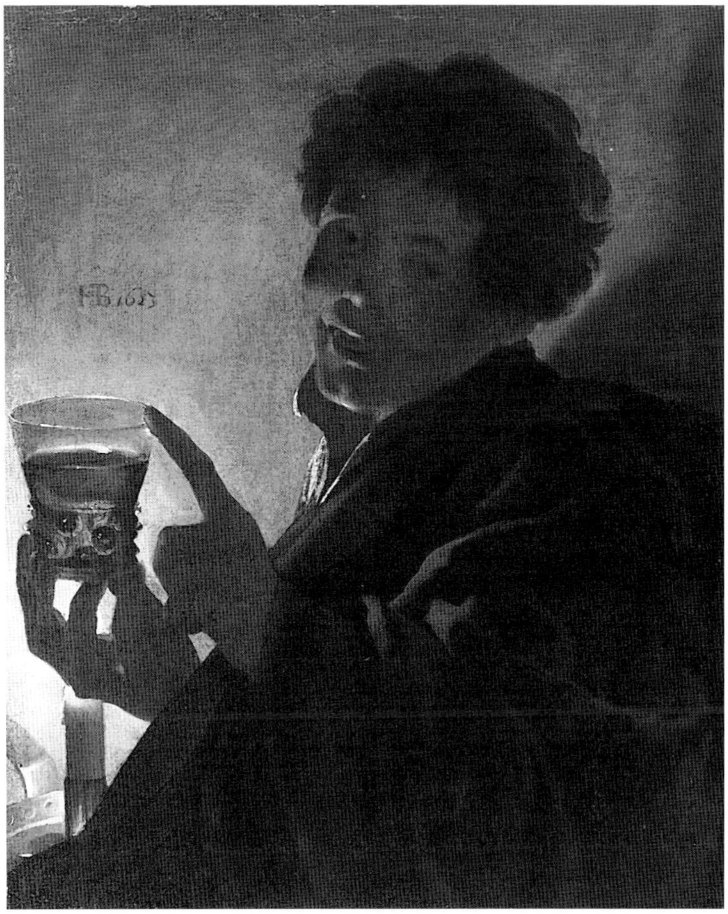

fig. 30 Hendrick ter Brugghen, *Laughing Boy with a Wine Glass*, 1623. Oil on canvas. 67.3 × 56.5 cm. North Carolina Museum of Art, Raleigh.

the seer Calchas and Iphigenia's uncle, concluding his account with the painter's brilliant decision to represent Agamemnon's unspeakable grief by showing him "covering his face, with hands or clothes."[37] By specifying a wide range of emotions in *Judas Returning the Thirty Pieces of Silver* and the *Raising of Lazarus*, Rembrandt adapted Timanthes' fabled skill to biblical painting.

A signature element in Rembrandt's expressive faces of the 1620s is the open mouth that flashes its teeth (cat. 12). Rembrandt must have been well aware of the clever use his contemporaries were making of this earthy device: Frans Hals' laughing children and Hendrik ter Brugghen's exuberant musicians gain individual life from their dental specifics and near-audible vocalizations (figs. 29, 30). Rembrandt, too, used the ploy to signal laughter, but more often in his works it registers pain, rage, or anguish (fig. 31). His versatility with the open mouth thus emulated the ancient accomplishment of Polygnotus, who, in Pliny's words, "made many improvements to technique, painting the lips parted so as to reveal the teeth, which brought expression to the face in place of the rigidity of former times."[38]

Antique challenge may even have been partially responsible for the radical change in Rembrandt's and Lievens' coloring, evident about 1626 to 1627, from Lastman's brightly lit, variegated palette to a more unified range, in which yellow and white highlights punctuate compositions in browns, blacks, and greens. The monochromatic color scheme and newly subtle chiaroscuro of

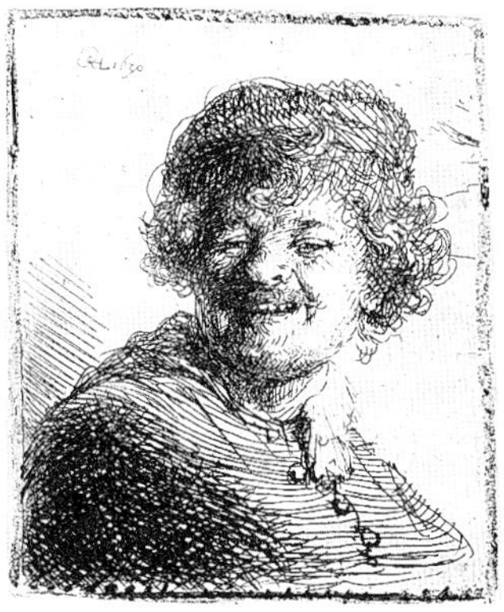

fig. 31 Rembrandt, *Self-Portrait Grinning*, 1630. Etching, 5 × 4.4 cm. British Museum, London. Bartsch 316.

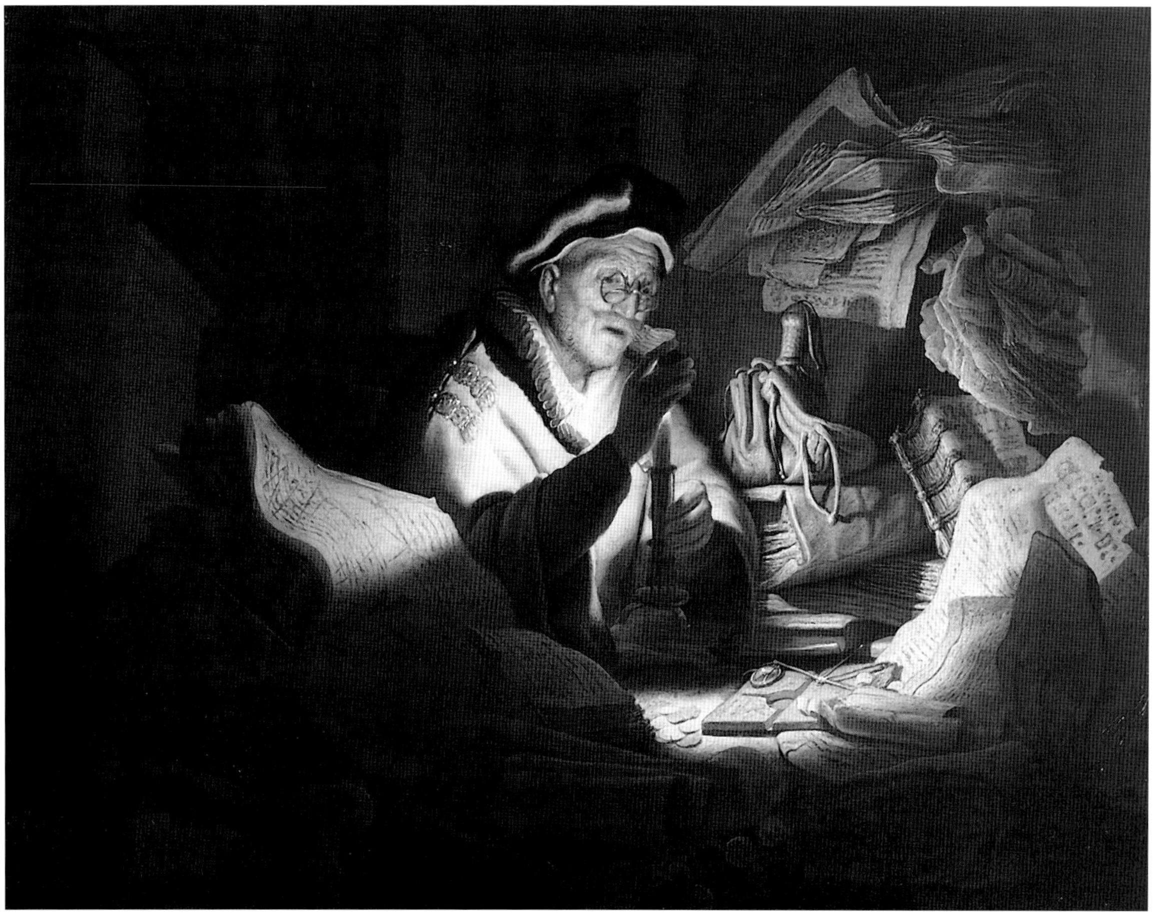

fig. 32 Rembrandt, *The Rich Man of the Parable,* 1627. Oil on wood, 32 × 42.5 cm. Staatliche Museen zu Berlin, Berlin.

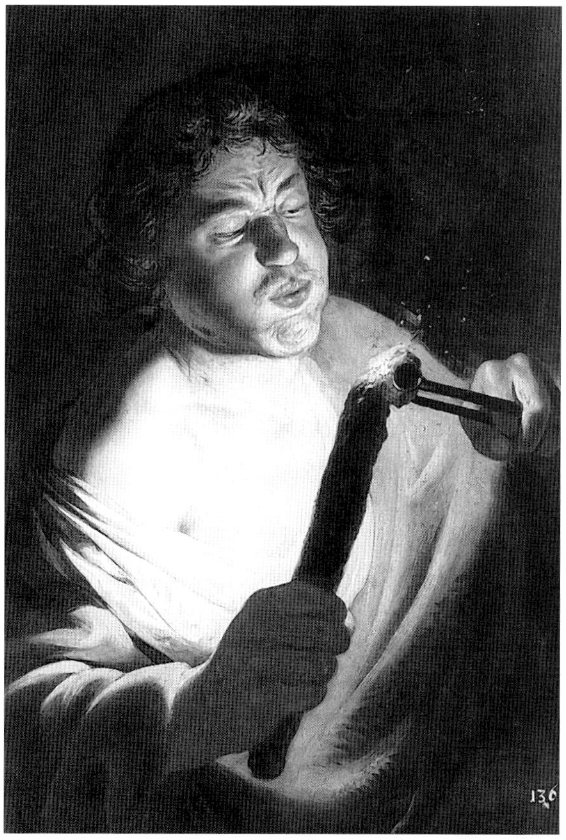

fig. 33 Jan Lievens, *Youth Blowing on a Torch,* ca. 1625–27. Oil on wood, 82 × 64 cm. Muzeum Narodowe, Warsaw.

Rembrandt's *Rich Man of the Parable* (fig. 32) and Lievens' *Youth Blowing on a Torch* (fig. 33) were occasioned by the nocturnal subjects and by the single light sources within the paintings. The then recent innovations of Gerard van Honthorst, whose work was admired by Huygens and Frederik Hendrik, were partly responsible for this subtle tonalism, and so was the success of the monochrome painting style introduced on the Dutch art market in the later 1620s. Yet its particular incarnation in the art of Lievens and Rembrandt suggests that they were cognizant of antique precedent.[39] Van Mander had expressed well the legendary talent of Antiphilus for painting the subtle effects of a single light source on an entire composition:

> Reading Pliny we find that the art of reflection was already applied in the past, by Antiphilus, who was no fool in painting a youth who was blowing hard and diligently to get a fire to burn; and the resulting shine made visible the interior of a fine house, and it made the blower's face light up softly.[40]

Lievens' *Youth Blowing on a Torch* directly acknowledges the antique source, but Rembrandt's *Rich Man of the Parable* offers the precise study of reflections in a surrounding domestic interior for which van Mander praised Antiphilus. The man's right arm pro-

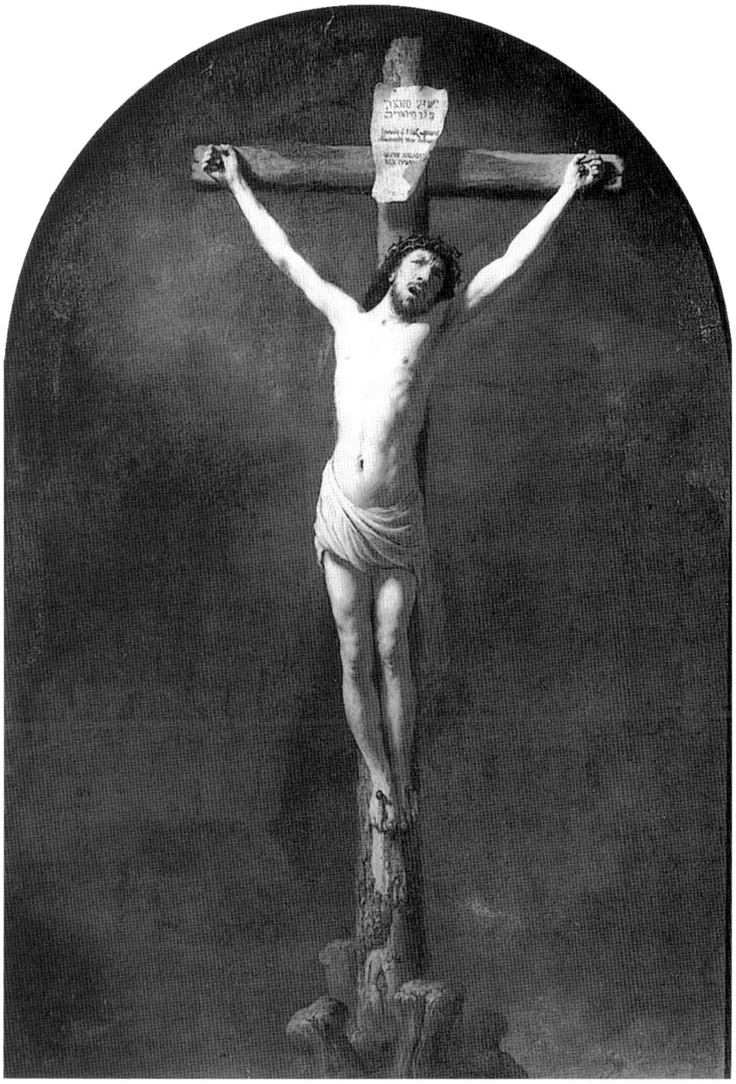

fig. 34 Rembrandt, *Christ on the Cross*, 1631. Oil on wood, transferred to canvas, 99.9 × 72.6 cm. Eglise parossiale, Le Mas d'Agenais.

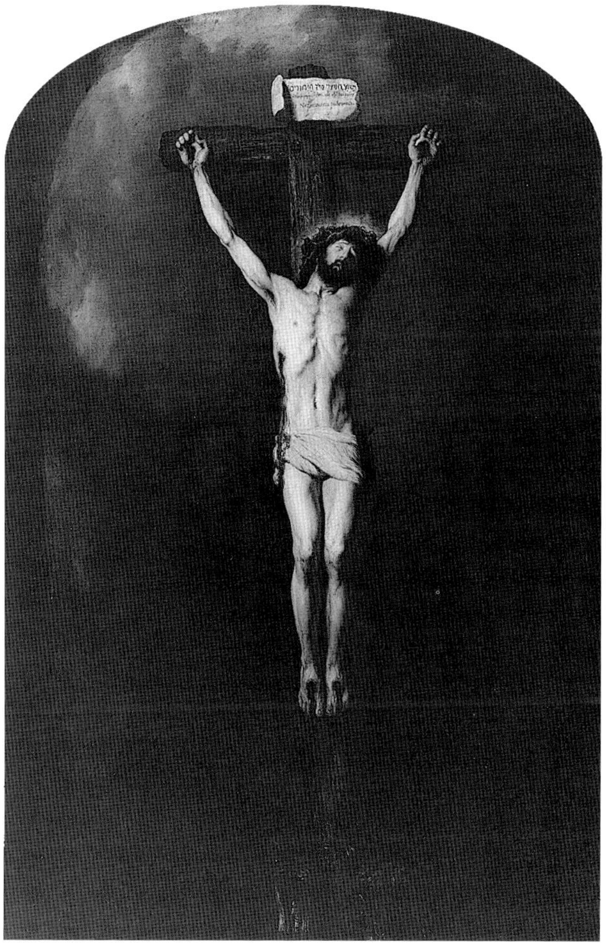

fig. 35 Jan Lievens, *Christ on the Cross*, 1631. Oil on canvas, 130 × 85 cm. Musée des Beaux-Arts, Nancy.

duces strong foreground shadows, while his glasses throw delicate lines onto his softly glowing face. The quirky shadows of the purse strings call attention to the soft leather binding of the book on which it rests. Pinpoint reflections highlight the tasseled clasps of the man's tabard, the wire rims of his glasses, the tip of his nose. The limited reach of the candlelight subordinates all inessential elements.

Stimulated by these records of antique accomplishment, artists in Renaissance Italy developed a distinguished tradition of artistic rivalry with peers past and present, as Huygens, Rembrandt, and Lievens must have known. Vasari's *Vite*, and van Mander's redaction of them, are richly larded with the tricks of artists undercutting and trumping each other. Vasari invented some of his stories to serve as metaphors for the artistic relationship between two artists, but others are grounded in historic competitions held to award commissions for significant public or private works. Most famous of these was the contest held in 1401–2 between Lorenzo

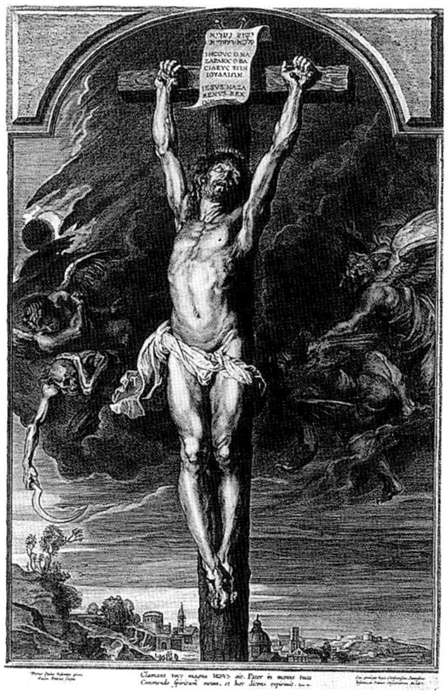

fig. 36 Paulus Pontius, after Peter Paul Rubens, *Christ on the Cross*, 1631. Engraving.

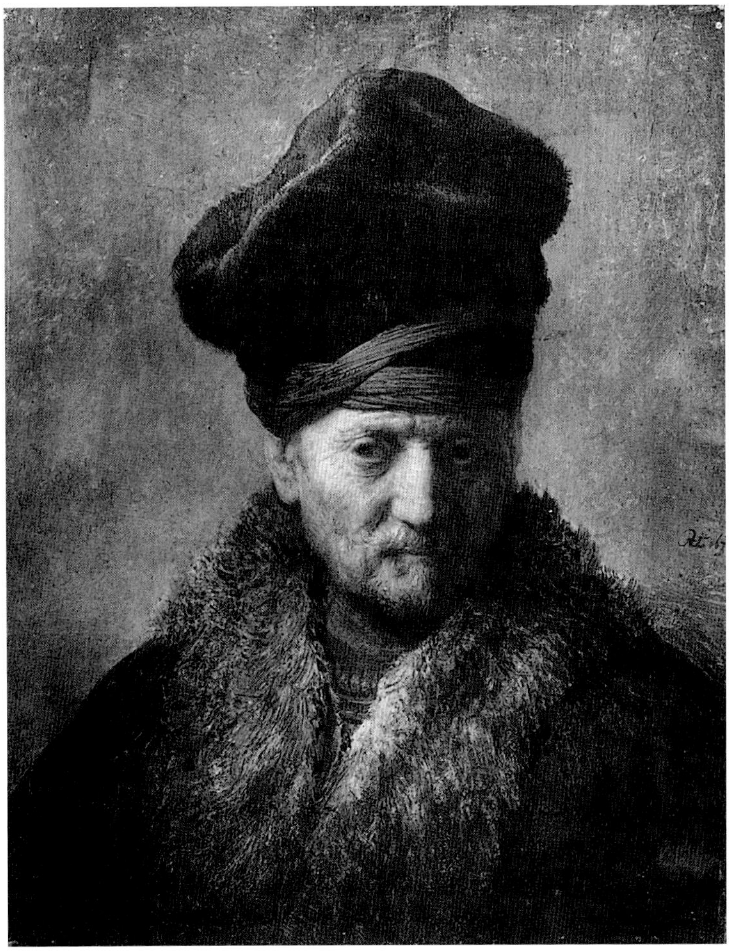

fig. 39 Rembrandt, *An Old Man in a Fur Cap (called Rembrandt's Father)*, 1630. Oil on wood, 22.2 × 17.7 cm. Tiroler Landesmuseum Ferdinandeum, Innsbruck.

his face. Soon, however, Rembrandt's images of himself began to serve more complex functions.

In a series of more than fifteen small self-portrait etchings, made between 1627 and 1630, Rembrandt appears to try out a wide range of sentiments, as if putting on so many masks (fig. 38 and cats. 1, 12, 13, 15). These small studies reflect contemporary drawing practice, as their origins in Rembrandt's small self-portrait drawings from the same period suggest (see figs. 1a, 1b). Half a century after their production, Rembrandt's pupil Samuel van Hoogstraten discussed the exercise of self-expression in his *Inleyding tot de hooge schoole der schilderkonst: anders de zichtbaere werelt*, a treatise published in 1678. Quite possibly transmitting his master's lesson, he recommended that artists learn to render the passions by trying out emotions in the mirror and fixing their reflections in drawings. Rembrandt's decision to apply this practice in etchings, which are by definition reproducible, suggests that they were intended for circulation and thus had a use beyond the studio. Early in his career they could advertise his capacity for capturing human expression, and they could simultaneously spread knowledge of the face he was already beginning to turn into fascinating art. They may even have encouraged a collecting habit in his first customers: just as modern collectors seek perfect series and specimens of first-issue stamps, designer watches, or small stuffed animals, owners of Rembrandt's self-portrait prints may have aimed to own all of his faces.[48] Eventually all etchings by Rembrandt became subject to just such obsessive collecting. By the end of the seventeenth century, print connoisseurs began to collect the Complete Work of Rembrandt, the way a lover of poetry might seek to own all of Shakespeare. Several collectors each owned more than four hundred of his prints, perhaps because they had sought to acquire impressions of all states.[49]

Compared with the contemporaneous self-portrait paintings in which Rembrandt poses with aristocratic gorget and wistful lovelock (fig. 6a), his early self-portrait etchings share a programmatic inelegance. A mere interest in capturing extreme emotion cannot explain why, in these quickly scribbled works whose scruffy line mimics the emotional states of their subjects, Rembrandt emphasized the puffy irregularity of his nose, or why he favored irritable, sleepy, and glowering sentiment: romantic pensiveness is a difficult emotion, too, and strong expression can happen to elegant faces. Identified directly with their author, these deliberately uncouth self-portrait prints "branded" Rembrandt's innovative mode of painting historical figures in an earthy, picturesque fashion. While contemporaries such as Lievens and Moyses van Wtenbrouck shared Rembrandt's interest in such a "low" mode of representation, Rembrandt's dedication to it in the first five years of his career was unmatched.

Half of Rembrandt's works of the 1620s present memorable images of old age. Often, the identities of these men and women justify their wizened faces: an old miser, the aging Tobit and Anna, prophets and apostles getting on in years—but Rembrandt's disproportionate and novel interest in older subjects calls for explanation. His anonymous old men and women are often supposed to represent his father and mother (figs. 39, 40, cat. 16), even though there is no known portrait of his mother, and none of the men resemble Rembrandt's drawing of his father (fig. 41). It is perfectly logical to assume that Rembrandt would have asked his mother to sit for him—in 1679, only ten years after his death, an inventory already identified a print as "Rembrandt's mother"—but if he did, her name appears to have been irrelevant to the first owners of any such pictures. In the early 1630s, for example, Sir Robert Kerr gave Charles I a painting presumed to be "Rembrandt's mother," but apparently for its pictorial interest rather than the identity of its subject: the royal inventory of 1639 identifies her only as "an old woeman." Two years later, a close version of this painting in the collection of Jacques de Gheyn III was described as "a painting of an old little *tronie*." *Tronie* was a generic term for "face," but in the seventeenth-century language of art it referred to bust-length paintings of single figures, usually male and of any age, flaunting interesting poses and facial features, inspired emotional expressions and fanciful costumes. The *tronie* thus became an ideal vehicle for the painter's study of human expression, composition, and light, and for the display of inventiveness, all central interests of

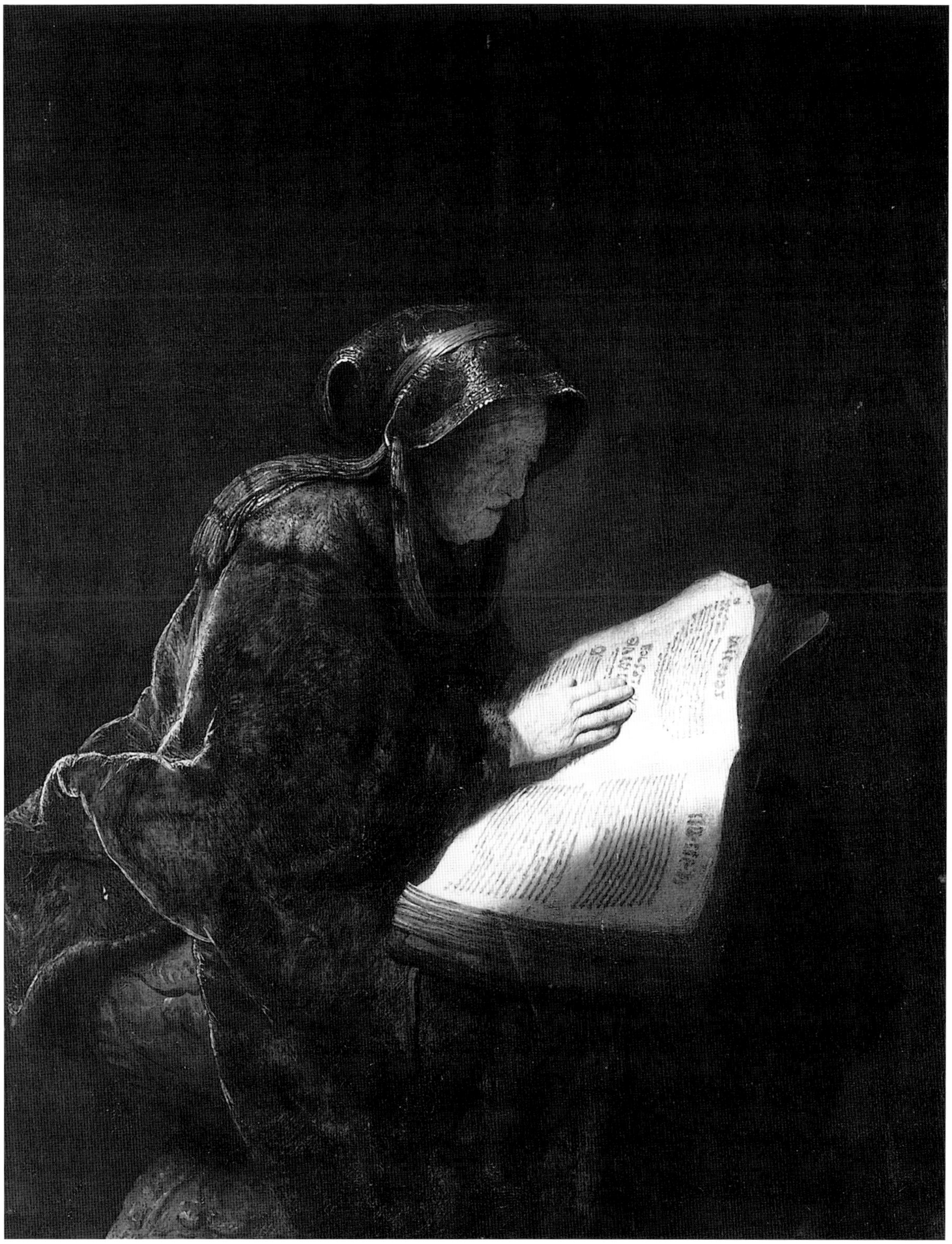

fig. 40 Rembrandt, *An Old Woman Reading (called Rembrandt's Mother)*, 1631. Oil on wood, 59.8 × 47.7 cm. Rijksmuseum, Amsterdam.

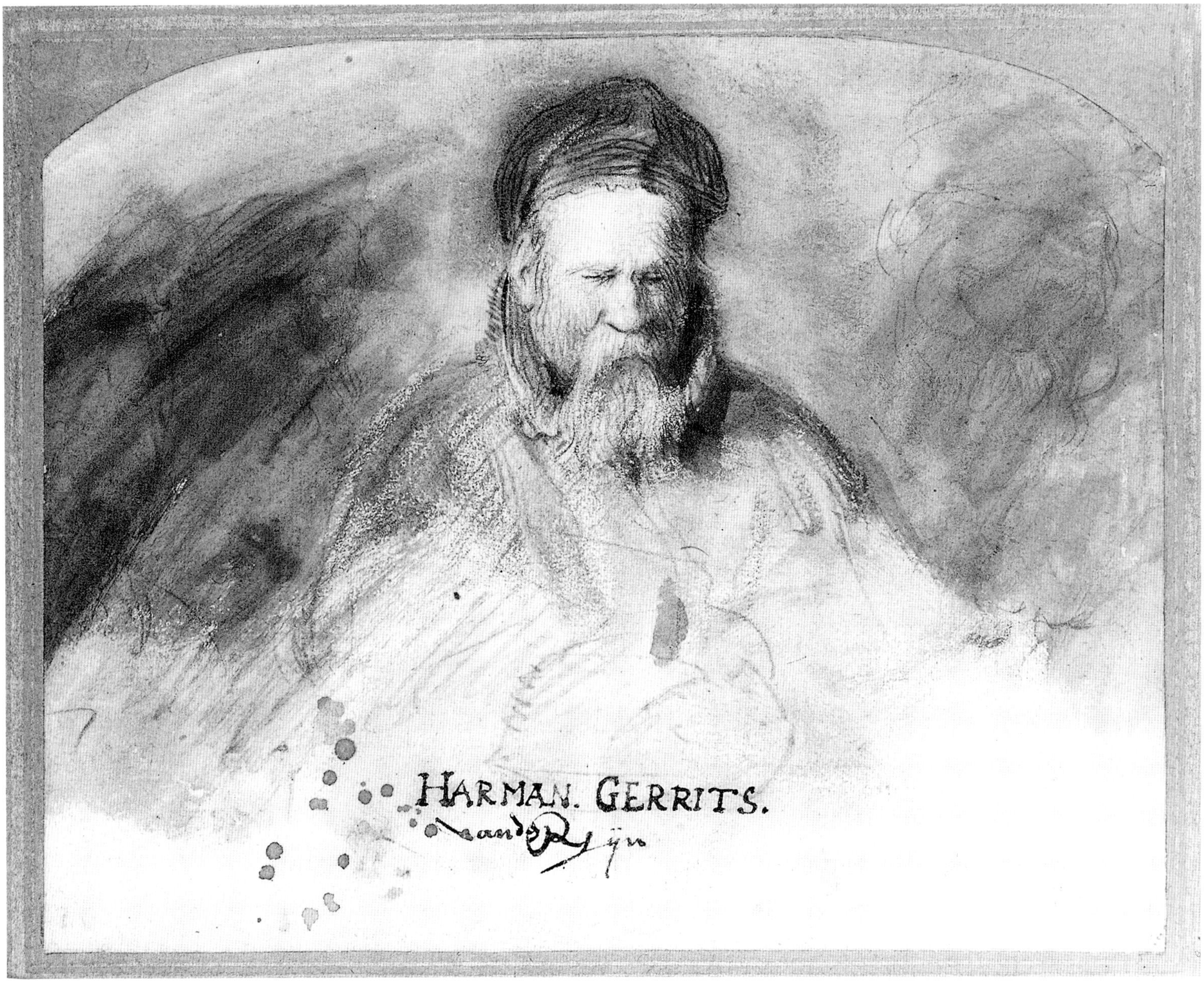

fig. 41 Rembrandt, *Harmen Gerritsz van Rijn*. Red and black chalk, brown wash, 18.9 × 24 cm. Ashmolean Museum, Oxford.

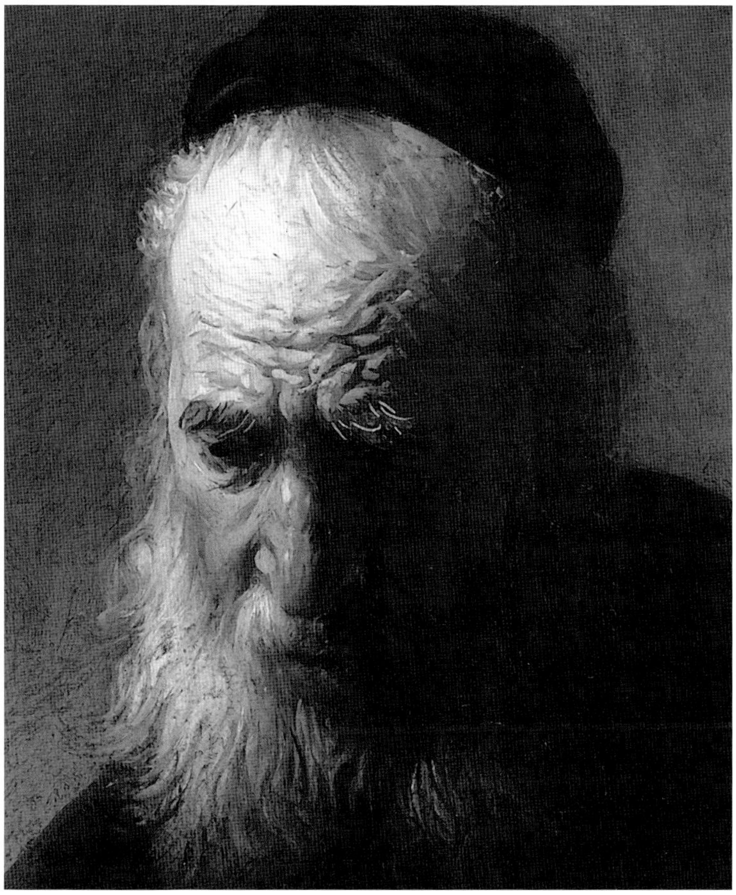

fig. 42 Rembrandt, *Old Man in Military Costume*, ca. 1631 (cat. 16, detail).

Rembrandt's history paintings, as we have seen. Rembrandt's self-portrait busts from around 1630 are such *tronies*, too. They show the painter in varied emotional states, and donning accessories and hairstyles that were the prerogatives of military officers and courtiers—attributes he could not have sported in life, but which were appropriate to the imaginative genre of the *tronie*.[50]

The physical effects of old age offered rewarding opportunities for *tronies* as well as history paintings, and Rembrandt relished both challenges. In *Tobit and Anna with the Kid* (fig. 48) he carefully differentiated the complexions of his protagonists. Tobit's brow is deeply furrowed in grief and the blue veins in his hands are set off against thin rolls of pale pink skin; Anna's facial skin is taut, though grooves radiate from her eyes, and her brownish hands are roughened by labor. Rembrandt's old *tronies* (fig. 42, cat. 16) have loosely painted, mottled skin that suggests tiny burst veins, uneven pigmentation, and unkempt stubble. It is difficult to understand the vogue for such virtuoso exercises in old faces and hands, but seventeenth-century texts about art suggest that the subject was seen as *schilderachtig*, a term best translated as "painting-like" or "worthy of painting"—an early instance of our "picturesque."[51] In the 1620s many Dutch painters sought out humble picturesque themes: country hovels and rainy days, beggars, disheveled peasant interiors, tobacco pouches and pipes, simple meals of herring and bread. They may have been stimulated by the famous accomplishments of the Greek painter Peiraikos, who, as Pliny wrote, had reaped the highest praise and best rewards for his pictures of "barbers and cobblers' shops, donkeys, food, and such things."[52] Moreover, these seemingly simple subjects, which required no knowledge of literature in order to be enjoyed, found ready takers on the rapidly expanding Dutch market for paintings. Eschewing any obvious religious content, they were also acceptable themes in a culture of Reformed proclivity. Only after mid-century, when Dutch collectors and painters became increasingly concerned that art should aspire to the standards of classical beauty espoused in Italy and France, would the vogue for lowly themes decline. In that period, the artist Jan de Bisschop spoke for many when he lamented the penchant of some Dutch painters—and he must have been thinking of Rembrandt and Lievens—for "misshapen, old, wrinkled" persons.[53]

"Misshapen" is certainly the adjective de Bisschop would have attached to Rembrandt's *Seated Nude* of about 1630 (fig. 43), for she is malformed, in comparison to the grand nudes of the classical tradition. In its technical range, from bare outlines to deep shadows, this etching demonstrates Rembrandt's facility with the print medium, but it is his uncompromising rendering of rolls of fat, double chin, sagging breasts, awkward extremities, and crude stocking marks that rivets attention. Her direct stare heightens her scandal: she is unashamed of her ungainly nudity. She lacks attributes that might justify her as a mythological or Old Testament figure, and she is no model in the studio either, for the mound on which she sits and the lightly drawn shrubbery to her right suggest a sylvan setting. She appears to be another of Rembrandt's picturesque exercises of this period, another of his exaggerated renderings of the utterly mundane. De Bisschop was virtually describing Rembrandt's etching when, in the course of his critique of *schilderachtige* motifs, he wrote a disdainful description of the nude women painted by artists of Rembrandt's generation. The *Seated Nude* is the quintessential "female nude with a fat and swollen belly, pendulous breasts, impressions of garters in the legs, and much more of such monstrosity."[54] Andries Pels in 1681 used almost precisely the same words, but applied them specifically to Rembrandt's nudes.[55] While Rubens favored a voluptuous female body type as well, he did so for narrative purposes, to suggest its fertility or seductiveness, and he ignored the female form's everyday imperfections. Rembrandt, by possibly conscious contrast, exaggerated the marks of living to such an extent that the woman's extravagant body became the print's theme. While such flouting of convention was distasteful to de Bisschop and others, Rembrandt's grotesque inventions were admired before the middle of the century. The print medium signals his expectation that his work would find ready buyers, and the great printmaker Wenceslaus Hollar honored it with an etched copy of 1635. In a sense, Rembrandt's early self-portrait etchings, produced and circulated in the period of his most singular dedication to wrinkled skin, flabby tissue, and gritted teeth, staked out his *schilderachtige* territory.

1 Orlers 1641, p. 375: "op dat hy tot zijne Jaeren ghecomen wesende de Stadt ende tgemeene besten met zijn wetentschap zoude mogen dienen ende helpen bevorderen...."

2 Ibid.: "en heeft daer toe gants geen lust ofte genegentheyt gehadt dewijle zijne natuyrlicke beweginghen alleen streckten tot de Schilder ende Teycken Conste; Waer omme zy luyden genootsaeckt geweest zijn haren Soon uyt de Schole te nemen, ende volgende zijn begeeren te brengen ende te besteden by een Schilder, omme by de selve te leeren de eerste fundamenten ende beginselen van dien."

3 Van Mander 1604, fols. 244v–245r, 262v; van Mander 1994, pp. 237–38, 309.

4 Schwartz 1985, p. 21, makes much of the civic guard duty exemption, going so far as to claim that Rembrandt enrolled in the university for this purpose at a time when he was already being trained as a painter. The available evidence strongly suggests that Rembrandt's first apprenticeship did not begin until 1621.

5 Leiden 1976, pp. 13–14.

6 For Rembrandt's *Saint Paul in Prison, Two Old Men Disputing, Saint Paul at His Writing Desk,* and the *Apostle Peter Kneeling* (cat. 18), see Corpus A 11, A 13, A 26, A 36. In the same period in Leiden, Jan Lievens painted four Evangelists and the *Apostle Paul,* all of which represent these figures as writers of the Scriptures; see Braunschweig 1979, nos. 10–13, 22.

7 The economic recession experienced by the Dutch Republic in the 1620s and 1630s, and its possible effects on artistic specialization in this decade, have been charted by Israel 1997. For the impressive development of art collecting in Leiden in the second half of the seventeenth century, when Gerrit Dou, Frans van Mieris and his sons, Jan Steen, and their many followers flourished there, see C.W. Fock, "Kunstbezit in Leiden in de 17de eeuw" in *Het Rapenburg: Geschiedenis van een Leidse gracht,* edited by T.H. Lunsingh Scheurleer et al., vol. 5a (Leiden, 1990), pp. 3–36, and Sluijter 1988.

8 Leiden 1976, p. 15.

9 Leiden 1976, pp. 17–18.

10 Hoogewerff, van Regteren Altena 1928.

11 Christopher White, *Rembrandt* (London, 1984), p. 13, represented prevailing opinion when he wrote that in van Swanenburg's studio Rembrandt "must have learnt the mechanics of painting, if little more."

12 Much is now known about the apprenticeships, tools, materials, and working processes of seventeenth-century painters, thanks in large part to the technical investigations conducted since 1969 by the Rembrandt Research Project, reported in the Corpus and van de Wetering 1997. Other detailed technical findings are gathered in London 1988.

13 Willem Martin, "Een 'kunsthandel' in een klappermanswachthuis," *Oud Holland* 19 (1901), pp. 86–88.

14 S. Muller, *Schildersvereenigingen te Utrecht, bescheiden uit het Gemeentearchief* (Utrecht, 1880), p. 76, no. 111, quoted, translated, and interpreted by E. van de Wetering, "Problems of apprenticeship and studio collaboration," in Corpus, vol. 2, pp. 45–90, esp. p. 50 note 51, p. 57.

15 For these requests and the eventual reinstitution of the painters' guild in Leiden, see Leiden 1976, p. 10.

16 Unacceptable as early works by Rembrandt, for example, are the *Three Singers, Operation,* and *Spectacles Seller* that constitute a partial series of the senses; see Corpus 1982, nos. B 1–B 3 [as neither accepted nor rejected]. Even taking into account the poor condition and extreme losses of these works, the handling and draftsmanship of the preserved parts do not cohere into a probable precursor of the type of painting Rembrandt made in 1625 and 1626, after his apprenticeship with Lastman; they are more easily understood as poor derivatives of Rembrandt's paintings such as the *Baptism of the Eunuch* and *Musical Allegory* of 1626 (Corpus A 5, A 7).

17 Orlers 1641, p. 375: "ende also hy gheduyrende den zelven tijt zoo seer toegenomen hadde dat de Const Lief-hebberen daerinne ten hoochsten verwondert waeren ende datmen genoechsaem konde sien dat hy metter tijdt een uytnemende Schilder soude werden." Compare, for example, van Mander's accounts of the prodigious early progress of Lucas van Leyden and Bartholomeus Spranger (Van Mander 1604, fols. 211r–211v, 268r–269v.

18 Orlers 1641, p. 375: "So heeft zijn Vader goet ghevonden hem te besteden ende te brengen by den Vermaerden Schilder P. Lastman, woonende tot Amsterdamme, op dat hy door den selven vorder ende beter mocht geleert ende onderwesen werden."

19 Cornelis de Bie, *Het gulden cabinet vande edel vry schilder const* (Antwerp, 1662), p. 234: "trachtende door een ander handelingh te sien wat vruchten ende verholen secreten in dese Const waren schuylende begaf hem daer naer by eenen Jeronimus van Diest uytnemende fray in het wit en swert te schilderen...." On van de Venne's grisailles, Annelies Plokker, *Adriaen Pietersz. van de Venne (1589–1662): de grisailles met spreukbanden* (Leuven, 1984) and Westermann 1999.

20 Houbraken 1718, vol. 1, p. 275.

21 Rembrandt received the funeral medal of the Guild of Saint Luke in Amsterdam in 1634, at least two years after he had moved to the city. Such medals were given to artists upon their entry into the guild. See Strauss, van der Meulen 1979, doc. 1634/10, p. 114.

22 Schwartz 1985, pp. 16–27, 33–39.

23 E. de Heer, "Jan Gillisz van Vliet, 'Plate cutter in Leiden'" in Amsterdam 1996, pp. 6–7, with further literature.

24 Corpus A 34. The provenance of the Mauritshuis painting makes this identification slightly more likely than the alternative possibility that the inventory refers to Rembrandt's earlier picture of the theme, now in the Kunsthalle in Hamburg (Corpus A 12). See The Hague 1997, no. 22.

25 The complexity of these attributions and of the documentary evidence is set out in Corpus, vol. 2, p. 839.

26 Corpus A 38, A 39.

27 For the arguments see Corpus A 24 and The Hague 1997, no. 21. The provenance of the painting points generally in this direction, but the identification is very much compromised by several paintings of this subject by Lievens, one now lost and two certainly from his years in Leiden before 1632.

28 Orlers 1641, p. 376.

29 See the provenance discussions of Rembrandt's *Bust of an Old Woman* (Windsor Castle) and *Self-Portrait* (Walker Art Gallery, Liverpool) in Corpus 1982, pp. 321, 330.

30 Exemplary accounts of the *nexus* between politics, public display, patronage, and collecting at the court of Frederik Hendrik and Amalia van Solms are the twin exhibition publications The Hague 1997 and *Vorstelijk vertoon aan het hof van Frederik Hendrik en Amalia* (exh. cat. Haags Historisch Museum, The Hague, 1997).

31 Jonathan Brown, *Kings and Connoisseurs: Collecting Art in Seventeenth-Century Europe* (Princeton, 1995); and The Hague 1997. In an apparent reference to Charles I's acquisition strategies, Huygens heaped envious scorn on the pretension of "the English, who consider themselves competent to judge [Rubens] just because they've bought a few foreign canvases." Huygens 1897, p. 72; Huygens 1987, p. 80.

32 Huygens 1897, p. 73; Huygens 1987, pp. 80–81.

33 This position has been argued most powerfully by Ernst van de Wetering, "De symbiose van Lievens en Rembrandt" in Leiden 1991, pp. 39–47.

34 Ernst van de Wetering, "Rembrandt's manner: Technique in the service of illusion" in Berlin 1991, pp. 12–39.

35 These are the words of the Leiden poet Dirk Traudenius, who in 1662 published a poem claiming that if Zeuxis were alive to see a painting by Dou, he would be taken in once more; see Sluijter 1988, p. 21. A shield similar to the one in Rembrandt's *History Painting* and Dou's *Painter in His Studio* appears in Dou's *Old Man Writing behind an Easel* (private collection; Sluijter 1988, fig. 22) and *Officer with Arms*

(Szépművészeti Múzeum, Budapest; E.J. Sluijter, *De lof der schilderkunst: Over schilderijen van Gerrit Dou (1613–1675) en een traktaat van Philips Angel uit 1642* [Hilversum, 1993], fig. 15), and in Adriaen van Gaesbeek's *Painter in His Studio* (private collection; *Leidse fijnschilders* [exh. cat. Stedelijk Museum De Lakenhal, Leiden, 1983], no. 17).

36 Van Mander 1604, fol. 28r; *Grondt*, chap. 6.64–65. See Miedema 1973, pp. 178–79. The source is Pliny the Elder, *Natural History*, book 35.63.

37 Van Mander 1604, fol. 26r; *Grondt*, chap. 6.40–43. See Miedema 1973, pp. 170–71.

38 Pliny the Elder, *Natural History*, book 35.58.

39 Van Honthorst's *Youth with a Torch*, probably painted around 1623, may have been a direct source for Lievens; see J.R. Judson, *Gerrit van Honthorst* (The Hague, 1959), no. 161, fig. 16. Orlers' inventory of 1640 included two copies of paintings of musicians by van Honthorst; see Leiden 1976, pp. 17–18.

40 Van Mander 1604, fol. 31r; *Grondt*, chap. 7.27. See Miedema 1973, pp. 190–91. The source is Pliny the Elder, *Natural History*, book 35.138.

41 Recounted by Italian biographers from Ghiberti to Vasari; not in van Mander. For the different accounts, see John Pope-Hennessy, *Italian Gothic Sculpture* (New York, 1985), pp. 205–7, and idem, *Italian Renaissance Sculpture* (New York, 1985), pp. 246–47.

42 This motive for the series is strongly implied by Schama 1999, pp. 242–94.

43 The "series" may indeed have started as just a pair of pictures inspired by Rubens' famous altarpieces of *The Raising of the Cross* and *The Descent from the Cross*, both painted about 1632–33. The first known mentions of the other three paintings occur only in Rembrandt's letters to Huygens of 1636. The etching of Rembrandt's *Descent*, made in 1633 by Jan van Vliet and printed, as Rubens' own engravings were, with a privilege, seems to confirm that the Passion series arose on Rubensian impulses shared by Huygens, Rembrandt, and the stadhouder and his wife.

44 *Libri appendiciarii Bibliothecae Scriverianae, ut et aliae raritates eximiae, picturae videlicet statuae marmoreae, &c.* (Amsterdam, 1663) [copy in Rijksuniversiteit, Leiden], "schilderyen," no. 3: "Twee braave groote stukken van Rembrant."

45 M. Wurfbain, in Leiden 1976, no. S26.

46 Among the other suggested subjects are Saul Giving Arms to David, Coriolanus, the Consul Cerealis and the German Legions, and the Clemency of Titus; for a summary of these and others, see Corpus 1982, p. 112. On balance, the Palamedes identification remains the most compelling, in my view.

47 Martin Kemp, "'Ogni dipintore dipinge se': A Neoplatonic echo in Leonardo's art theory" in *Cultural Aspects of the Italian Renaissance: Essays in Honour of Paul Oskar Kristeller*, edited by C.H. Clough (Manchester, 1976), pp. 311–23.

48 *The Cultures of Collecting*, edited by John Elsner, Roger Cardinal (London, 1994).

49 William W. Robinson, "'This passion for prints': Collecting and connoisseurship in Northern Europe during the seventeenth century" in Boston 1980, pp. xliii–xliv.

50 On Rembrandt's creative use of costume in his self-portraits, see de Winkel 1999. For *tronies*, see Lyckle de Vries, "Tronies and other single figured Netherlandish paintings,' *Leids Kunsthistorisch Jaarboek* 8 (1989), pp. 185–202.

51 B. Bakker, "'Schilderachtig': Discussion of a seventeenth-century term and concept," *Simiolus* 23 (1995), pp. 147–62.

52 Pliny the Elder, *Natural History*, book 35.112. On these lowly themes in Dutch painting of the 1620s, see R.L. Falkenburg, "'Schilderachtig weer' bij Jan van Goyen" in *Jan van Goyen* (exh. cat. Stedelijk Museum De Lakenhal, Leiden, 1996), pp. 60–69.

53 Jan de Bisschop, *Paradigmata graphices variorum artificum* (The Hague, 1671); see van Gelder, Jost 1985, vol. 1, p. 228; vol. 2 (dedication to Jan Six): "en dat meer schilderachtich sij en voor de konst verkieselijck een mismaeckt, out, verrimpelt mensch."

54 Ibid: "een vrouwe-naeckt met een dicken en gheswollen buyck, hangende borsten, kneepen van kousse-banden in de beenen, en veel meer sulcke wanschaepenheyt." De Bisschop's words were closely echoed by van Hoogstraten 1678 (p. 64).

55 Pels 1681, pp. 35–36: "Slappe borsten, / Verwrongen handen, ja de neepen van de worsten / Des ryglijfs in de buik, des kousebands op 't been" (Sagging breasts / Twisted hands, even the sausage pinches / in the corset of the stomach, and in the garter on the leg.)

56 On the portrait of Jacques de Gheyn III and his collection, see Melbourne 1997, no. 8. For the pendant portrait of Maurits Huygens, see Corpus A 57.

57 Israel 1997; J.M. Montias, "Works of art in seventeenth-century Amsterdam: An analysis of subjects and attributions" in *Art in History/History in Art: Studies in Seventeenth-Century Dutch Culture*, edited by D. Freedberg, J. de Vries (Santa Monica, 1991), pp. 331–72.

58 Strauss, van der Meulen 1979, doc. 1629/1.

59 Ibid., doc. 1631/4.

60 J. M. Montias, "Cost and value in seventeenth-century Dutch art," *Art History* 10 (1987), pp. 455–66; E. J. Sluijter, "Jan van Goyen als marktleider, virtuoos en vernieuwer" in *Jan van Goyen* (exh. cat. Stedelijk Museum De Lakenhal, Leiden, 1996), pp. 38–59; R.L. Falkenburg, "Onweer bij Jan van Goyen: Artistieke wedijver en de markt voor het Hollandse landschap in de 17de eeuw," *Nederlands Kunsthistorisch Jaarboek* 48 (1997), pp. 117–61; Westermann 1999.

61 J. K.S. Moes, B.M.A. de Vries, eds., *Stof uit het Leidse verleden: Zeven eeuwen textielnijverheid* (Utrecht, 1991; Leidse Historische Reeks, vol. 5).

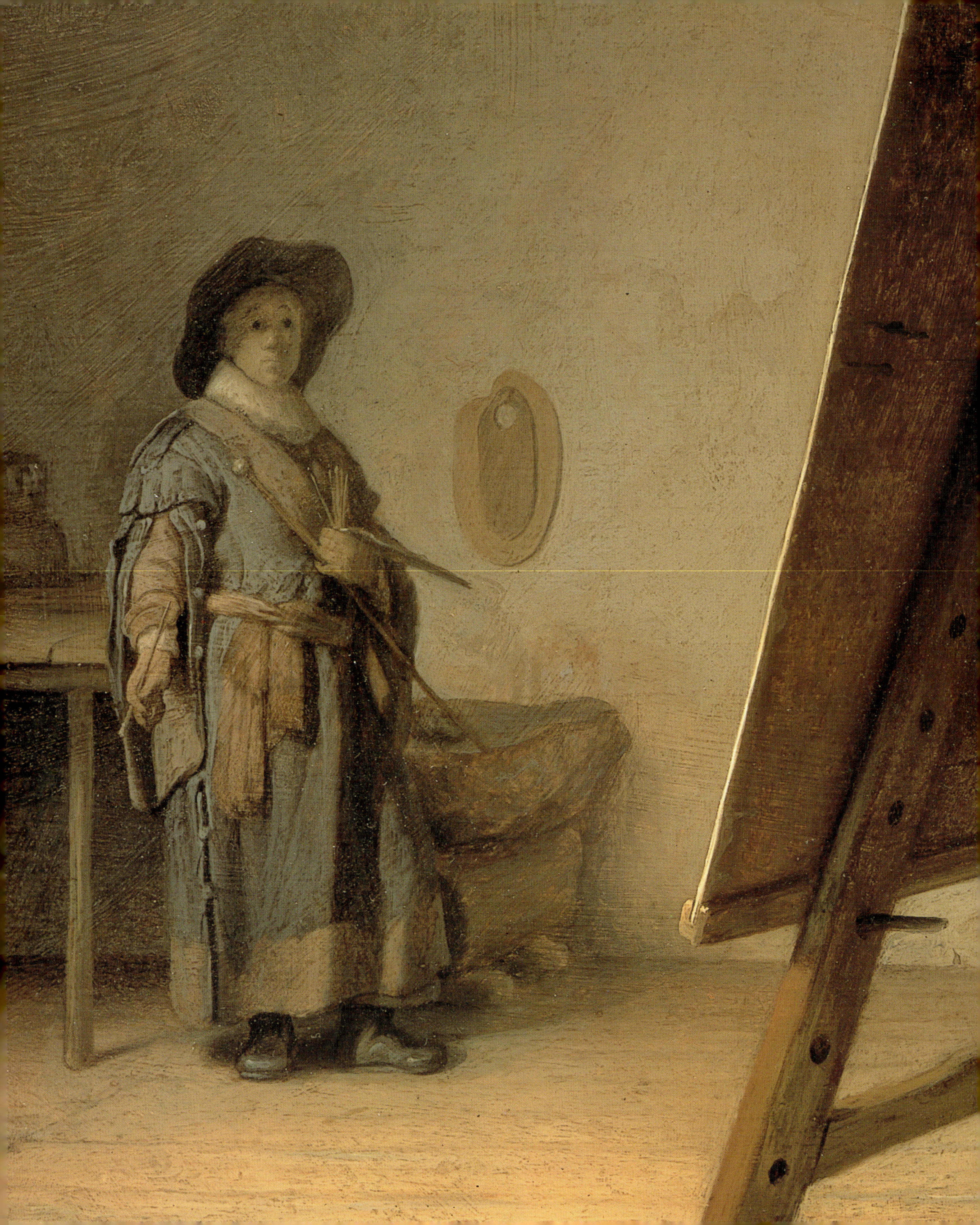

Christopher White

Rembrandt's Technique during the Leiden Years

At the age of about nineteen Rembrandt returned from Amsterdam and set up on his own as a fully-fledged artist. It may well be, as local tradition has it, that he shared a studio with fellow-artist Jan Lievens, one year his junior, who had also returned to Leiden from Amsterdam, about a year earlier. Whatever their working arrangement, there can be no doubt that they were in close communication over their art, which they were pursuing in an entirely independent manner from other local artists. (Their early works, particularly drawings, have sometimes been confused in the past.) They had both undergone training in the studio of Pieter Lastman, a leading history painter in Amsterdam, who unquestionably had a great impact on the manner of both their drawing and painting. Before that, according to the Leiden writer Jan Jansz Orlers, Rembrandt had spent three years in the studio of the little-known Leiden painter Jacob Isaacsz van Swanenburg, an artist of an older generation who painted architectural scenes and diableries in the style of Hieronymus Bosch. Apart from the basic technique of painting, it is difficult to imagine what else he could have imparted to Rembrandt, although it should be pointed out that he had spent a number of years in Italy, and thus might have passed on some knowledge of Italian art to the younger man.

Such is the impact of Rembrandt's early work produced in Leiden, much of it unquestionably original in outlook, that an understandable assumption has developed that his technique in drawing, etching, and painting was no less of his own invention. For example, in 1969, in a round-table discussion of Rembrandt's painting technique, it was said, without contradiction from the other participants, that "each painting may have been a technical creation as well as a pictorial one."[1] But recent research into the master's technique, especially in the field of painting, has proved that the situation is considerably more complicated. In many respects Rembrandt did introduce technical variations of his own when it suited him, but he also followed contemporary techniques and practices.

fig. 44 Rembrandt, *The Artist in His Studio*, 1629 (cat. 4, detail).

Drawing

Drawing played a fundamental role in Rembrandt's practice as an artist from his earliest days, and we have a substantial number of studies that can be attributed to his Leiden years. Although not all are now accepted, Otto Benesch catalogued no less than sixty-three sheets from this period.[2] As can be seen from these works, Rembrandt employed traditional techniques that, to look no further, he would have found in use in the studio of Pieter Lastman, many more of whose drawings certainly existed than the handful known today.[3] And his master's example would have remained before his eyes, since the inventory of Rembrandt's possessions drawn up in 1656 includes two albums of sketches by Lastman, one in pen and the other in red chalk.[4]

Despite the fairly common use of blue paper in Holland during the seventeenth century (it was much favored by Venetian Renaissance artists and, not surprisingly, by the Dutch artists who worked in Italy), Rembrandt eschewed the attractions of color and confined himself to white papers that varied in texture, thickness, and tone. (One group of drawings, executed around 1629 to 1630, appears to have been done on an Italian white paper.[5]) But following Lastman's example, he occasionally prepared the paper with a colored wash, a method he sometimes used for his landscape drawings and his etchings later in his career. No less than five chalk drawings of a bearded old man from this early period (fig. 45; Benesch 18, 20, 39, 41), were executed on a white paper prepared with a pale yellow wash.[6] Nearly all of Lastman's known chalk drawings are on white paper prepared with different colored washes.[7]

Although Rembrandt later abandoned chalk almost entirely in favor of pen and ink, he used it regularly during the Leiden period. There are a number of drawings in both black and red chalk. The latter, which a later pupil, Samuel van Hoogstraten, specifically recommended for drawing "faces, hands or entire nudes from life,"[8] was much favored by Rembrandt at the time for

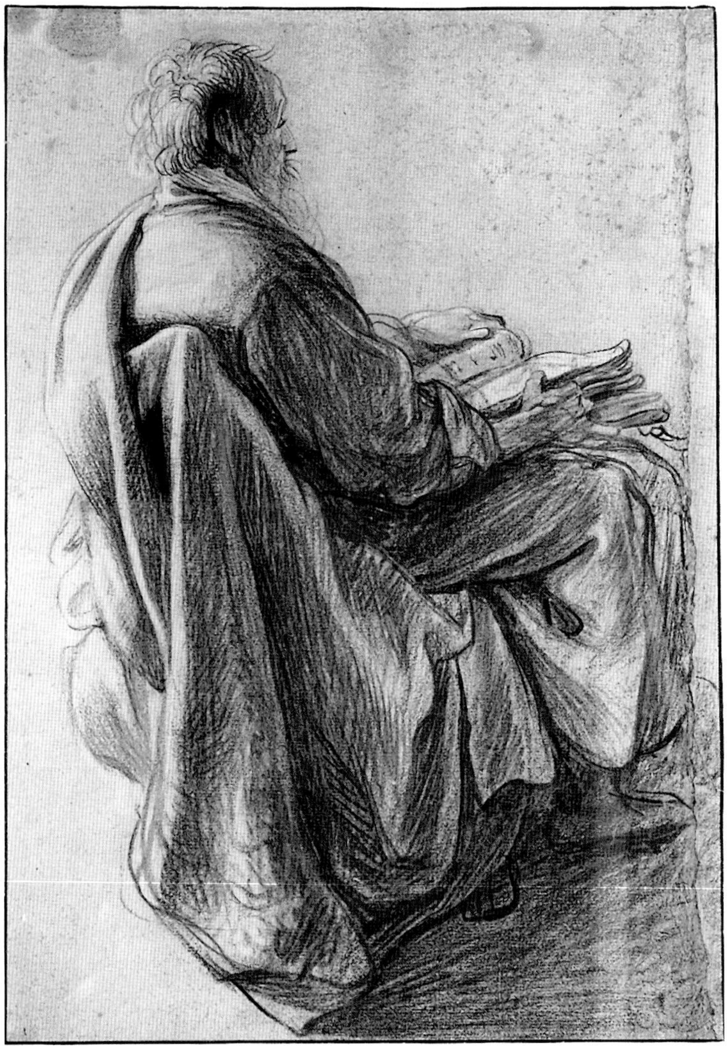

fig. 45 Rembrandt, *Old Man in a Chair*, ca. 1628. Red chalk and brush on tinted paper, 29.5 x 21 cm. Staatliche Museen zu Berlin, Berlin. Benesch 7.

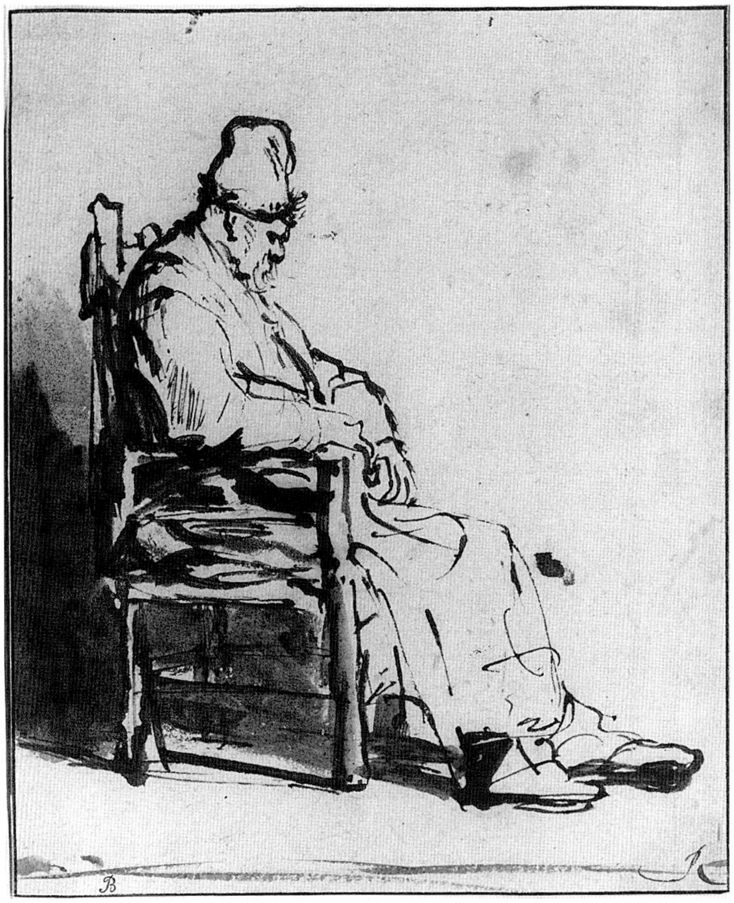

fig. 46 Rembrandt, *Seated Old Man in Profile*, ca. 1626. Pen and brush on paper, 15.2 x 12.8 cm Musée du Louvre, Paris. Benesch 49.

more worked-up figure studies. Following the example of Lastman, Rembrandt sometimes used a combination of black and red chalk, as in three of the studies of a bearded old man (fig. 45 and Benesch 18, 41), and in the portrait of his father (Benesch 56). As a further enrichment to the appearance of the drawing (once again following Lastman's example), he also introduced highlights by the addition of white gouache, the effect of which is particularly apparent in one of the most finished of the studies of a bearded old man (fig. 45), where the light falls on the subject's back and on the open book resting on his knees. He also used white gouache as a means for making corrections, as can be seen in one of the drawings connected with the painting *Judas Returning the Thirty Pieces of Silver* (fig. 24), in which one of the figures (now again visible as a pentimento) was blocked out.

But if in his use of chalk Rembrandt followed other artists, including Lastman, he employed it very much in his own manner. Compared to Lastman's more linear drawing, in which the outline of the figure is clearly established, Rembrandt's method was immediately more variable, as can be seen in the freely sketched study of a *Standing Archer* (Kupferstich-Kabinett, Dresden; Benesch 3), one of his very first chalk drawings. In some chalk studies, such as that of the *Old Man with Arms Extended* (fig. 2a), which was used in the etching *Peter and John at the Gate of the Temple* (cat. 2), and the *Standing Beggar* (Rijksmuseum, Amsterdam; Benesch 30), he merely roughed-in the outline of the figure, creating a sense of form and light with very free, open strokes. In other studies he produced a much higher degree of finish, as in the bearded old man (fig. 45). Even compared to the chalk drawings of Lievens, which he developed in a similar manner from Lastman's example, and which he also drew on paper prepared with a yellowish wash, Rembrandt succeeded in being more pictorial and suggestive, very soon achieving an entirely personal style.[9] The occasional trick of wetting the chalk can be seen as typical of his inventiveness in adapting his materials to his purpose.

Pen and ink was a commonly used technique for drawing in the sixteenth and early seventeenth century, but it became less so in Holland in the latter part of the seventeenth century. Rembrandt used pen and ink with much the same freedom as he drew with chalk, although less often during the Leiden period. Developing what he had seen in Lastman's drawings, but adopting a freer attitude towards the delineation of outline, he exploited the flexibility of the quill pen in order to create a varied, richly expressive line. This is apparent in the eloquent study *Beggar Couple with a Dog* (Benesch 22), in which the depiction of shadows is evocative of etchings by Jacques Callot, an important influence during the early years. Closer to Lastman's drawing style, the *Seated Old Man in Profile* (fig. 46), which, it has been claimed,[10] may be the artist's earliest drawing, shows his determination to achieve flexibility and freedom from his pen; in this instance he also employed the brush to work over some of the outlines.

In keeping with contemporary practice, Rembrandt often used a brush to add washes to pen lines. (Occasionally, as in the portrait of his father [fig. 41] and studies for the etchings of *Saint Paul* [Louvre, Paris; Benesch 15] and *Diana* [British Museum, London; Benesch 21], he added wash to a chalk drawing.) Probably reflecting what he had heard from his master's lips, Samuel van Hoogstraten recommended the use of pen and ink "to sketch your first thoughts on the paper, and a brush, which is damp with water, to create shadows with washes."[11] Although one finds fewer such drawings during the Leiden period — his earliest compositional study, for the *Raising of the Cross* (Museum Boijmans Van Beuningen, Rotterdam; Benesch 6), is in chalk — the two studies for *Judas Returning the Thirty Pieces of Silver* (fig. 58 and Benesch 8) are excellent examples of his ability to realize the pictorial possibilities of combining pen and brown ink and freely applied brown wash. The yellow-brown ink used in these two studies, as well as in other studies of the period, was a special compound, which left grains of pigment visible in the lightly brushed areas.[12] Rembrandt again used this ink in the only landscape drawing executed while he was still in Leiden (Fitzwilliam Museum, Cambridge; Benesch 57a); it helps to create the effect of light playing over the buildings.

Painting

Recent research has revealed much new information about Rembrandt's painting technique.[13] If he is no longer considered the wizard he was once thought to be, he is revealed as an artist who, as part of the current tradition, gradually turned existing materials and processes to his own increasingly personal purposes. The Leiden years saw a clear start on this journey — and it is possible that Rembrandt's studio, site of such experiments, may be recorded in the painting of the *Artist in His Studio* (fig. 44; cat. 4). And it is now clear that in this search for a new painting technique, he worked closely, if not side by side, with Jan Lievens.

With three exceptions (to be mentioned below), the paintings produced in Leiden were executed on panel.[14] In this practice Rembrandt was following the example of his master, Pieter Lastman, who rarely painted on canvas, a support that Rembrandt only started to use after his move to Amsterdam. Examination of

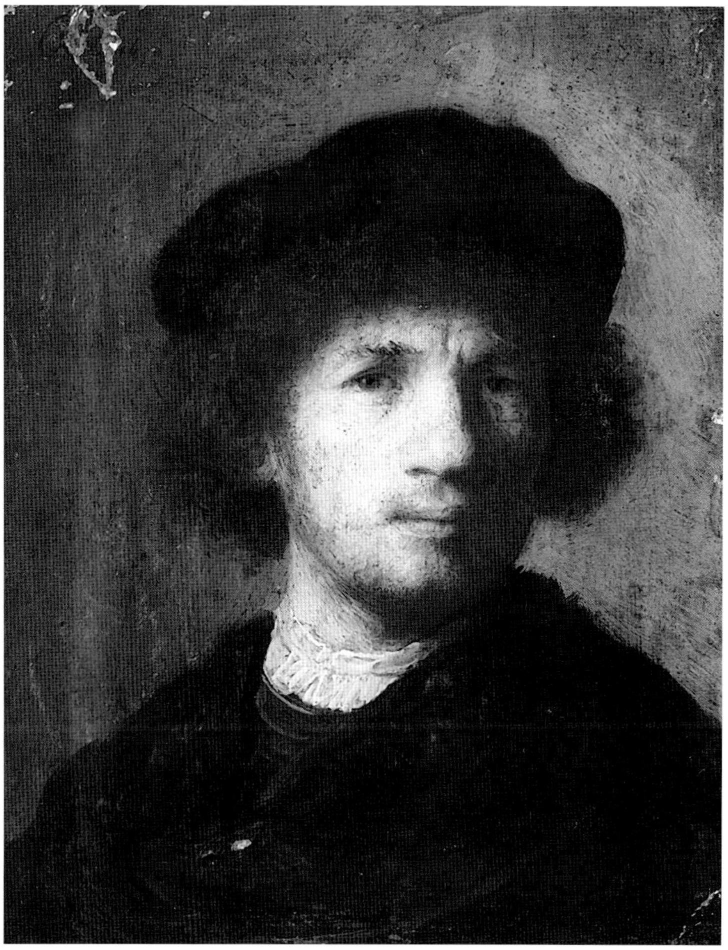

fig. 47 Rembrandt, *Self-Portrait*, 1630. Oil on copper, 15 × 12.2 cm. Nationalmuseum, Stockholm.

the make-up of these panels has proved that they were no different from those used by his contemporaries, and that they were cut to standard sizes, which were commercially available.[15] Most of the panels used by Rembrandt in Leiden were oak, which had in the main been imported into the Netherlands from the Baltic. Only in later years did Rembrandt vary the type of panel he used.

An analysis of Rembrandt's grounds for panel paintings reveals basically the same composition found elsewhere at the time: a first layer of chalk and glue, a mixture already employed by Netherlandish fifteenth and sixteenth century artists, followed by a priming consisting of a thin coat of oil paint. Rather than carry out such preliminary work in the studio, he may well have purchased panels with a ground already laid professionally. From scientific research, Ernst van de Wetering has been able to conclude that "the young Rembrandt in Leiden experimented neither with the appearance nor with the compositions of his grounds."[16]

Exceptions to the paintings on panel include three works executed on copper: a *Self-Portrait* dated 1630 (fig. 47), an *Old Woman Praying* (Ferdinandeum, Salzburg; fig. 8a), and a *Laughing Soldier* (Mauritshuis, The Hague; Corpus B 6). Despite the reservations of the

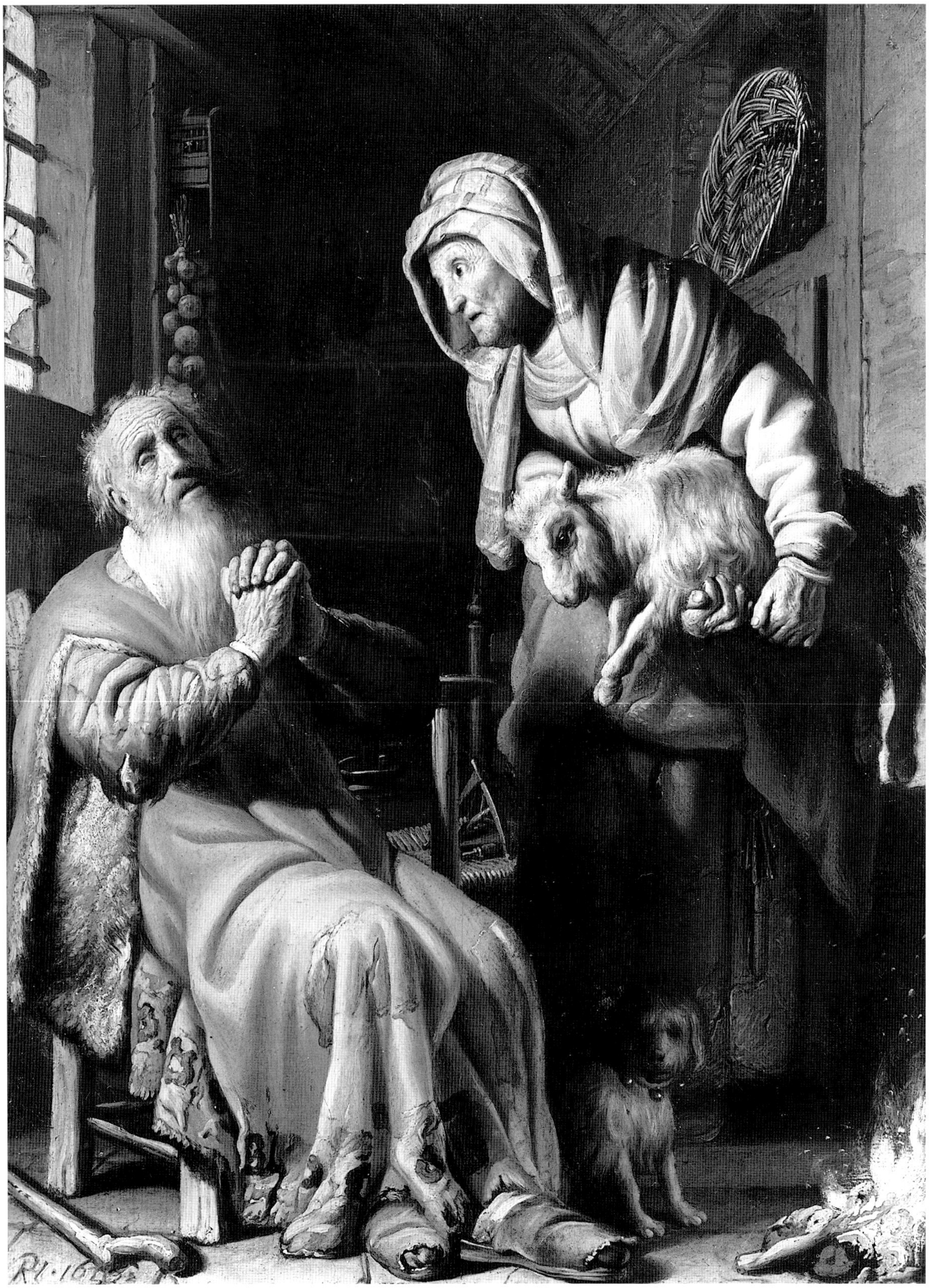

fig. 48 Rembrandt, *Tobit and Anna with the Kid*, 1626. Oil on wood, 39.5 × 30 cm.
Rijksmuseum, Amsterdam.

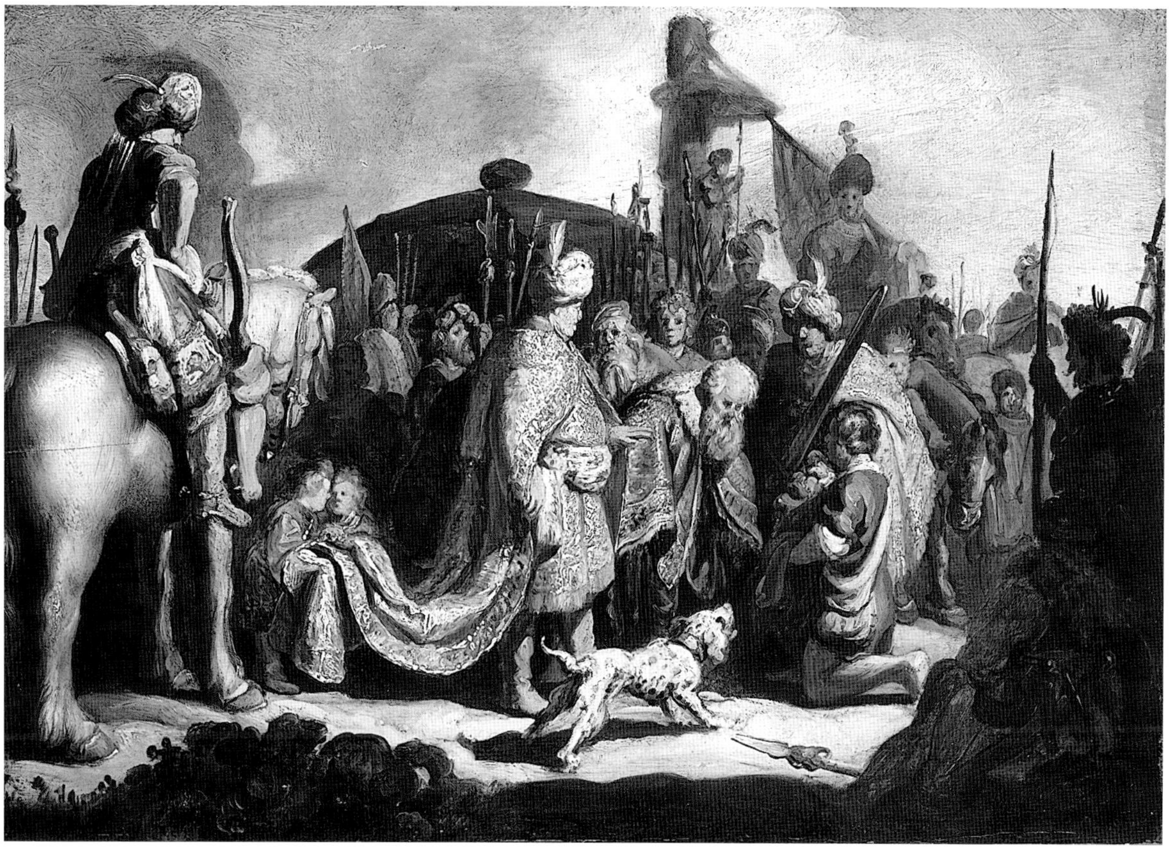

fig. 49 Rembrandt, *David Presenting the Head of Goliath to Saul*, 1627. Oil on wood, 27.2 × 39.6 cm. Kunstmuseum, Basel.

Rembrandt Research Project in the case of two of these works, they are now generally accepted as by Rembrandt.[17] The use of copper as a support was not unusual at the time, but what distinguishes Rembrandt's three works is the application of a thin layer of gold leaf on the chalk and glue ground. This technique was extremely unusual, and so far it has not been discovered in the work of any other artist. Undoubtedly Rembrandt intended to create a glow beneath the surface of the painting, an effect that is particularly visible in the self-portrait in Stockholm, owing to the wearing of the paint surface.

When Rembrandt started to work on his panels, he did not draw in chalk on the panel, as Rubens often did and Lastman did at least once, but instead painted freely in monochrome, apparently over lightly brushed-in lines, to indicate the general composition. This procedure accords with the first two recognized stages of producing a painting in the seventeenth century, "invention" followed by "dead coloring," to be completed with the "working-up" with color in full detail; for the last stage, it seems that Rembrandt followed a set pattern, usually, but not invariably, working from the back to the front of the picture, reserving space for the foreground figures.[18] Thus far Rembrandt was largely following contemporary practice.

One can see more originality in the way he developed or changed the composition in the course of working (to be discussed below) and in his handling of paint. To begin with, his brushwork was clearly modeled on Lastman, but he quickly developed his own more expressive manner in which the varied surface of the paint was molded to suggest the different textures of the materials represented. This was a feature not found in Lastman but that was increasingly used by Rembrandt and Lievens during their Leiden years.

One of Rembrandt's earliest paintings, *Tobit and Anna with the Kid* (fig. 48), dated 1626, already shows a wonderful range of textures precisely suggested by the paint—wrinkled flesh, animal hair, various costume materials, fur lining, flames, wickerwork, and so on. At the same time he was able to set all this detail convincingly within a rich pattern of light, made more subtle by its origination from two sources—the window on the left and the fire in the lower right. One of his favorite tricks, possibly done with the end of the brush, was to scratch lines into the wet paint, revealing the ground, in order to depict details such as hair and fur collars; this was done quite extensively in the early *Historical Subject*, dated 1626 (fig. 26).

It may well be that Lievens, rather than Rembrandt, was the pioneer in developing this system of manipulating paint for optical effects, since Samuel van Hoogstraten goes out of his way to praise the former as an "expert in seeking wonders in smeared pigments,

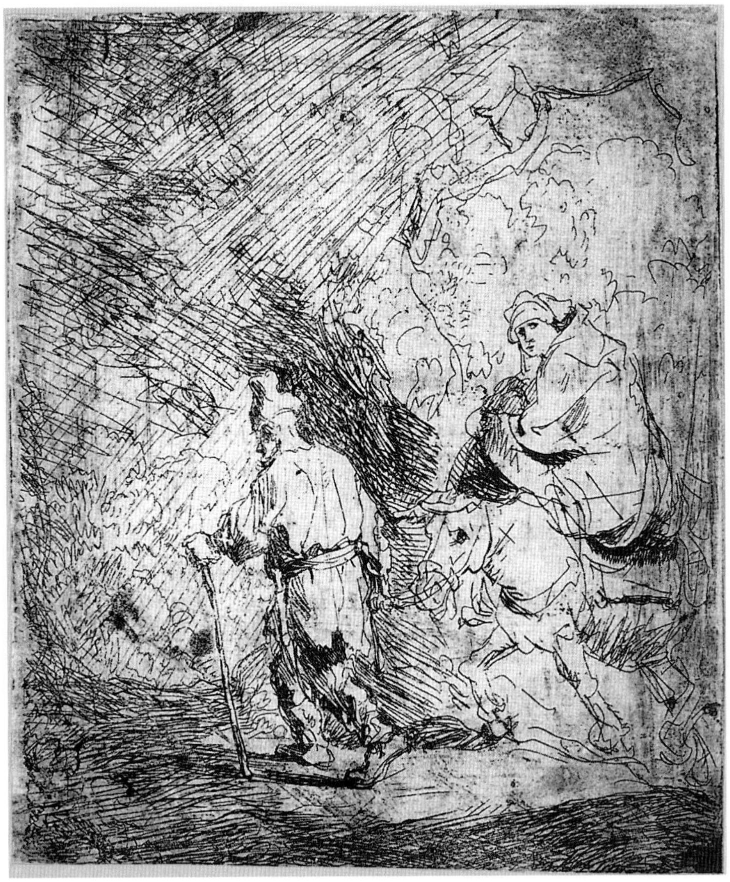

fig. 50 Rembrandt, *Flight into Egypt*, ca. 1627. Etching, 14.6 × 12.2 cm. British Museum, London. Bartsch 54.

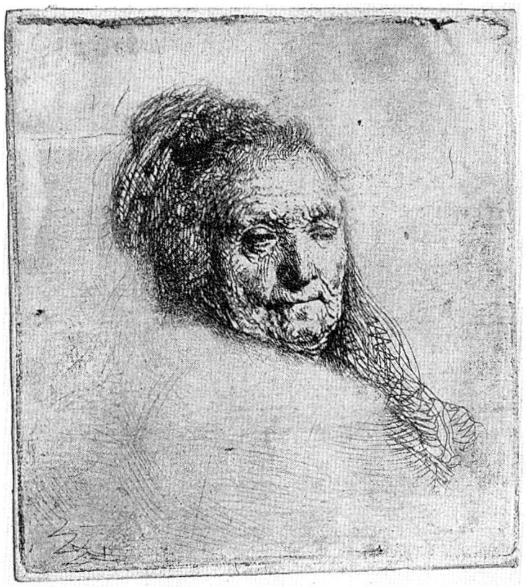

fig. 51 Rembrandt, *An Old Woman (called Rembrandt's Mother)*, 1628. Etching, 6.6 × 6.3 cm. British Museum, London. Bartsch 354 (1st state).

varnishes and oils."[19] And as part of this process, both young artists may have taken to grinding their own colors in order to get the right consistency, so essential for the different textures they sought. Perhaps some evidence that this took place is the grinding stone clearly visible in the background of *Artist in His Studio* (fig. 44; cat. 4).

Depending on the painting's purpose, it may be that in *David Presenting the Head of Goliath to Saul* (fig. 49), dated 1627, Rembrandt was experimenting in varying the degree of finish, in much the same way he was to do in his etchings two years later. Although it has the general appearance of an oil sketch, and is unlike any other work of these years, the picture is fully realized, in both form and color. It is — or was, since it has been cut at the bottom — approximately the same size as several other Leiden pictures, such as *Tobit and Anna with the Kid*. If it is not a preliminary sketch for an unknown work, as has sometimes been argued — and for which there is some material evidence (see below) — it is distinguished from other finished works of the period by its looser, much freer touch in handling, and by the presence of some thickly-painted areas executed wet-in-wet.

Rembrandt's earliest works, among them *Tobit and Anna with the Kid,* were rich in local color, but after 1629 he became increasingly preoccupied with creating a pattern of chiaroscuro, suggestive of air and space. The same feature can be seen in his etchings of these years, for example, *Christ Disputing with the Doctors* (cat. 9) of 1630, which will be discussed below. In the same year he painted *Jeremiah Lamenting the Destruction of Jerusalem* (cat. 14), in which the color is less varied and more subdued, but the sense of depth and atmosphere is greatly enhanced. Yet he still used a varied patina of paint, although one more directed at catching highlights — such as those on the richly embroidered borders of the old man's clothes, the costly carpet, and the silver-gilt vessels beside Jeremiah — than at describing individual textures, as seen in earlier works. The handling of paint, with the introduction of further refinements, was to play an ever more fundamental part in Rembrandt's painting, increasingly setting him apart from his contemporaries.

Etching

Rembrandt appears to have taken up the practice of etching very soon after his return to Leiden, and it was to grow into an independent medium, distinct in purpose from his painting. Although there are, as will be seen, parallels between the two media, his etching gradually took on its own personal language.

Apart from a few plates from early in his career, very probably executed by Jan van Vliet after Rembrandt rather than by the master himself, Rembrandt was not interested in reproductive printmaking. Almost from the start, he showed as much, if not more, initiative in refining existing techniques as he had done in painting and drawing.[20] His master in etching, if he in fact had one, remains unknown; Lastman got no closer to the process than producing some preparatory drawings for etchings carried out by an anonymous printmaker. But as models there were, of course, numerous earlier printmakers, such as Andrea Mantegna, Albrecht Dürer, Lucas van Leyden, Jacques Callot, and Antonio Tempesta, whose works Rembrandt closely studied in different and specific ways. But it is one thing to study the finished result, and quite another to have the benefit of an experienced practitioner to teach various "tricks of the trade," which in the case of etching have a touch of alchemy about them. In matters of technique the most inventive and experimental artist of an earlier generation was unquestionably Hercules Segers. But although there was only one direct contact in the work of the two artists—when later in his career Rembrandt reworked Segers' plate of *Tobias and the Angel*, transforming the subject into a *Flight into Egypt* (Bartsch 56)—Segers appears to have acted as a general inspiration to the younger artist in his freer, more inventive attitude to technique and working methods.[21]

From the existing copper plates etched by Rembrandt it is possible to determine that he used copper of a standard thickness, which could have been obtained from the usual sources.[22] However, he showed unorthodoxy from the beginning in his habit of cutting down or even cutting up a plate if he was not satisfied. The small plate of *Christ Disputing with the Doctors*, 1630, which will be discussed below, was reduced in size in the course of work. In the case of the earlier *Flight into Egypt* (fig. 50), he took the subject no further than a sketch, before cutting up the plate and retaining only two small pieces; on one he reworked the figure of Saint Joseph into a study of a tramping peasant, and on the other he etched a small self-portrait (Bartsch 5). Another plate was cut up into five pieces, which contained separate, individually developed studies of various men (Bartsch 366). He was also experimental in the manner in which he printed from his plates, often, as in the first two states of *Christ Disputing with the Doctors* (figs. 53, 54), leaving the edges rough, as if he had postponed polishing because he was eager to see the results.

Many professional etchers in the seventeenth century, such as Callot, used a hard ground on their plates, which allowed them to achieve the clean, regular rhythm of an engraved line made with the burin. From a recipe published in England in 1660 and described as "the Ground of Rinebrant of Rein,"[23] it seems that Rembrandt used a softer ground, which allowed him to draw with much greater freedom, thereby realizing the essential difference between an engraved and an etched line. As will be seen, it also made the act of working with the etching needle closer to drawing with the pen. Where acids were concerned, Rembrandt had a number of options, but since nearly all his plates are very finely bitten, he probably used mordant, which bites slowly and gives the precision he sought, rather than nitric acid, which works fast, but spreads beneath the ground, widening and coarsening the lines.

Rembrandt's Leiden years were marked by his attempt, not entirely successful, to establish etching as an independent medium distinct from painting and drawing, and as a result he very quickly went his own way, producing work quite unlike that of his contemporaries. It is significant that although many of his Leiden plates were very small and were no more than sketches, they amount to more than a quarter of his etched oeuvre, which was produced over some thirty-five years. What must be Rembrandt's first etching is, by his standards, the conventionally executed, cleanly bitten plate of the *Circumcision*,[24] which the inscription states was published in Leiden by J.P. Berendrecht; about the same time the latter published an etching in a very similar style by Jan Lievens of *John the Evangelist* (Hollstein 9), an acknowledgement that the young artists were establishing themselves in their home town. Essentially linear in style, both works had the general appearance of engraving, an effect sought by many contemporary etchers. Rembrandt quickly turned away from this manner and aimed at the effect of drawing, as can be seen in his experimental *Flight into Egypt* (fig. 50) of about 1627. Etched on a roughly surfaced plate, which as far as the loosely drawn lines would allow sought greater tonal contrasts, this work already has much of the unique character that Filippo Baldinucci in 1686 admired in Rembrandt, who "with certain scrawls and scribbles and irregular strokes and without outline" achieved "a deep chiaroscuro of great vigor" and "a picturesque flavor."[25]

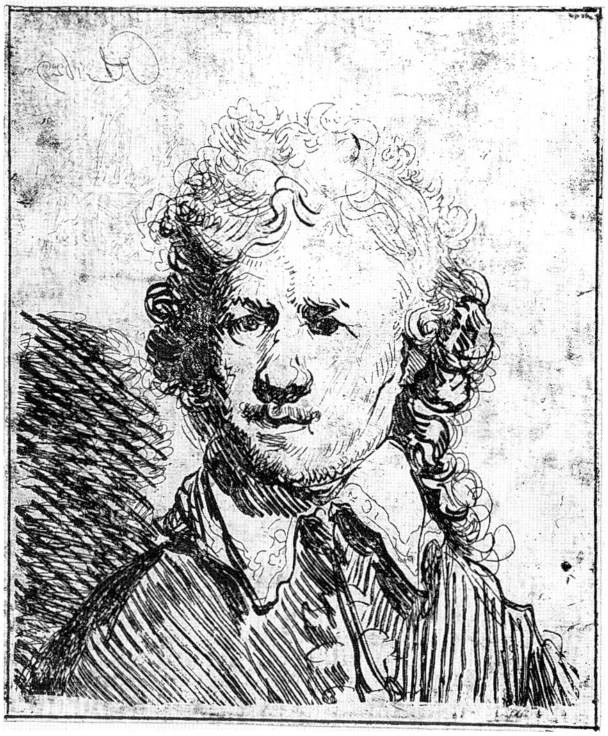

fig. 52 Rembrandt, *Self-Portrait*, 1629 (cat. 1).

In 1628, the year of his first dated etchings, Rembrandt produced two small plates of his *Mother* (fig. 51 and Bartsch 352) that are far more finished than previous works. Both are very minutely hatched with a loose, open stroke typical of true etching, and the features of the face were drawn in with the delicacy and precision of silverpoint drawings seen at the time in the work of older artists such as Hendrick Goltzius and Jacques de Gheyn. But clearly Rembrandt felt constricted by the small scale required for such finely drawn work, and in the following year he produced several much larger plates, such as *Peter and John at the Gate of the Temple* (cat. 2), which are very different in appearance; the rough execution and the degree of foul biting suggests that they were all intended as experiments.[26] Unquestionably the most original and experimental is the *Self-Portrait* (fig. 52; cat. 1), dated 1629, for which he used an already worked, scraped-down plate. (As in his painting, particularly in his self-portraits, Rembrandt was always reluctant to waste good copper, panel, or canvas.) In order to get the weight and width of a drawn as opposed to an etched line, which would allow him to work on a larger scale, he used a double-pointed instrument, very probably a quill-pen, instead of the conventional etching needle. This technique produced much bolder lines, but although it resulted in a powerful image, it could not serve as a satisfactory recipe for the future, since the widely bitten lines did not hold the ink consistently.

The next year he returned to very small plates executed in the same fine manner used for his portraits of his *Mother* (fig. 51 and Bartsch 352). The carefully worked up *Christ Disputing with the Doctors* (cat. 9; figs. 28–30), which aimed for the chiaroscuro of a monochrome painting rather than the effect of a drawing, set the pattern for the immediate future. But his plates, while maintaining the degree of finish, gradually increased in size to works such as the two later portraits of his *Mother* (Bartsch 343 and 348) and two nudes, a *Naked Woman Seated on a Mound* (fig. 43) and *Diana at the Bath* (Bartsch 201), all executed about 1631, culminating in the monumental *Raising of Lazarus* (Bartsch 73), possibly already begun before he left Leiden. These were essentially etchings done in emulation of a monochrome painting; a true etcher's style was yet to be developed.

By the time Rembrandt moved permanently to Amsterdam in 1631, his existing oeuvre of nearly one hundred plates can be said to have already justified Baldinucci's tribute to "the most bizarre manner which he invented for engraving on copper with acid," which was "all his own, neither used again by others, nor seen again."[27]

Working method

Rembrandt distinguished himself from other artists in the way he conceived and evolved his subjects. The actual act of working on panel, canvas, or copper was often either no more than a first stage in developing an idea not precisely formulated in his mind or a process that stimulated him to modify the work in the course of execution. But in claiming this, it has to be borne in mind that, at least in the medium of paint, because of the concentration of current research on Rembrandt, we know much more about his technique and procedure than we do about those of other artists of the period.

Rembrandt's attitude had a direct bearing on his conception of the role of drawing.[28] For many if not most artists, drawing was primarily a means of preparing a painting or print. In Rembrandt's case, drawings that closely relate to paintings or prints form only a very small proportion of his total drawn oeuvre. During the Leiden years there are two undoubted such working drawings, both for etchings and both of which were indented for transfer: *Saint Paul* (Louvre, Paris; Benesch 15) and *Diana at the Bath* (British Museum, London; Benesch 21). But the latter drawing appears to have started as a straightforward study from the nude model that was subsequently transformed into a specific subject. The three compositional studies for the painting *Judas Returning the Thirty Pieces of Silver* (fig. 58 and Benesch 6, 8), to be discussed below, are rare examples of the kind of working drawing found so frequently in the work of Rubens, but even here they are unusual since they were made during the course of painting. (One of these, Benesch 6, contains a compositional sketch for another composition, the *Raising of the Cross*, on the other side of the sheet.)

The role of drawing changed over the course of Rembrandt's career, but during the Leiden years the larger proportion was devoted to figure studies. At the outset of his career, drawing served as his method of familiarizing himself with the diversity of the human figure as well as studying the range of facial expression. These studies provided a bank of knowledge to which he could subsequently refer, either taking over a figure unchanged or modifying it according to need. As already mentioned, the largest group were the chalk drawings of bearded old men. Whether or not it had been made with this purpose from the start, the most highly finished of these (fig. 45) was used for one of the figures in the painting of *Two Scholars in Conversation* (fig. 20). Another (Benesch 20) was only used some years later, when it served for the figure of Jacob in the oil sketch *Joseph Telling His Dreams* (Corpus A 66), and the subsequent etching of 1638 (Bartsch 37). A more freely sketched figure of an old man with arms outstretched served as the figure of Saint Peter in the etching *Peter and John at the Gate of the Temple* (see fig. 2a and cat. 2). Other studies had less tangible connections. A pen drawing of an elderly couple in profile, walking (Benesch 22), of about 1629, finds some echoes in the etching of the same subject (Bartsch 165) of a year or two later. Although one can find more connections with paintings or etchings in this early group than in the drawings he made after he moved to Amsterdam, it must be concluded that his emphasis was not on making preparatory studies.

Unlike many other artists, both past and contemporary, Rembrandt usually went to work directly on the panel, canvas, or copper without the aid of preparatory drawings. He was definitely one of those artists, as described by Karel van Mander, who "are used to drawing fluently by hand on their panels what they have already seen painted in their mind's eye."[29] This sometimes led him to work in stages, as well as to make substantial modifications as he proceeded. This method does not appear to have been used by either Lastman or Lievens, who both seem to have been fully

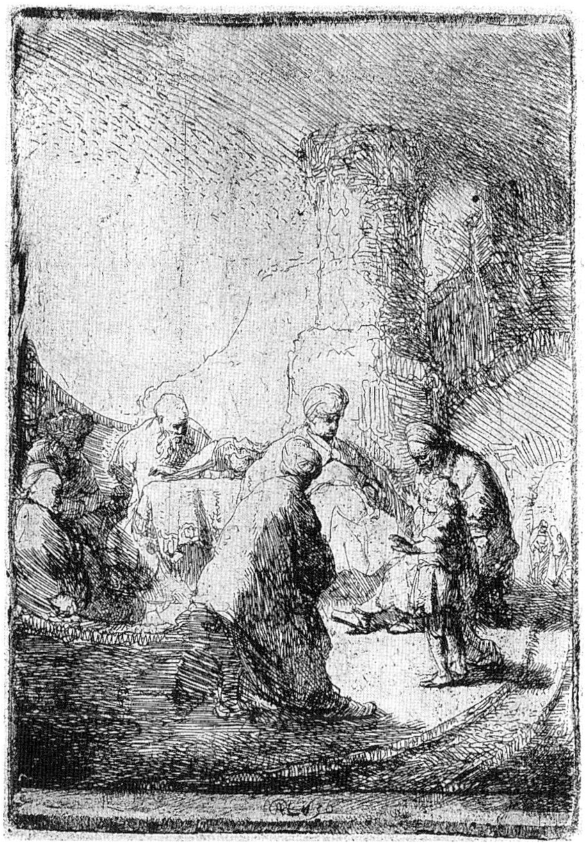

fig. 53 Rembrandt, *Christ Disputing with the Doctors* (1st state), 1630. Etching, 10.8 x 7.8 cm. British Museum, London. Bartsch 66.

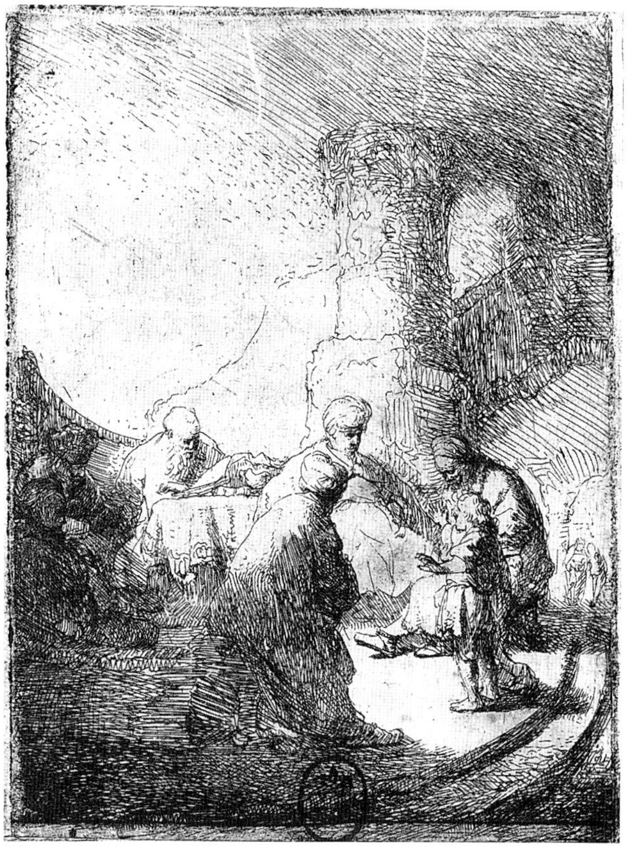

fig. 54 Rembrandt, *Christ Disputing with the Doctors* (2nd state), 1630 (cat. 9).

prepared before they started painting; the X-radiograph of at least one painting by the latter, to be mentioned below, confirms this conclusion.

Thanks to impressions taken during execution, the practice of working in stages has always been clear in Rembrandt's etchings; although different working states of plates by other artists are known, Rembrandt was unique in proceeding quite so regularly state by state. The wish to stop and look at what he had done was essential to the way he worked. But whereas biting one area of a plate after another was relatively straightforward, making corrections to what was already there was more troublesome, since it required careful scraping down and burnishing of the copper. One method he adopted in order to avoid the necessity of making corrections was, before finally committing himself, to draw in chalk a possible solution on an impression from the unfinished plate. For example, on an impression of the first state of one of the small portraits of his mother of 1628 (Bartsch 352), he drew with chalk the hood and suggestions of the shoulders, which at this stage was the only completed part of the etching; this solution apparently did not please him, and he cut down the plate so that the subject was, in its finished form, confined to a study of the head.

His practice of working by stages is illustrated in the other portrait of his mother (fig. 51) dated 1628. In the first state he drew in the

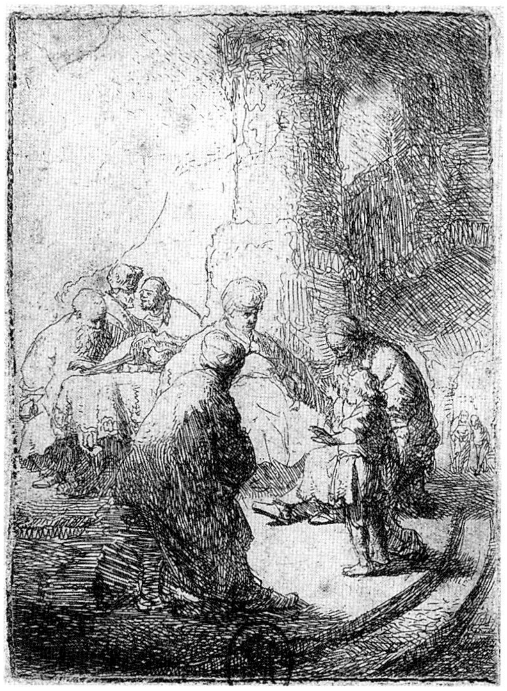

fig. 55 Rembrandt, *Christ Disputing with the Doctors* (3rd state), 1630. Etching, 8.9 x 6.8 cm. British Museum, London. Bartsch 66.

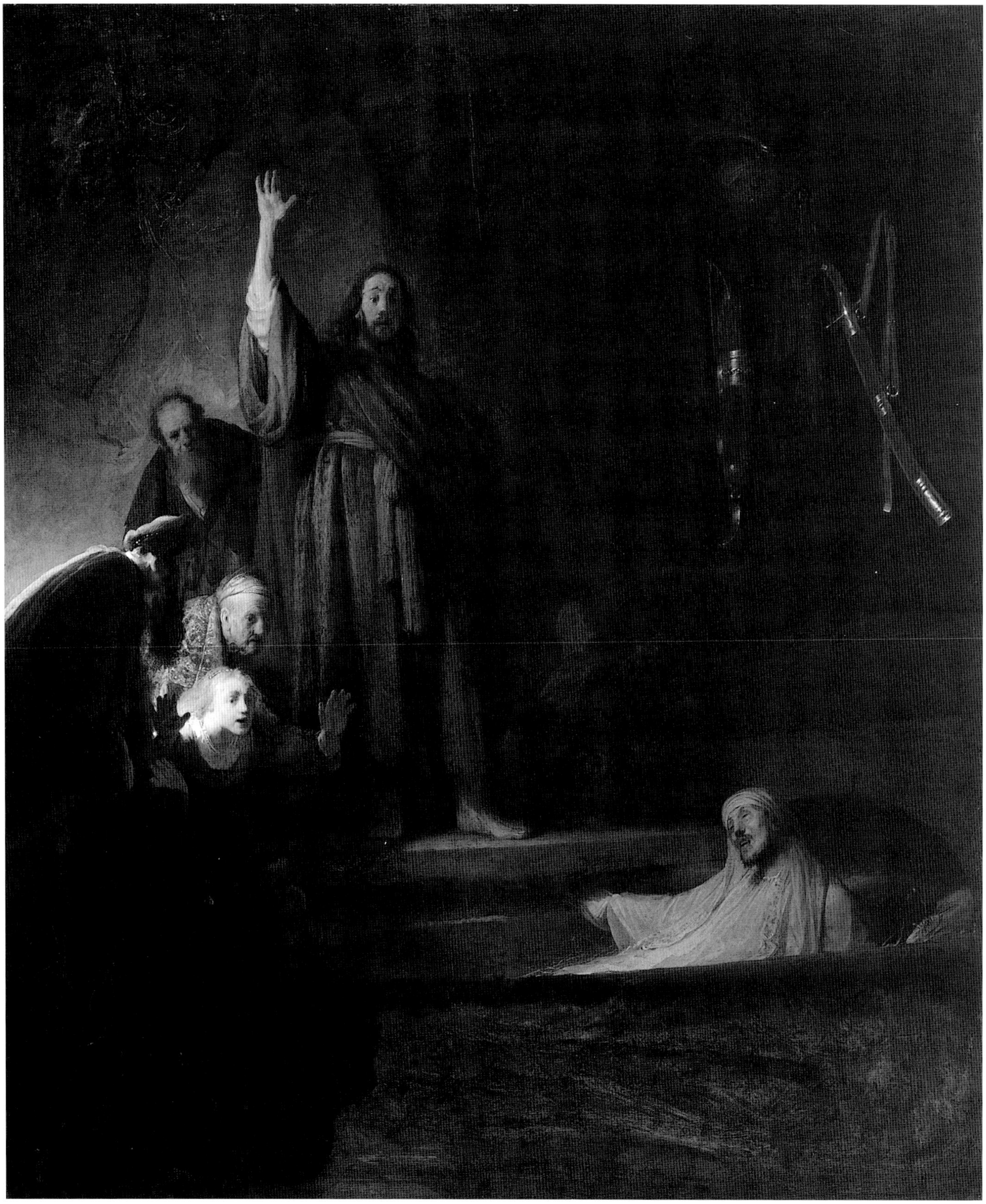

fig. 59 Rembrandt, *The Raising of Lazarus*, ca. 1630. Oil on wood, 96.4 × 81.3 cm.
Los Angeles County Museum of Art.

when the same degree of scientific research has been carried out on the work of Rembrandt's contemporaries. In the meantime it can be supported by at least one example. Jan Lievens was working on a similar composition of the *Raising of Lazarus* (fig. 72) at about the same time as Rembrandt was developing his painting, but X-radiographs of the former do not reveal that any changes were made during the course of execution.[36]

By the time Rembrandt made his final move to Amsterdam, probably sometime in 1631, he had established himself as a name to reckon with. The six formative years in Leiden saw both a realization of his potential to become a great and original artist, and his thorough mastery of the various techniques of painting, drawing, and etching, which he succeeded in molding to his own purposes. It is difficult to think of another artist in the history of art who had a greater feel for the intrinsic qualities of each medium in which he worked, and who so quickly went about achieving it.

1 Stated by the conservator Richard Buck; Chicago 1973, p. 94.
2 Benesch 1973, vol. 1. For recent discussions of the Leiden drawings, see, for example, Schatborn 1985; Schatborn 1989; Martin Royalton-Kisch, *Drawings by Rembrandt and His Circle in the British Museum* (London, 1992).
3 Rembrandt's drawing technique was discussed in Otto Benesch, *Rembrandt: Selected Drawings* (London, 1947). See also, for example, *Dutch Figure Drawings from the Seventeenth Century* (exh. cat. Rijksmuseum, Amsterdam; National Gallery of Art, Washington, 1981–82). For Lastman's drawings, see Peter Schatborn, "Tekeningen van Pieter Lastman" in Amsterdam 1991, pp. 132–75.
4 Strauss, van der Meulen 1979, p. 377, nos. 263 ("Een dito [boeckie], vol schetsen van Pieter Lasman"), 264 ("Een dito van Lasman met root krijt").
5 Schatborn 1989, p. 125.
6 For a list of these drawings, see Schatborn 1985, p. 24 note 6.
7 See Amsterdam 1991, nos. 30–36.
8 Van Hoogstraten 1678, p. 31: "Maer tot het teykenen van tronien, handen, of geheele naekten na't leven, moogt gy gesmijdich root krijt op wit papier gebruiken."
9 For Rembrandt and Lievens, see Leiden 1991.
10 Schatborn 1989, p. 118.
11 Van Hoogstraten 1678, p. 31: "uw eerste gedachten op't papier te schetsen, en de schaduwen met een pinseel, en't zelve vocht met water, aen te zabberen".
12 This was observed in Schatborn 1985, under no. 5.
13 The most extensive study of Rembrandt's painting technique, to which this essay is much indebted, has been carried out by Ernst van de Wetering (van de Wetering 1997); his conclusions (see chapter 2 for the Leiden years) are largely developed from his contributions to the Rembrandt Research Project (Corpus 1982). For other valuable contributions to the subject, see M. Ainsworth et al., *Art and Radiography: Insights into the Genesis of Paintings by Rembrandt, Van Dyck and Vermeer* (New York, 1982); and New York 1995, vol. 1, by H. von Sonnenburg.
14 *Christ on the Cross* (Le Mas d'Agenais; fig. 34), dated 1631, was transferred from wood onto canvas.
15 Van de Wetering 1997, p. 14, in which research on the types and sizes of the panels is discussed.
16 Van de Wetering 1997, p. 21.
17 For the most recent discussion of the technique of Rembrandt's three paintings on copper, see Isabel Horovitz, "The materials and techniques of European paintings on copper supports" in *Copper as Canvas: Two Centuries of Masterpiece Paintings on Copper 1575–1775* (exh. cat. Phoenix Art Museum et al., 1998–99), p. 79, no. 46. See also W. Froentjes, "Schilderde Rembrandt op goud," *Oud Holland* 84 (1969), pp. 233–37; and de Vries et al. 1978, pp. 49–55.
18 This is a simplification of a more complicated situation; see van de Wetering 1997, pp. 23–44.
19 Van Hoogstraten 1678, p. 238: "In d'aengesmeerde verwen, vernissen en olyen wonderen te zoeken, van *Jan Lievens* dapper t'huis." See van de Wetering 1997, pp. 173–78 for a detailed discussion of this phenomenon.
20 For Rembrandt's etching technique, see White 1999. For more on earlier and contemporary printmakers, see Münz 1952 and Ackley 1980.
21 For Rembrandt and Segers, see White 1999, pp. 5–6.
22 For an examination of Rembrandt's plates, see Hinterding 1993.
23 Münz 1952, p. 208.
24 White, Boon 1969, vol. 18, p. 165 [no. S398, ca. 1626]; repr. vol. 19, p. 277.
25 Baldinucci 1686, p. 80: "con certi freghi, e freghetti, e tratti irregolari, e senza dintorno, facendo però risultare dal tutto un chiaro scuro profondo, e di gran forza, ed un gusto pittoresco fino all'ultimo segno".
26 It has been suggested that these particular works were executed on zinc plates; see White 1999, p. 6.
27 Baldinucci 1686, p. 80: "fu una bizzarrissima maniera, ch'egli s'inventò, d'intagliare in rame all'acqua forte, ancor questa tutta sua propria, ne più usata da altri, ne più veduta".
28 See, for example, Jeroen Giltaij, "The function of Rembrandt's drawings," *Master Drawings* 27 (1989), pp. 111–17.
29 Van Mander 1604, Grondt chap. 12.4: "Gaen toe, en uyt der handt teyckenen veerdich / Op hun penneelen, t'ghene nae behooren / In hun Ide' is geschildert te vooren." See Miedema 1973, vol. 1, pp. 252–53.
30 See Corpus 1982, pp. 31–33.
31 See Corpus 1982, p. 131.
32 For a clear description of the different stages of evolution of this painting, see London 1988, no. 1.
33 In addition to the discussion under Corpus A 30, see Los Angeles 1991. Van de Wetering 1997, p. 41, suggests that the existing subject may even have been painted over another subject.
34 See White 1999, figs. 31–33.
35 This was suggested in Corpus 1982, no. A 30, but disputed by Richard Rand in Los Angeles 1991, p. 17.
36 Los Angeles 1991, p. 35, fig. 4.

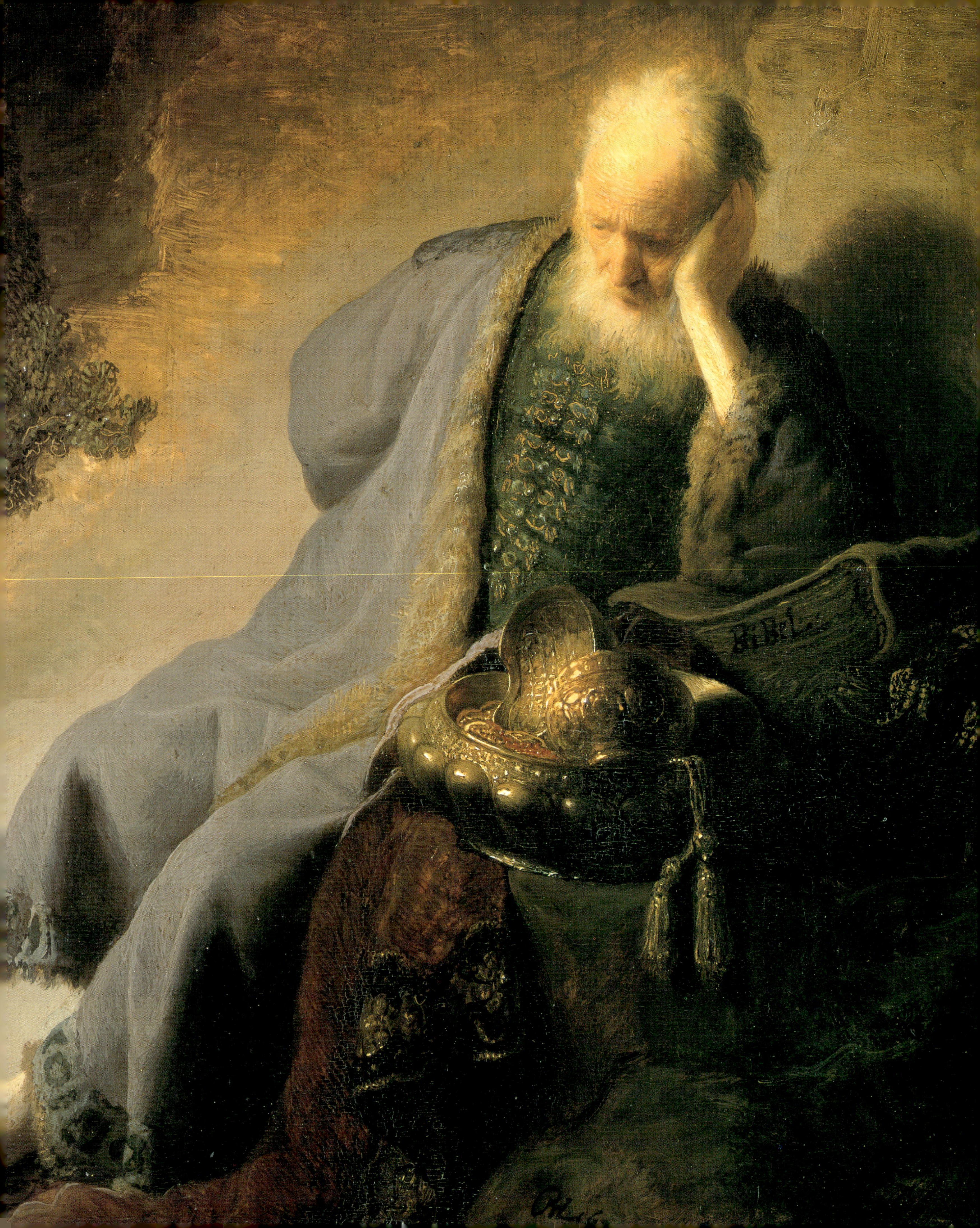
BiBel

Alan Chong

The Myth of Young Genius: Understanding Rembrandt's Early Career

This exhibition explores the emergence of Rembrandt as a fully mature artist at the end of his stay in his native Leiden. Or, put in different terms, it adumbrates the moment when Rembrandt became recognizable as Rembrandt, the great artist now familiar to us. From the beginning of his career, Rembrandt was a personality, not simply a remarkably talented artist or an attribution assigned to individual works of art. And as he commanded the attention of critics and writers, he also stirred controversy. The critical response to Rembrandt's early career has not been fully treated, perhaps because scholars have tended to survey the critical writing of specific periods.[1] However, the critical history of Rembrandt's training, education, and early patronage may have had an impact on the understanding of the nature of artists generally.

The earliest descriptions of Rembrandt suggest that he possessed prodigious natural abilities. In January 1628, when Rembrandt was twenty-one, the lawyer Arnold Buchelius jotted a brief line in his diary, "Also, a miller's son in Leiden is esteemed highly, although prematurely" (Molitoris etiam Leidensis filius magni fit, sed ante tempus).[2] Although Buchelius did not seem to know or remember Rembrandt's name, he captured an early aspect of his celebrity: his father's occupation. Buchelius also injected a note of censure by suggesting that Rembrandt was a precocious talent who had gained recognition before his skills were fully developed. Perhaps, too, he thought that Rembrandt's abilities were not being directed and trained properly.

The secretary to stadhouder Frederik Hendrik, Constantijn Huygens (fig. 61), wrote a short account of Jan Lievens and Rembrandt in his autobiography of 1631 (see Appendix). Like Buchelius, Huygens emphasized that Rembrandt's father was a miller, and thus came from a simple background. Much more enthusiastic about the artist's accomplishments, Huygens called Lievens and Rembrandt

fig. 60 Rembrandt, *Jeremiah Lamenting the Destruction of Jerusalem* (cat. 14, detail).

> a notable pair of youths from Leiden. Were I to say that they were the only ones among all mortals who have equaled what I have formerly described [in biographies of earlier artists], I would still be greatly underestimating the merits of these men. And were I to say that they would surpass them in a short time, I would not be adding anything to what the best connoisseurs have already predicted for each of them, based on such astounding beginnings.

Huygens already speaks of "Rembrandt" without a surname—a practice the artist himself would adopt in his signatures after 1633—as though he recognized the artist's celebrity status. In Huygens' text, Lievens is called "Johannes Lievens" and even the acknowledged masters Rubens and Michelangelo are referred to by their last names.

Huygens reported that Lievens and Rembrandt came from humble backgrounds, were self-taught, and practiced their profession with exceptional diligence. However, he warned that because they had refused to visit Italy their education would remain incomplete and their art short of perfection. He also fretted that they may have been working too hard for their own good. Although Huygens' comments remained unknown until his autobiography was discovered at the end of the 1800s, his observations were echoed by many contemporary observers; many of his themes had a surprising longevity in critical writing. Almost all critics agreed that Rembrandt was an extraordinary talent, although the shifting nature of criticism meant that his actual work was appreciated in very different ways.

Huygens' description of Rembrandt and Lievens is a remarkable document that can be appreciated as a subtle work of Latin literature, rather than as just a few interesting observations on Rembrandt's early painting, *Judas Returning the Thirty Pieces of Silver* (fig. 24). The passage on the two Leiden artists culminates Huygens' discussion of the artists he studied with or met, and is therefore integral to his autobiography. The commentary on

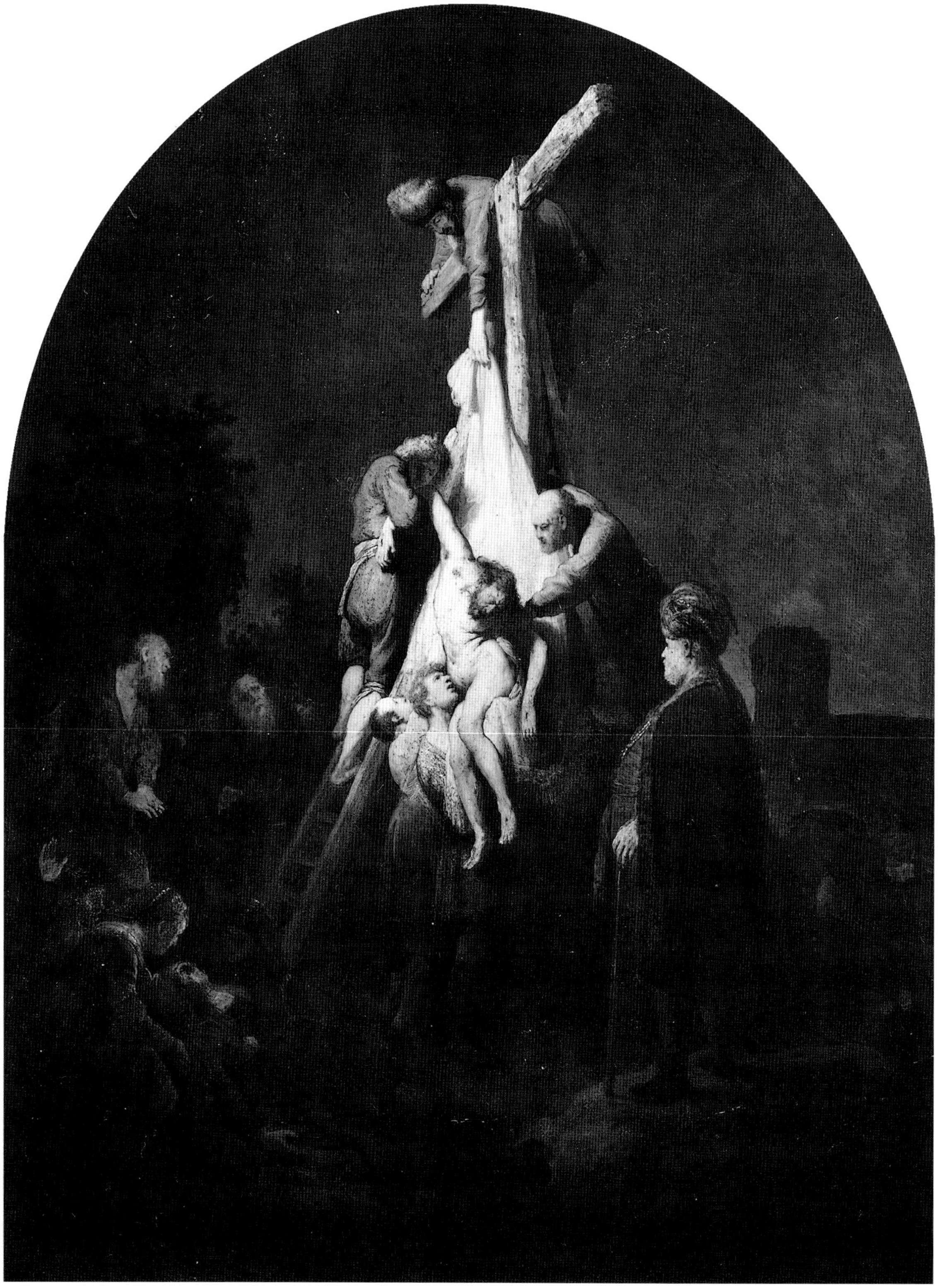

fig. 65 Rembrandt, *Descent from the Cross*, ca. 1633. Oil on wood, 92 × 69.3 cm.
Bayerische Staatsgemäldesammlungen, Munich.

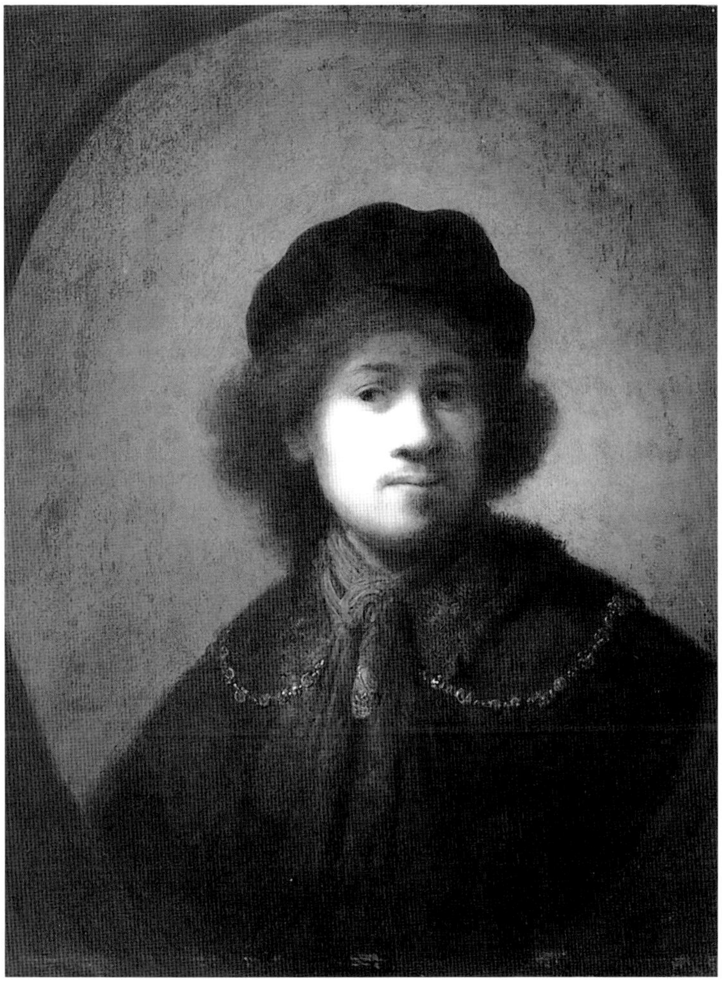

fig. 66 Rembrandt, *Self-Portrait with Beret*, 1630. Oil on wood, 69.7 × 57 cm. Walker Art Gallery, Liverpool.

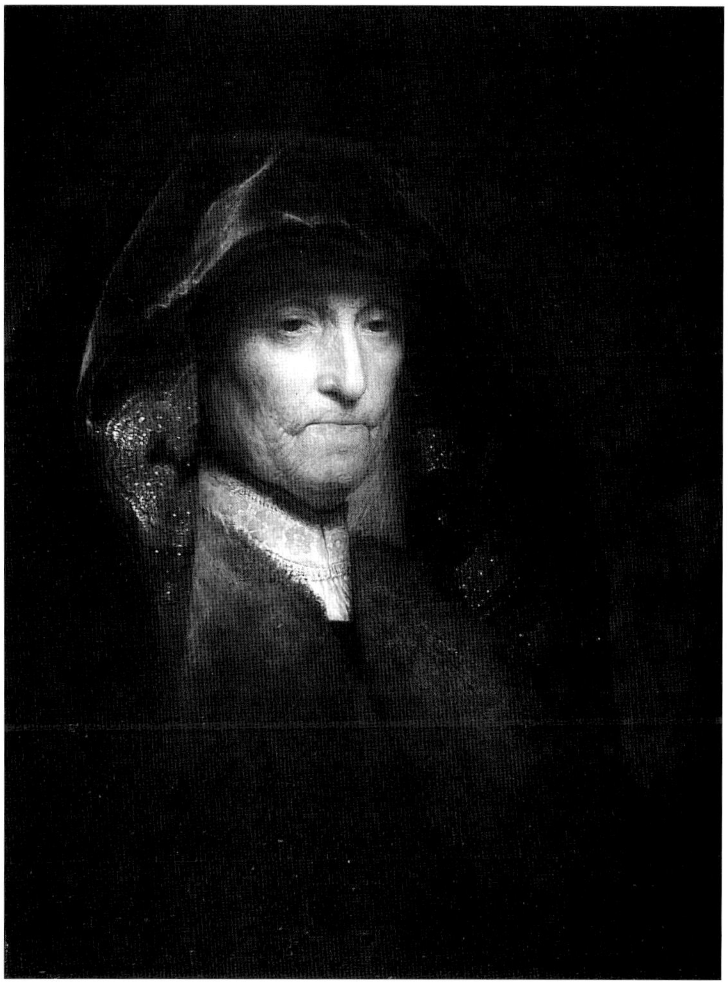

fig. 67 Attributed to Rembrandt, *An Old Woman*, ca. 1630. Oil on wood, 61 × 47.4 cm. Royal Collection, Windsor Castle.

commissioned by the court on Huygens' advice. Painted within a year of each other, the three paintings show compelling women in very different, almost deliberately varied roles. The innocent Proserpina is an unwilling abductee, while Delilah, the treacherous seductress, is presented as a woman in nearly the opposite relationship. Finally, Minerva, surrounded with objects representing learning and power—correctly called "Melancholy" in the 1632 inventory—presents a contemplative and stoic image of female power. These often overlooked images are surprisingly powerful and sophisticated, and represent the most prestigious commissions Rembrandt received during his Leiden residency. More attention has been paid to the painting of *Judas Returning the Thirty Pieces of Silver* (fig. 24) because of Huygens' eloquent evocation of the emotional power of the work, yet we have no idea who owned the picture nor what other connoisseurs thought of it. These early acquisitions paved the way for one of the most significant commissions of Rembrandt's career, the series of six paintings of Christ's Passion ordered by the stadhouder Frederik Hendrik and executed in the years 1633 to 1639 (fig. 65). Painted after Rembrandt's move to Amsterdam, they document the artist's attempt to master religious painting in terms acceptable to international connoisseurs and the Dutch court, and to rival the most prominent artist of his time, Peter Paul Rubens.

Further validation of Rembrandt's early career ambitions, and indeed of his status as an artist, came from perhaps the most sophisticated and dedicated collector of paintings in the seventeenth century. Two early paintings by Rembrandt entered the collection of Charles I soon after they were painted: a self-portrait of about 1630 (fig. 66) and *An Old Woman* (fig. 67).[55] In 1629, during a diplomatic mission to the Netherlands, Sir Thomas Kerr might have become acquainted with Rembrandt's work. By 1633, Kerr had given the two paintings by Rembrandt, as well as a work by Lievens, to Charles I.[56] It is not known whether Kerr met Rembrandt personally, or whether the paintings were a gift from the stadhouder, but the two paintings have something of the status of official gifts, and it is even possible that Huygens played some role in the transaction.[57]

It is especially significant that a self-portrait of the young Rembrandt entered the royal collection at this time. The inventory of Charles I's collection, drawn up 1637–40, makes it clear that

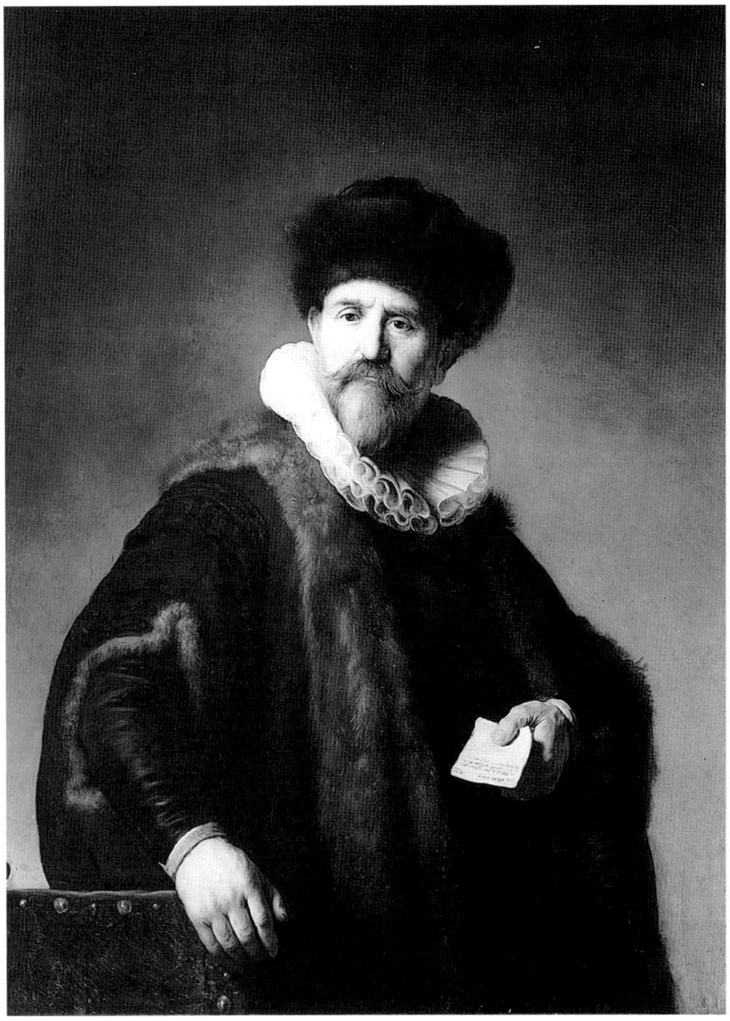

fig. 68 Rembrandt, *Portrait of Nicolaes Ruts*, 1631. Oil on wood, 116.8 × 87.3cm. Frick Collection, New York.

the portrait is Rembrandt's "owne picture & done by himself." Rembrandt's numerous explorations of his own visage, ranging from the informal to the pretentious, found a surprisingly early and extremely prestigious client. Ironically, this self-portrait was acquired by the most sophisticated collector in Europe before Rembrandt had actually produced a true commissioned portrait —the very type of portrait for which the early self-portraits are nowadays thought to be preparatory. The painting of the old woman is equally personal and intimate—a moving character study typical of Rembrandt's early work, although an attribution to Lievens has recently been suggested.[58] It is remarkable that the English gift, consisting of a simple self-portrait and a study of an old person, represents more clearly Rembrandt's early activity than the acquisitions of the Dutch court.

Rembrandt's portrait of Nicolaes Ruts (fig. 68) is the artist's earliest surviving commissioned portrait and one of the first works known to have been made after Rembrandt's arrival in Amsterdam. Painted in November 1631, it evinces great calculation and effort. The three-quarter length composition is far more ambitious than any of Rembrandt's earlier character studies and self-portraits, and the attention to the textures of fabric and fur is painstaking. Grand and imposing, the portrait employs the devices and calculated hauteur of Rembrandt's seniors in Flanders, Rubens and van Dyck.

Aside from the documentary evidence of Rembrandt's success in attracting important patrons in the period 1629 to 1631, critics also stressed the role of the market in shaping Rembrandt's early career. As early as 1641, in a volume devoted to Leiden's glory, Jan Orlers discussed the reasons for Rembrandt's move to Amsterdam, obviously feeling the need to explain why an important artist had to leave town. "Because his art and work greatly pleased and delighted the citizens and residents of Amsterdam, and he was often asked to make portraits or other pieces there, he decided to move from Leiden to Amsterdam."[59]

Arnold Houbraken told a rather dramatic tale of the young Rembrandt journeying to The Hague sometime before 1630 in order to show a painting to a gentleman who bought the work for a hundred guilders.[60] Although Houbraken's fanciful story is meant to show that Rembrandt was preoccupied with money, it does indicate that even in 1718 Houbraken still knew that patrons in The Hague were important for the discovery of Rembrandt's work. This anonymous gentleman is surely a reference to Constantijn Huygens. Houbraken continued, "Now this brilliant beginning showed him the future possibility of profit and his interest was encouraged by connoisseurs, and thus he received much work."[61] Echoing Orlers, he further reported that in order to continue painting portraits and other pieces, it was necessary for Rembrandt to go frequently to Amsterdam and eventually to move there.

Early works in seventeenth and eighteenth century commentary

Huygens' extended commentary on *Judas Returning the Thirty Pieces of Silver* remained unpublished for centuries, but other early works by Rembrandt attracted attention in the seventeenth century. In 1641, the French painter Claude Vignon reported that he had appraised Rembrandt's painting *The Ass of Balaam,* a work dated 1626 (fig. 69):

> And in Amsterdam, my greetings to Mr. Rembrandt, and bring back something by him. Also tell him that yesterday I valued his painting of the prophet Balaam which was bought from him by Signor Lopez; this piece will be sold with the others mentioned above.[62]

The letter indicates that Rembrandt commanded a measure of international respect. The owner of this picture was Alphonso Lopez, an art dealer representing France in Holland, who had bought Raphael's celebrated portrait of Baldassare Castiglione (now in the Louvre) in Amsterdam in 1639. Vignon's comments demonstrate that even Rembrandt's juvenilia was readily recognized and respected by foreign connoisseurs more than a decade after it was painted.

In 1718 Arnold Houbraken mentioned several works by Rembrandt, including a relatively early painting, *Christ in the Storm on the Sea of Galilee*, dated 1633 (fig. 70), which he had seen in the Hinloopen collection in Amsterdam. Houbraken focused on the painting as an example of Rembrandt's early style—the first surviving critical appraisal of the artist's early manner as distinct from his late work:

> Indeed there are still to be seen in the most prominent art cabinets many of his works of art which are thoroughly painted and completed.... And I have noticed that in his early period he had much more patience to work out his works of art in detail than afterwards.[63]

Another early discussion of Rembrandt's youthful paintings is found in Charles Rogers' short biography of Rembrandt written in 1778: "At this time he finished his Pictures as high as Mieris, yet with great Force and Fire."[64] While the comparison of Rembrandt's early style with the work of Frans van Mieris seems far-fetched,

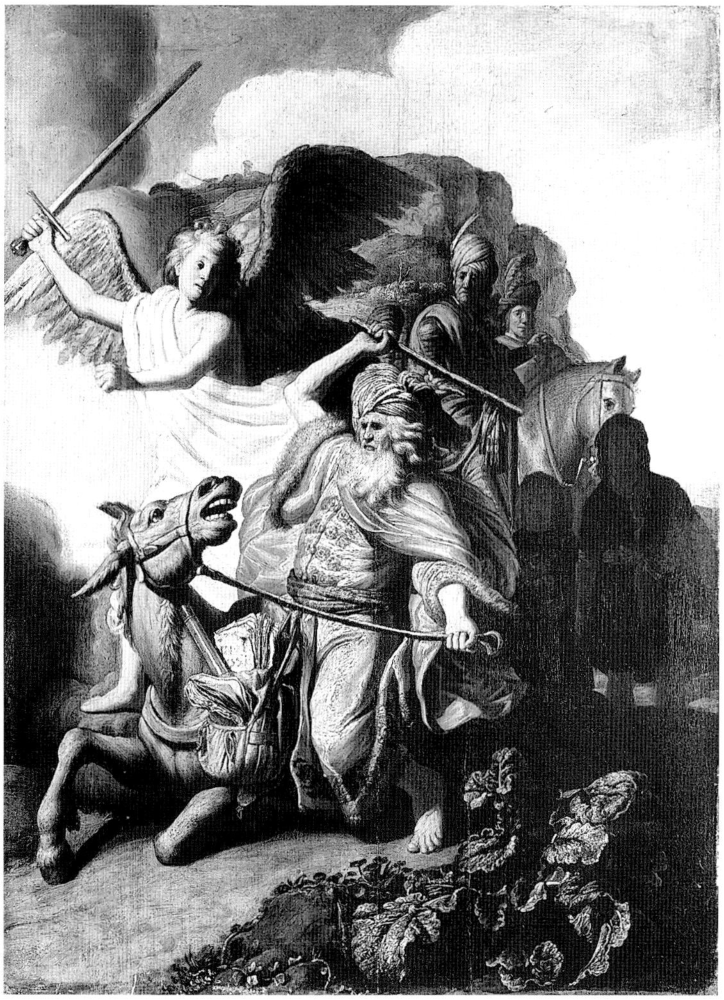

fig. 69 Rembrandt, *The Ass of Balaam*, 1626. Oil on wood, 65 × 46 cm. Musée Cognacq-Jay, Paris.

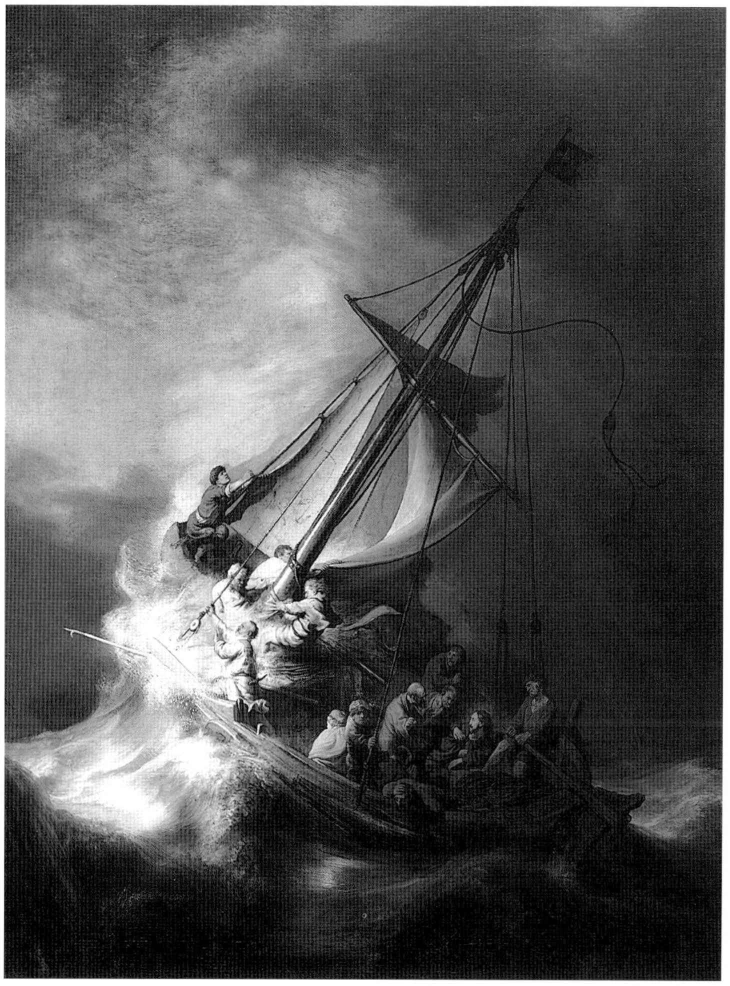

fig. 70 Rembrandt, *Christ in the Storm on the Sea of Galilee*, 1633. Oil on canvas, 160 × 127 cm. Isabella Stewart Gardner Museum, Boston.

Rogers at least shows an understanding of Rembrandt's development. In his catalogue of Rembrandt's paintings published in 1836, John Smith echoed these characterizations of Rembrandt's early style. Rembrandt had "a neat and careful manner of handling, accompanied by firmness and precision of touch," although Smith also called Rembrandt's early method "a system of laborious finishing."[65] Gustav Waagen wrote that in Rembrandt's paintings before 1633, "a clear daylight prevails, the colour of the flesh is warm and clear, but true to nature, the touch already masterly and free, but very careful, and, to a certain point, fused."[66]

It is only in the 1790s that early paintings by Rembrandt began to attract the careful attention of connoisseurs. Beginning in 1790, the art dealer Jean-Baptiste Pierre Lebrun published a large series of engravings in order to illustrate less familiar aspects of Netherlandish painting. Thus, while he reproduced no mature works by Rembrandt, two purportedly early paintings were included: *The Presentation in the Temple*, dated 1627 (Kunsthalle, Hamburg), and *Man Writing by Candlelight* (fig. 71), from Rembrandt's circle and certainly similar to early works by the artist.[67] The *Presentation in the Temple* had attracted considerable attention when it was auc-

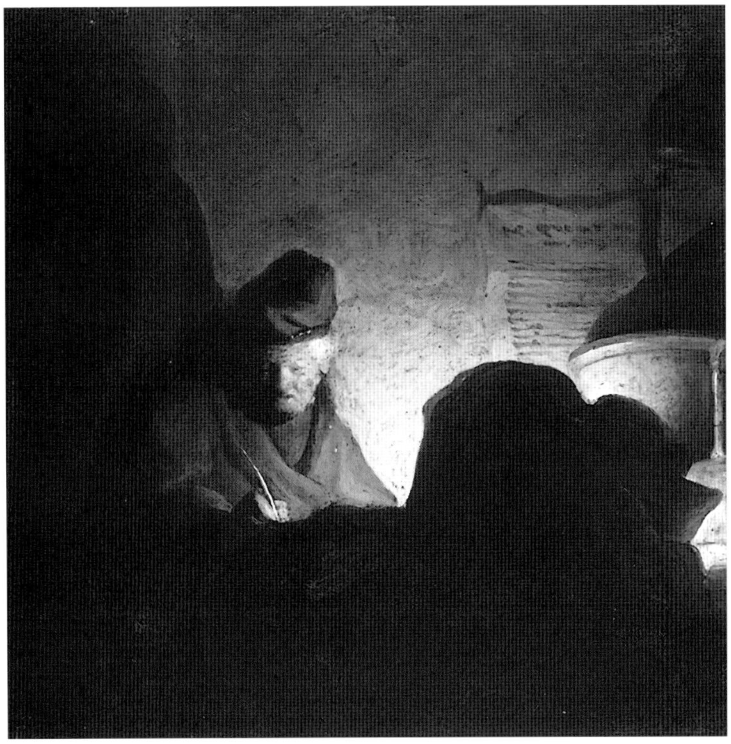

fig. 71 Attributed to Rembrandt, *Man Writing by Candlelight* (p. 133, cat. 20).

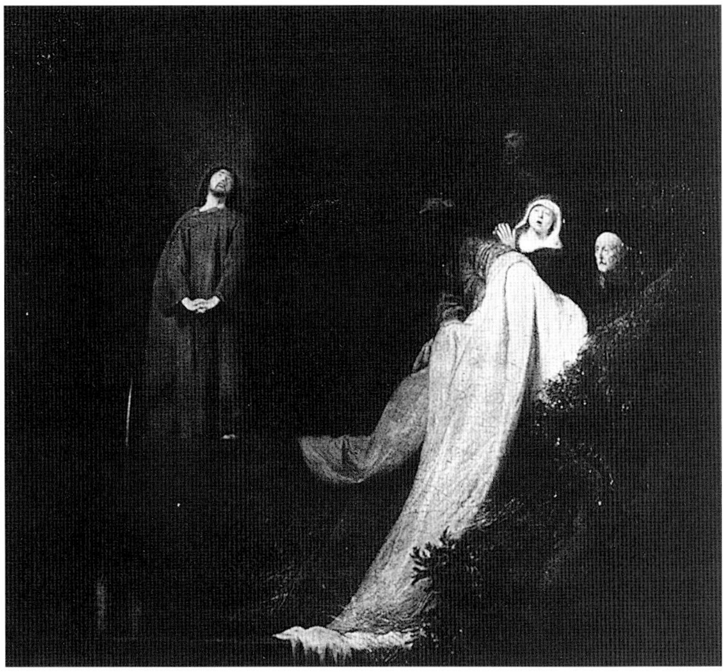

fig. 72 Jan Lievens, *The Raising of Lazarus*, 1631. Oil on canvas, 103 × 112 cm. Brighton Museum and Art Gallery, Brighton.

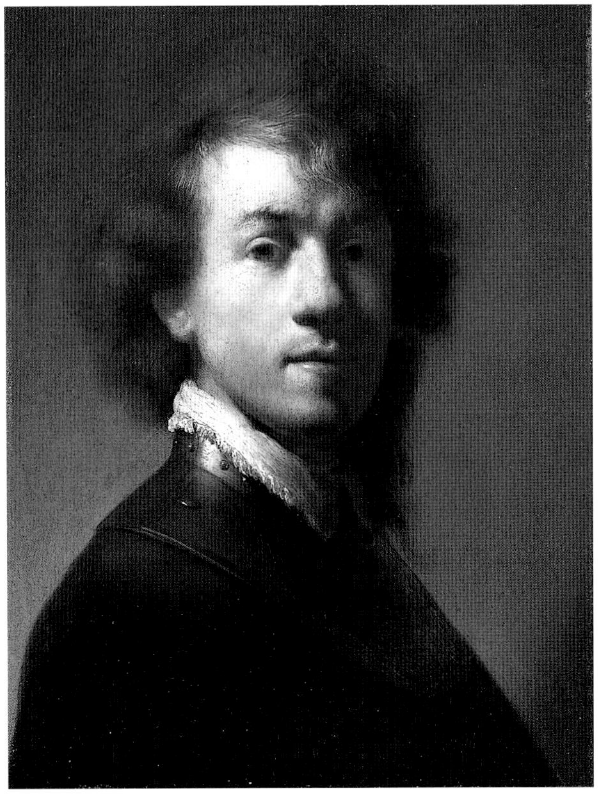

fig. 73 Circle of Rembrandt, *Portrait of Rembrandt in a Gorget* (cat. 6).

tioned in Paris in 1770 and 1774; around this time, Jan Stolker made a fantasy portrait of Rembrandt showing the artist in his studio surrounded by etchings and with this painting propped up on an easel (drawing, British Museum, London).[68]

Henry Fuseli was acquainted with a few early paintings by Rembrandt, but interestingly much preferred Jan Lievens' *Raising of Lazarus* of 1630 (fig. 72) to any of Rembrandt's works of this period, including perhaps Rembrandt's contemporaneous painting of the subject (fig. 59). While celebrating Rembrandt as perhaps the greatest storyteller in art, Fuseli noted the exception of "the raising of Lazarus by Lievens, a name comparatively obscure, whose awful sublimity reduces the same subject as treated by Rembrandt and Sebastian of Venice, to artificial parade or common-place."[69]

Portrait of Rembrandt in a Gorget

Napoleon's invasions of the Netherlands and Germany in the 1790s and the accompanying seizures of important collections of art had the bizarre side-effect of bringing together a large number of Rembrandt's paintings. Hung in the Louvre and reproduced in elaborate volumes, early works by Rembrandt could receive scholarly scrutiny. When the French military brought the Dutch stadhouder's beautiful *Portrait of Rembrandt in a Gorget* (fig. 73; cat. 6) to Paris, it was catalogued as by "van Vliet," surely a reference to J.G. van Vliet, who was known to have produced prints in the early 1630s after Rembrandt paintings.[70] At first, the portrait was not even exhibited at the Louvre, and when it was shown, it was labeled "H. van Vliet."[71] This prescient de-attribution was ignored, and the entire episode forgotten, when the painting was returned to Holland in 1815.

The insightful Maxime Du Camp, in 1857, was also disturbed by the portrait's qualities. "For me, this is a very primitive work, perhaps by the young artist when still living in the mill in Leiden ... strong in execution but dry, hard, a little ordinary, like green marble, rather strange for Rembrandt.... One almost could say it is like a van der Werff seen through a lens.... I take it for a Rembrandt, but I have never seen another in this manner."[72] A few years later, Adolf von Wurzbach stated that the painting was not by Rembrandt. Although Wilhelm Bode disagreed, he also accepted the Nuremberg version of the self-portrait (fig. 6a) as a genuine Rembrandt.[73] The controversy resurfaced a century later when Claus Grimm argued forcefully that the Nuremberg self-portrait was the only version by Rembrandt and that the portrait in the Mauritshuis was by a follower.[74]

The Song of Simeon

In contrast to the lukewarm response to the *Portrait of Rembrandt in a Gorget,* the stadhouder's *Song of Simeon* (fig. 74) commanded excitement and praise from the 1790s on. When the painting was seized by the French, it was immediately hung in the Louvre. Antoine Filhol, in the *Galerie du Musée Napoléon*, wrote, "One recognizes Rembrandt in this painting. One also sees the bizarre nature which characterizes many of his compositions." Filhol continued with comments on Rembrandt's early manner of painting: "It is of a very firm execution and more finished than is common in the productions of this painter. This has led to doubts as to its originality for some art lovers who have attributed it to van Vliet, Rembrandt's student... but we believe they are in error... it merits the distinguished place it occupies in the gallery."[75] John Smith, in 1836, considered the painting Rembrandt's "first work of any importance"; it is "replete with expression, as well as delicacy of finishing and effect."[76]

In his extensive monograph on Rembrandt written in 1854, Eduard Kolloff noted that little was known of Rembrandt's early work, but he felt certain that the *Song of Simeon* was Rembrandt's first true masterpiece. He observed that it already revealed all of the essential characteristics of the artist's mature style, and could be seen as representing the emergence of the real Rembrandt.

> The application of the paint is already impasto-like, although thinner than in the later pictures, and the master seems especially well versed in the richness and artistic blending of alternating tones. But the entire conception and expression of feeling of this painting are as little youthful as is the workmanship, which wonderfully combines clarity of color with brilliance of effect and, in retrospect, cedes little to the magical diffusion of light and shadow and the multiple half tints of the master's late paintings.[77]

When Maxime Du Camp visited the Mauritshuis, he was equally struck by "the luminous effects, which have an extraordinary power." "The architecture is rendered by simple striations which allow the wood of the panel to be seen... the grand stairway in the back is drawn in half tints with the luminous shadows at which Rembrandt excelled." Rembrandt possessed "the science, now lost, of opposing shadow and light, which gives vigor to the main parts of the picture, one never overwhelming the other; it is the splendor and the brutal sincerity of these little figures idealized by the force of truth."[78] Carel Vosmaer, writing in 1868, stressed the originality of Rembrandt's picture: "It has nothing in common (especially in intimacy and personality), with the religious painting of the old Italians, Flemings, and Dutch."[79]

A few years later, Théophile Thoré described with remarkable clarity what Rembrandt had achieved in his Leiden period. For him, the same painting was the pinnacle of Rembrandt's early career, a judgment that many share today.

> This little marvel, the first in the chronology of the oeuvre, already fully reveals, by the fullness of touch, and the originality of the overall effect, the true style of Rembrandt, which characterizes his beginnings as well as his maturity.[80]

Thoré also noted that precise, "cold" details distinguish Rembrandt's early paintings from later works. *Anatomy of Dr. Tulp* (fig. 75), dated 1632, allowed Thoré to clearly distinguish between Rembrandt's Leiden and Amsterdam periods.

These nineteenth-century critics admired themselves for being able to discern signs of Rembrandt's maturity—his true style—in his youthful efforts. Some writers seem to have truly believed that the *Song of Simeon* was a work of genuine emotional power, but most saw it as an important first step towards something else. The painting proves to be an interesting test case for the new respect for Rembrandt's work from his Leiden period. While it is an indication of what would come later, the painting slowly emerged as a compelling work of considerable interest in its own right.

Jeremiah Lamenting the Destruction of Jerusalem

Other paintings also inspired respect in the course of the nineteenth century. Although hardly ever seen by connoisseurs because it was in a private collection in Saint Petersburg, *Jeremiah Lamenting the Destruction of Jerusalem* (cat. 14) was already fully published in 1800 and reproduced shortly afterwards in a folio edition. The catalogue praises the "air of profound reflection on the vanities of the world represented by the gold and silver vessels." It also shows an understanding of Rembrandt's early style: "made with a magic touch that has a little hardness, it has the air at a certain distance of the most precious finish."[81] In 1864, Gustav Waagen was able to confirm that the painting was dated 1630. He, too, opined that the luminous, golden painting predicted, but did not quite achieve,

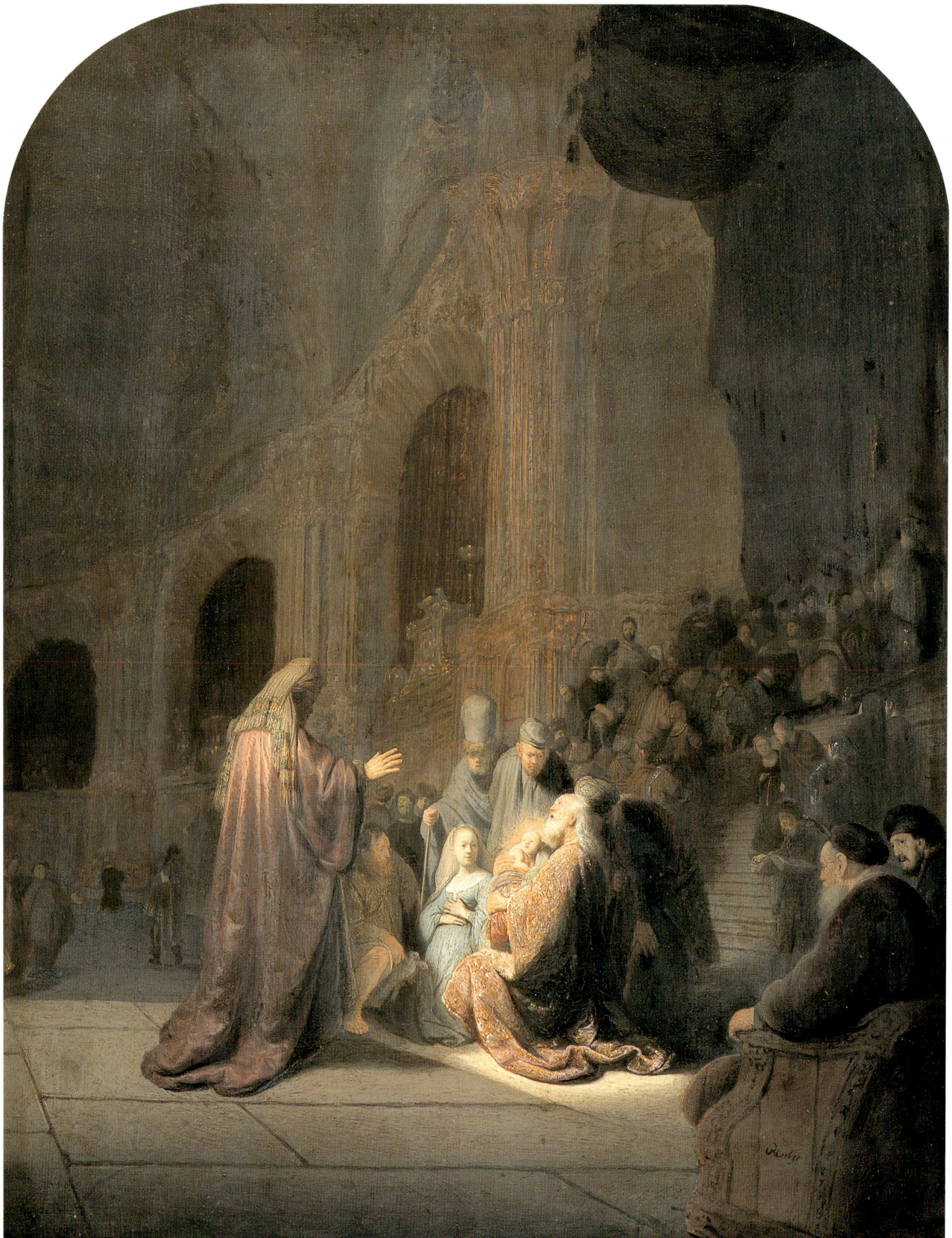

fig. 74 Rembrandt, *The Song of Simeon*, 1631. Oil on wood, 61 × 48 cm.
Mauritshuis, The Hague.

greatness. "It promises something, but does not yet achieve it."[82] Wilhelm Bode was more enthusiastic: "It is a real jewel among Rembrandt's youthful works, which suffers nothing in comparison with most of his later creations."[83]

Bode, director of the Berlin museums, was the scholar most responsible for the modern scholarly understanding of Rembrandt's early career. Carel Vosmaer's early attempts to examine Rembrandt's origins and early career were severely hampered by lack of material, while Kurt Bauch's later efforts did not significantly advance Bode's work.[84] In publications of 1881, 1883, and 1897, Bode catalogued all the essential aspects of the early Rembrandt. His task was no doubt made easier by the presence of several major early works in German collections, in particular, the early paintings made for the stadhouder (figs. 62, 63, 64) which had lain forgotten in Berlin storerooms for more than a century. As early as 1881, Bode also noted the importance of the works of 1627 in Stuttgart and Berlin (figs. 18a, 32), as well as the depictions of Jeremiah, Paul, and Peter (cat. 14, fig. 14a, cat. 18). Bode also believed that both versions of Rembrandt's self-portrait in a gorget in Nuremberg and The Hague (fig. 6a and cat. 6) were genuine, an opinion re-endorsed only a century later.[85] Bode was a persuasive advocate for the appreciation of Rembrandt's Leiden period. A viewer, he wrote, might be

> repelled by the unfamiliar elements, the evidences of the "prentice hand" more or less apparent in all such youthful essays, and finds himself entirely out of sympathy with them. On the other hand, they shew, even at this early period, such marked individuality, such a radical departure from established precedent, such a notable endeavour to give depth and force to the motive… and discard the vicious methods of his teachers, that every work, no matter how trivial in scope and subject, has a deep interest for the student.[86]

Self-Portrait, 1629

Several German museums purchased early paintings by Rembrandt in the late nineteenth century, but the grand American collectors of the Gilded Age were not at all attracted to such works. They generally preferred the sooty, spackled pictures of the artist's maturity or, more commonly, the highly emotional pictures by Rembrandt's students and followers which were then believed to be by the master himself.

Isabella Stewart Gardner was one significant exception. In the mid-1890s she set about forming a significant art collection. In January 1896, Bernard Berenson sent her a photograph of a self-portrait by

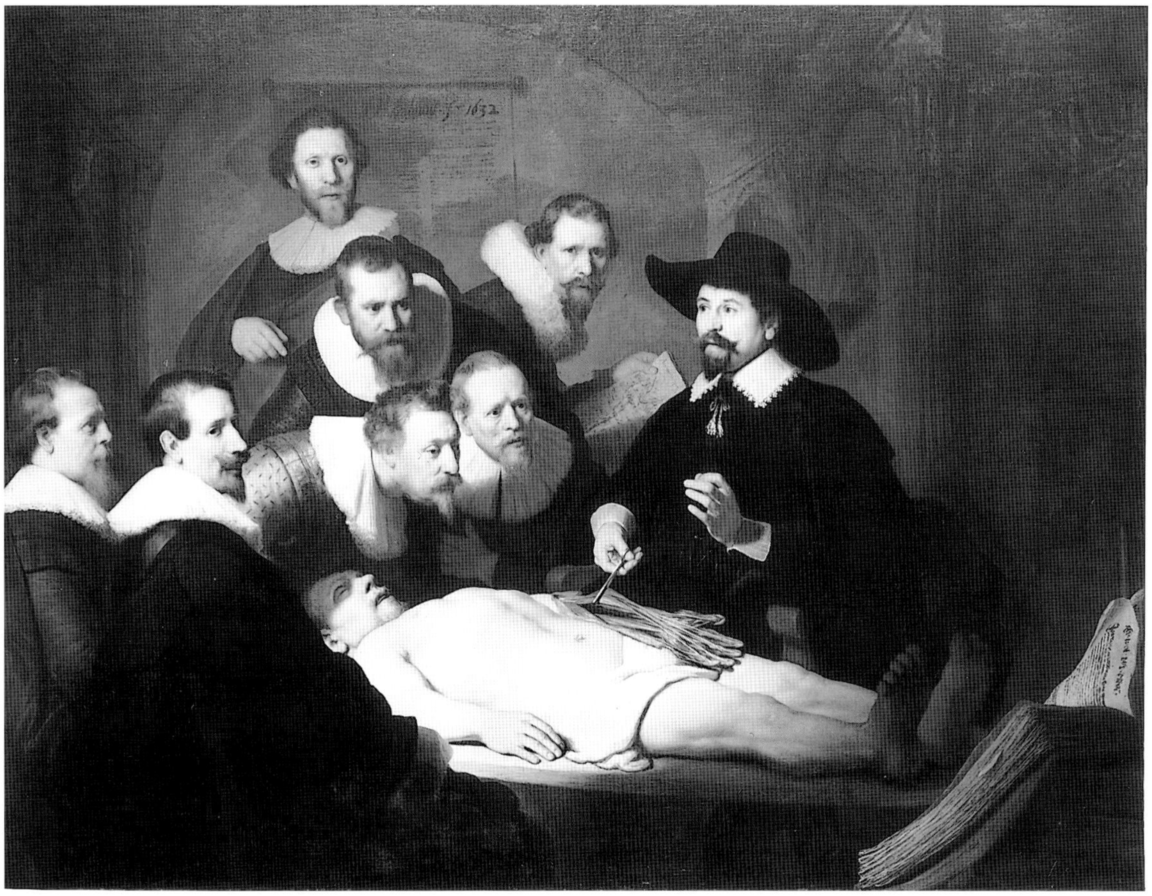

fig. 75 Rembrandt, *The Anatomy of Dr. Tulp*, 1632. Oil on canvas. 169.5 × 216.6 cm. Mauritshuis, The Hague.

catalogued as "the picture done by Rembrandt. being his owne picture & done by himself in a Black capp and firrd habbitt with a litle goulden chaine uppon his Shouldrs." [margin: "Given to the King by my Lo: Ankrom"]. *An Old Woman* is described as "an old woeman with a greate Scarfe uppon her heade with a peaked falling band, In a Black frame" [margin: "Done by Rembrant & given to the kinge by my Lo: Ankrom"]. Source: Millar 1960, p. 57, no. 87; p. 60, no. 101.

56 A label on the back of *An Old Woman* states that it was presented to the king by Kerr, who was created Earl of Ancram in 1633 (Millar 1960, p. 60; Corpus A 32).

57 Orlers 1641, p. 377 states that a painting by Lievens (now lost) depicting a life-size figure wearing a red cap, studying by a fire, was given by the Prince of Orange to the English ambassador, probably Kerr, who in turn gave it to Charles I. See discussion in London 1999, p. 132.

58 Corpus, vol. 2, pp. 839–40; W. Liedtke, in New York 1995, vol. 2, p. 10; London 1999, p. 132. Although the condition of the picture does not allow for a firm attribution, it seems closer to Rembrandt's work than Lievens'.

59 Orlers 1641, p. 375: "Dewijle dat zijne Konst ende arbeyt, de Borgeren ende Innewoonderen van Amsterdamme ten hoochsten behaechde ende aengenaem was, ende dat hy veeltijden versocht werde omme 'tzy Conterfeytselen ofte ander stucken aldaer te maecken, zoo heeft hy goet ghevonden hem van Leyden te transporteren naer Amsterdamme..."

60 Houbraken 1718, vol. 1, p. 255.

61 Houbraken 1718, vol. 1, p. 256: "Thans deed hem dit blikend beginsel de hoop van geldwinning vooruit zien, en zyn konstdrift op die wyze gespoort nam zodanig toe in de Konst dat hy aan alle konstkenneren genoegen gaf... Dus kreeg hy... de handen vol werk."

62 Strauss, van de Meulen 1979, p. 212, doc. 1641/6: "e in Amsterdamme mi saluti anche il sig. Rembrant, e porti seco qualcosa del suo. Gli dica pure, che io feci ieri la stima del suo quadro del profeta Balam, che comprò da lui il sig. Lopez, il qual quadro si vendrà fra quelli sopradetti."

63 Houbraken 1718, vol. 1, p. 260: "Egter zyn 'er nog vele zyne konstsukken, welke in 't geheel doorschildert en uitgevoert zyn, in de voornaamste Konstkabinetten te zien... En ik heb opgemerkt dat hy in zyn vroegen tyd wel meer gedult gehad heeft om zyne konststukken uitvoerig te bewerken dan daarna."

64 Rogers 1778, vol. 2, p. 215.

65 Smith 1836, pp. xxxv, xv.

66 Waagen 1860, vol. 1, p. 341.

67 Lebrun 1792.

68 The drawing by Jan Stolker (1724–1785) is reproduced in Scheller 1961, fig. 1 and Corpus 1982, p. 155, fig. 6.

69 Fuseli 1831, vol. 3, pp. 130–31 ["Aphorisms," no. 170]; also mentioned on p. 86.

70 Boyer 1970, p. 156 [1796 inventory, no. 149: "Tête, dite Rembrandt" by van Vliet].

71 F. P. J. Pommereul, *De l'art de voir dans les beaux arts* (Paris, 1798 [an 6]), section: "État des objets d'art envoyés aux divers musées français, et conquis par les armees de la République pendant la guerre de la liberté," p. 294 [the portrait was not exhibited]. Filhol, Lavallée 1804, vol. 1, pl. 29 [engraving by Alexis Chataigner, as H. van Vliet].

72 Du Camp 1857, p. 363: "Suivant moi, c'est une oeuvre toute primitive, peut-être même du jeune artiste lorsqu'il était encore dans son moulin à Leyde. Peut-être même est-ce son portrait... C'est étonnant d'effet, c'est même très-fort d'exécution, mais sec, dur, un peu commun, dans une gamme de vert marmoréen, assez étrangère à Rembrandt.... On dirait presque un van der Werff grossi par une lunette... je la tiens pour Rembrandt; mais je n'en ai jamais vu qu'une autre de cette manière-là."

73 A. von Wurzbach, in *Zeitschrift für bildenden Künste* 10 (1875), pp. 381–83. W. Bode, in *Zeitschrift für bildenden Künste* 11 (1876), pp. 125–26. Bode 1883, no. 114 [the Nuremberg portrait as Rembrandt]. In 1897, Bode listed the Nuremberg painting as possibly also genuine (Bode 1897, no. 16).

74 Grimm 1991, pp. 21–26 [as possibly Isack Jouderville, after Rembrandt's self-portrait in Nuremberg].

75 Filhol, Lavallée 1804, vol. 5 (1808), no. 325: "On reconnait Rembrandt dans ce tableau. On y retrouve également la bizarrerie qui caractérise la plupart de ses compositions, et lui fait sacrifier souvent les convenances au desire de produire de l'effect ... L'ensemble est en pittoresque ... il est d'une exécution très-ferme et plus arrêtée que ne le sont communément les productions de ce peintre. Cette circonstance a fait douter quelques amateurs de son originalité, et les ont entraînés à l'attribuer à Van-Vliet, élève de Rembrandt ... mais nous les croyons dans l'erreur ... et mérite le rang distingué qu'il occupe dans la Galerie." See also Boyer 1970, p. 156.

76 Smith 1836, p. xv.

77 Kolloff 1854, p. 434: "Die Farbenauftrag ist bereits pastos, indess schwächer als in spätern Bildern, und der Meister scheint im Reichthum und in künstlicher Verschmelzung der abwechselnden Töne sich besonders geübt zu haben. Aber die ganze Auffassung und der Ausdruck der Gefühls in diesem Bilde ist ebenso wenig jugendlich als die treffliche Ausführung, welche Klarheit der Farbe mit Brillanz der Wirkung verbindet, und hinsichtlich der magischen Vertheilung von Licht und Schatten und aller mannichfaltigen Zwischentinten den Bildern aus der spätern Zeit des Meisters nicht viel nachgibt."

78 Du Camp 1857, pp. 361–62.

79 Vosmaer 1868, pp. 16–17: "Cette composition plus importantes que les oeuvres antérieures, est déjà une oeuvre très originale. Il n'a rien de commun (si ce n'est l'intimité et la personalité) avec la peinture religieuse des anciens Italiens, Flamands, Hollandais."

80 Thoré 1858, pp. 193–94: "Cette petite merveille, la première dans l'ordre chronologique de l'oeuvre, révèle déjà pleinement, par l'ampleur de la touche et l'originalité de l'effect général, le style propre à Rembrandt, celui qui le caractérise, aussi bien à son origine que dans sa maturité."

81 Stroganoff cat. 1807, n.p.

82 Waagen 1864, p. 404: "Im lichten Goldton dieser frühen Zeit, in einem trefflichen Impasto fleissig ausgeführt, die Umgebung indess etwas unbestimmt. – Das Bildniss eines Mönchs. Verspricht etwas, ist indess jetzt zu sehr versunken."

83 Bode 1881, p. 63: "Es ist ein wahres Juwel unter den Jugendwerken Rembrandt's, das auch neben den meisten späteren Schöpfungen deselben nich verliert."

84 Carel Vosmaer, *Rembrandt Harmens van Rijn, ses précurseurs et ses années d'apprentissage* (The Hague, 1863); Vosmaer 1868. Bauch 1933; Bauch 1960.

85 Bode 1881; Bode 1883, pp. 359–99. The only significant error is Bode's misreading of the date in the *Holy Family* in Munich as 1631 rather than 1636.

86 Bode 1897, vol. 1, chap. 1.

87 Hadley 1987, p. 47.

88 *Catalogue from the Collection of Charles T. Yerkes, Chicago, U.S.A.* (Chicago, 1893), no. 48. The *Raising of Lazarus* (ibid., no. 47) is now in the Art Institute of Chicago; see Corpus 1982, pp. 306–7.

Catalogue

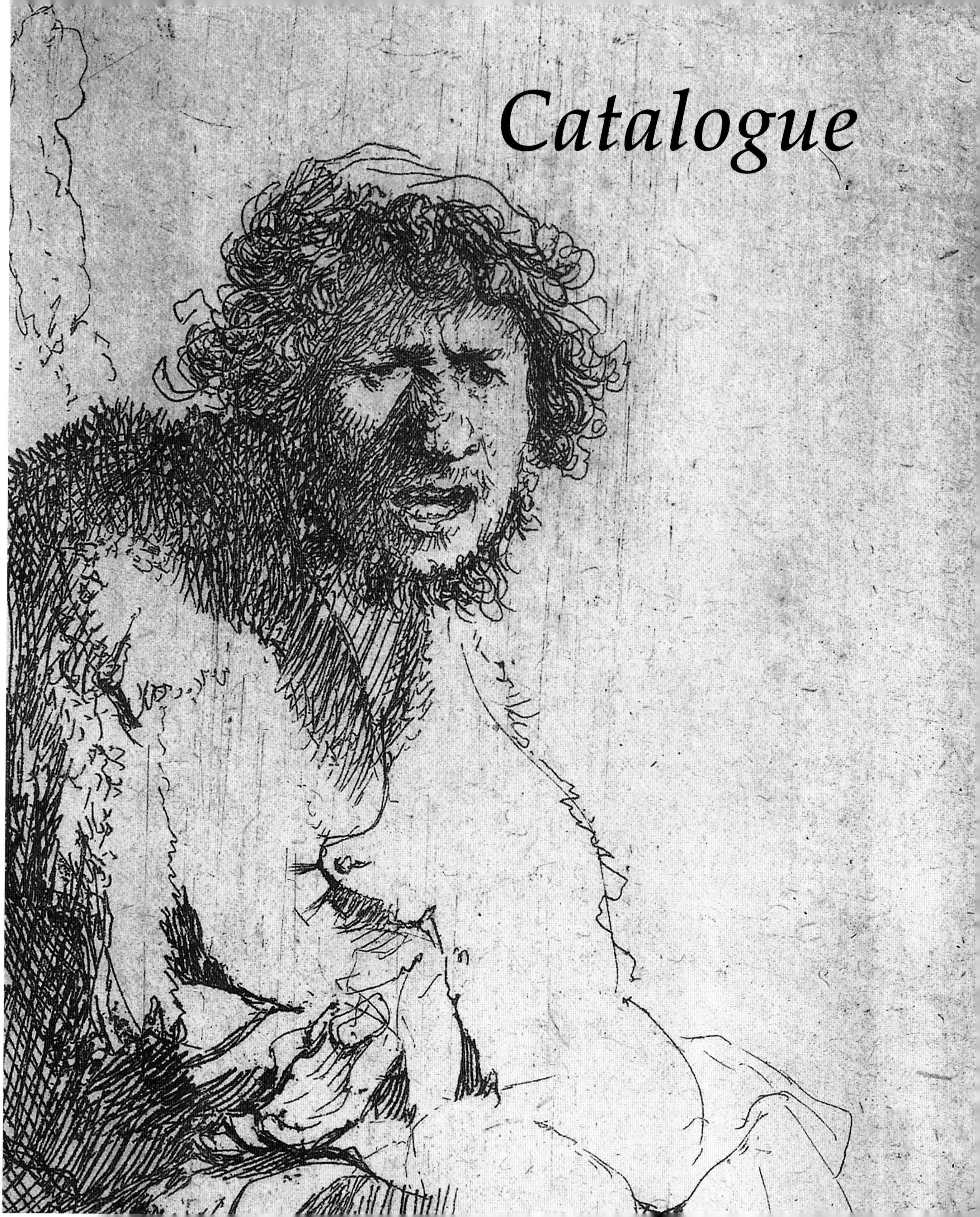

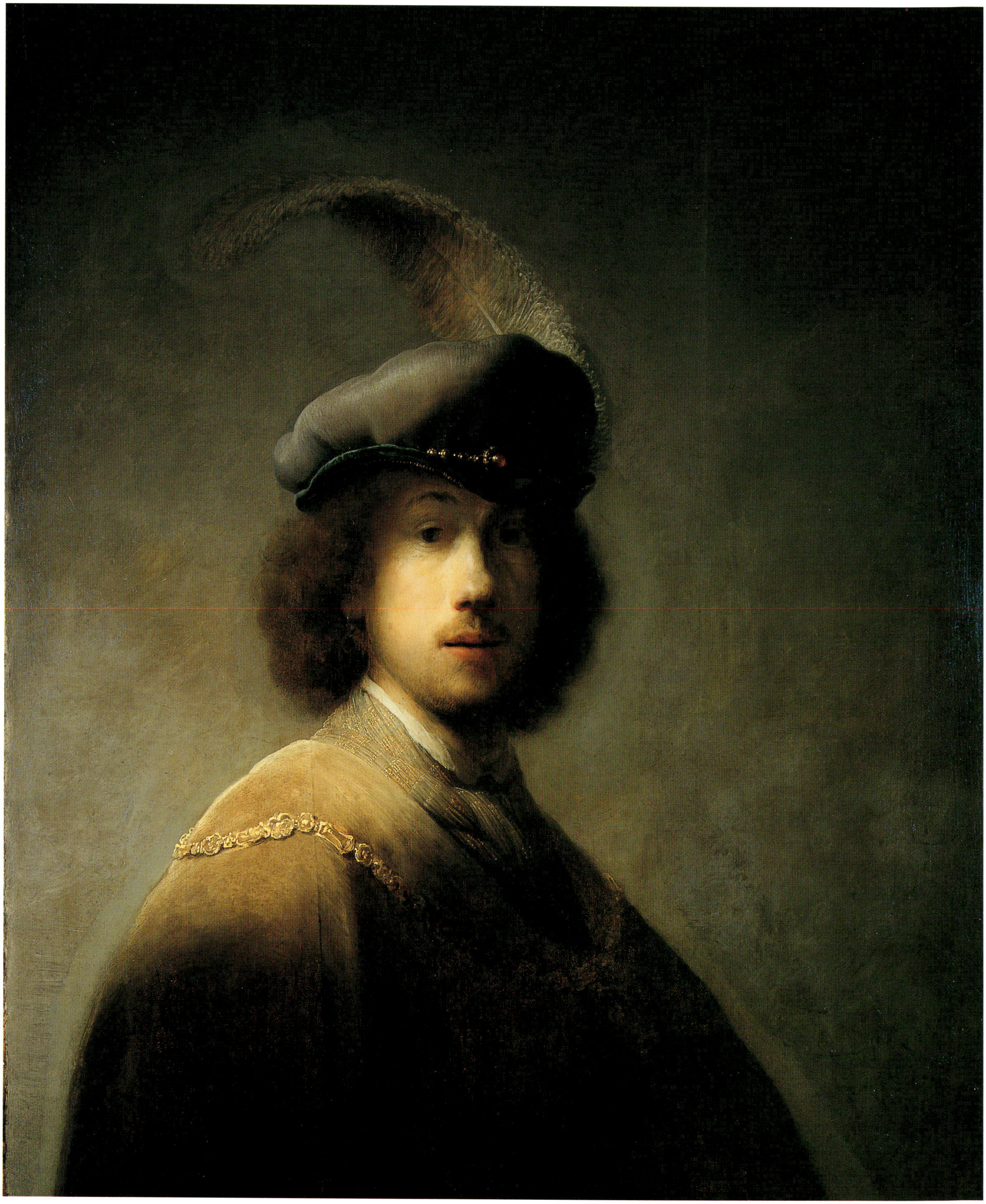

5
Rembrandt
Self-Portrait 1629

oil on wood, 89.7 × 73.9 cm, signed lower right: RHL [monogram] …9
Isabella Stewart Gardner Museum, Boston

Rembrandt's production of self-portraits is without parallel in the history of European art. More than twenty etchings and sixty paintings in which he portrayed his own features survive, and his face appears in numerous other works not formatted like traditional portraits. Many of these images are not especially flattering. The large number of self-portraits made between 1628 and 1634 tend to fall into two categories: direct, passive studies of Rembrandt's facial features; and paintings of heads based generally upon his features that explore either emotional expressions or types of costuming. These costume studies may also have been intended as advertisements for his ability to paint various types of portraits for the market. Therefore, a totally veristic presentation of his face was often irrelevant. The technical accomplishment of a painting like this one was no doubt intended to demonstrate his mastery to the public.

In this work, the largest self-portrait made up to 1629, Rembrandt was particularly concerned with costume and with the sophisticated rendering of textures and fabrics. Indeed his own features are somewhat generalized; his elongated face appears softly pear-shaped, his nose has been made more aquiline, his eyes have been widened and brought closer together. In portraying himself in the noble tradition of half-length portraits of the previous century, Rembrandt has taken great care in the articulation of his velvet mantle—wonderfully highlighted on his shoulder—and the oriental silk scarf with gold threads. He has painted the evocatively impastoed chain and the jewels on the bonnet with meticulous attention to detail. Infrared photographs indicate that he carefully drew the chain before beginning to paint it. And he has used fuller brushstrokes to depict the long feather in the cap. The passages of glossy surface and controlled brushwork are quite distinct from the loose, open brushwork found in other paintings by Rembrandt of this period. (Unfortunately, surface wear on the face and hair have compromised some of the modeling.) Was Rembrandt demonstrating his ability to rival the fine, glossy technique of his colleague Jan Lievens? The range of textures suggested is remarkable, from the velvet of the mantle to the silk of the scarf, from the feather to the stubble of his light, delicately highlighted, beard.

It has been argued that the chain makes no specific allusion to the nobility of his profession since such chains are common in Rembrandt's work, especially his studies of heads.[1] Nor does the chain resemble the ornamental necklaces of honor given by princely patrons to court painters such as Titian and Rubens, who depicted them in their self-portraits. Nonetheless, some general allusion by the ambitious Rembrandt to the nobility of the painter's profession cannot be excluded. Similarly, caution should be applied in attempting to interpret the feather in his cap. There is no particular reason to believe that the feather is a vanitas allusion since such caps are common historical costumes in seventeenth-century Dutch paintings, and various feathered hats with distinctive characteristics appear in many of Rembrandt's self-portraits.

Rather, this self-portrait appears to be a demonstration piece, a tour-de-force. It may not be coincidental that in the same year it was painted, 1629, Rembrandt met the English ambassador to Holland, Sir Robert Kerr. At that time, or shortly afterwards, Kerr acquired one of Rembrandt's self-portraits to present to Charles I (fig. 5a). It was also about this time that Constantijn Huygens, secretary to the stadhouder, visited the studio of Rembrandt and Lievens in Leiden.

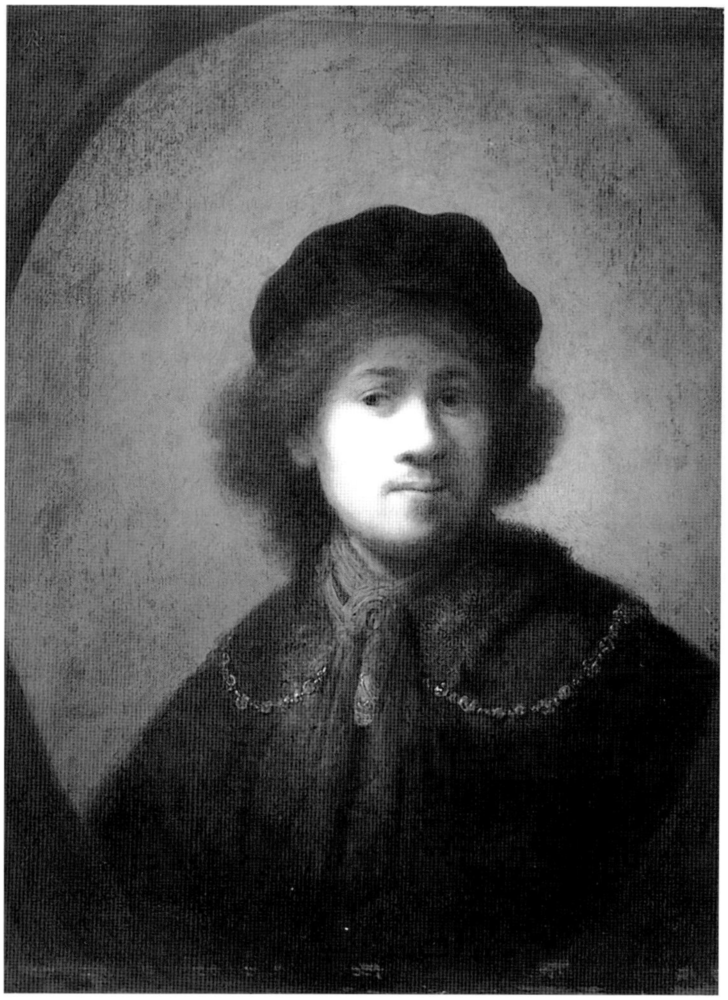

fig. 5a Rembrandt, *Self-Portrait with Beret*, 1630. Oil on wood. 69.7 × 57 cm. Walker Art Gallery, Liverpool.

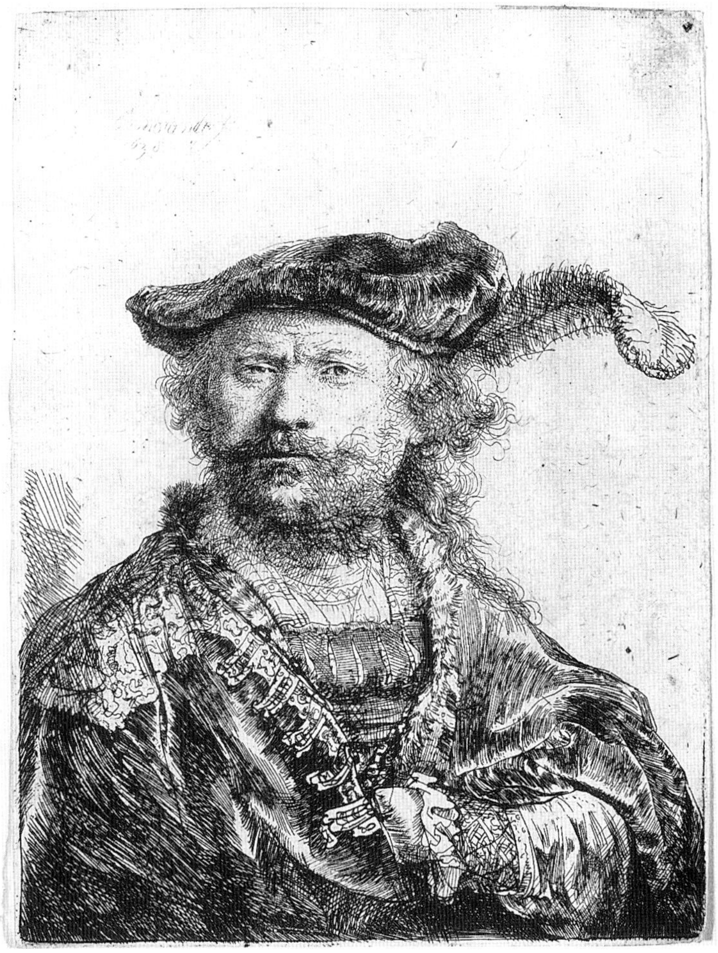

fig. 5b Rembrandt, *Self-Portait*, 1638. Etching, 13.4 × 10.3 cm. British Museum, London. Bartsch 20.

Although Rembrandt could have known Italian portraits through prints or drawings, he was probably more influenced by Northern portraits. Among these were the series of portrait engravings by Hendrick Hondius published in 1610; they feature, among others, notable fifteenth and sixteenth-century painters. The handsomely attired Jan Gossaert, for example, is shown wearing a beret. The portrait in the Gardner Museum anticipates to a remarkable degree the type of self-portrait Rembrandt was to execute a decade later, for example his etched self-portrait with feathered beret of 1638 (fig. 5b).

The portrait is painted on an oak panel. X-rays reveal that the portrait we now see is painted over a larger, more broadly based figure, which continues significantly higher up than the self-portrait. Traces of this figure are visible on the surface. Just as the artist reused copper plates for his etchings, so he often reused expensive oak panels.

This painting was the first by Rembrandt that Isabella Stewart Gardner acquired and, according to the first director of the museum, she later stated that it was this purchase that prompted her to create a museum collection.

HG

1 E. Buijsen, in London 1999, p. 99.

6

Circle of Rembrandt

Portrait of Rembrandt with a Gorget ca. 1630

oil on wood, 37.9 x 28.9 cm
Mauritshuis, The Hague

Until recently, this painting was universally accepted as an early, very beautiful self-portrait by Rembrandt. However, certain unusual characteristics have long been noticed. In particular, the smooth, polished brushwork and narrow range of color do not resemble other paintings by Rembrandt around 1629–30, its presumed date. In 1982, the Rembrandt Research Project, while accepting the work as genuine, conceded that it "to some extent stands alone among the works from around 1629."[1]

In 1795 Napoleonic forces removed this painting from the stadhouder's collection in The Hague and took it to Paris. At that time, French experts changed the attribution to "Van Vliet," no doubt a reference to the printmaker J.G. van Vliet, who was known to have made several etchings after early works by Rembrandt. In 1874, Alfred von Wurzbach wrote that the painting was not by Rembrandt. Two years later Wilhelm Bode refuted this conclusion; Bode also considered the version of the portrait in Nuremberg to be authentic (fig. 6a), although he tempered this conclusion somewhat in his catalogue raisonné of 1897.[2]

Claus Grimm, in 1991, revived the notion that the portrait in the Mauritshuis was not by Rembrandt himself, but a version based on the painting in Nuremberg, which had long been dismissed as a copy. Grimm tentatively suggested that the version in The Hague was by Isack Jouderville.[3] This theory was greeted with surprise and almost total disbelief, no doubt because such a prominent and beloved painting was being eliminated from Rembrandt's oeuvre.[4] However, study and scientific examination conducted in preparation for an exhibition in 1999, when both works were shown together, seemed to confirm the theory that the portrait in Nuremberg was painted by Rembrandt around 1629, and that the version in the Mauritshuis was copied soon afterwards by a follower. Experts at the Mauritshuis further believe that the painting might be by Gerrit Dou, Rembrandt's first pupil, who began his training in 1628 at the age of fourteen.

Infrared examination of the painting in The Hague revealed an underdrawing (fig. 6b), which was very likely executed in black chalk or charcoal.[5] Although the hair is loosely sketched, the eyes, nose, and mouth are carefully drawn. A system of repeating lines is employed for the torso and gorget; and curiously, another pair of eyes is found below and to the right of the present ones. This part of the underdrawing appears to be a preliminary outline of the composition perhaps made using a tracing of the Nuremberg portrait. Underdrawing of this sort has no known precedent in Rembrandt's genuine paintings and is not found in the Nuremberg

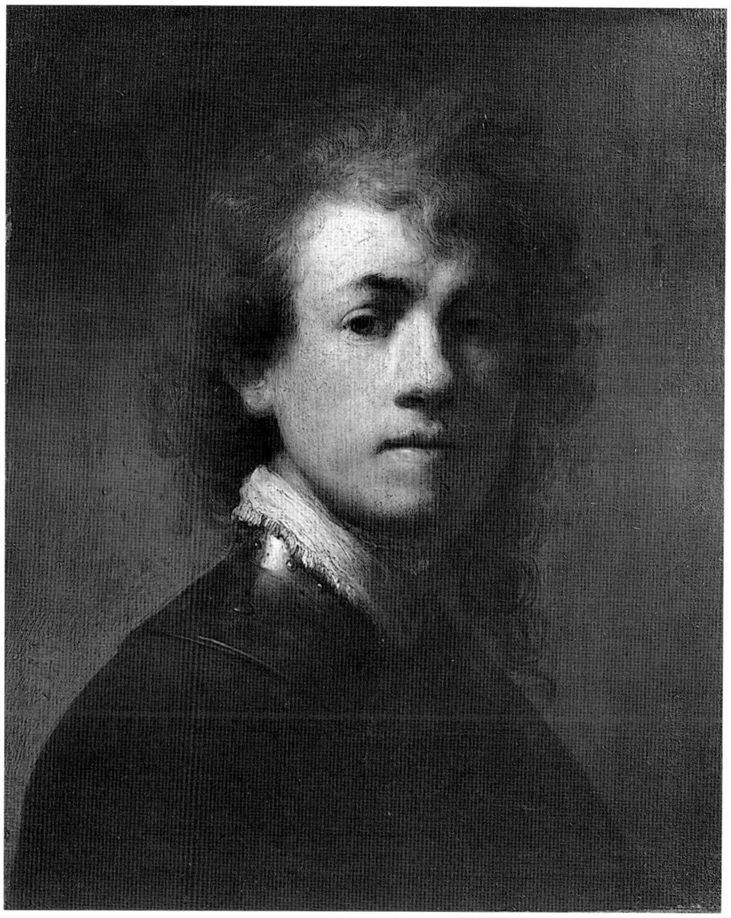

fig. 6a Rembrandt, *Self-Portrait with Gorget*, ca. 1629. Oil on wood, 38.2 x 31 cm. Germanisches Nationalmuseum, Nuremberg.

version. However, some early paintings by Gerrit Dou, in particular *An Old Woman Reading a Lectionary* of around 1631 (Rijksmuseum, Amsterdam), exhibit similar underdrawing with parallel lines.[6]

It should be stressed that the underdrawing in the Mauritshuis portrait cannot indicate conclusively that the artist was Dou, but it does show that the Nuremberg portrait was its model. The Nuremberg painting is quickly and energetically brushed, and the paint layers are built up in varying thicknesses, as is typical of Rembrandt's work of around 1629.[7] The unruly hair is thinly painted, allowing the warm brown underpaint to show through.

The Mauritshuis painting is more consistently and evenly brushed. The paint has been very carefully applied and covers the surface of the picture rather flatly so that underlayers do not show through. The transitions from brightly lit areas to shadow are sharply delineated, whereas Rembrandt typically used translucent layers of paint to achieve subtle gradations of shadow. There is also the troubling feeling that the portrait is too beautiful: the face is thinner, the skin and lips are glossy and perfect, and even the nose is less aggressively bulbous. And compared to the Nuremberg ver-

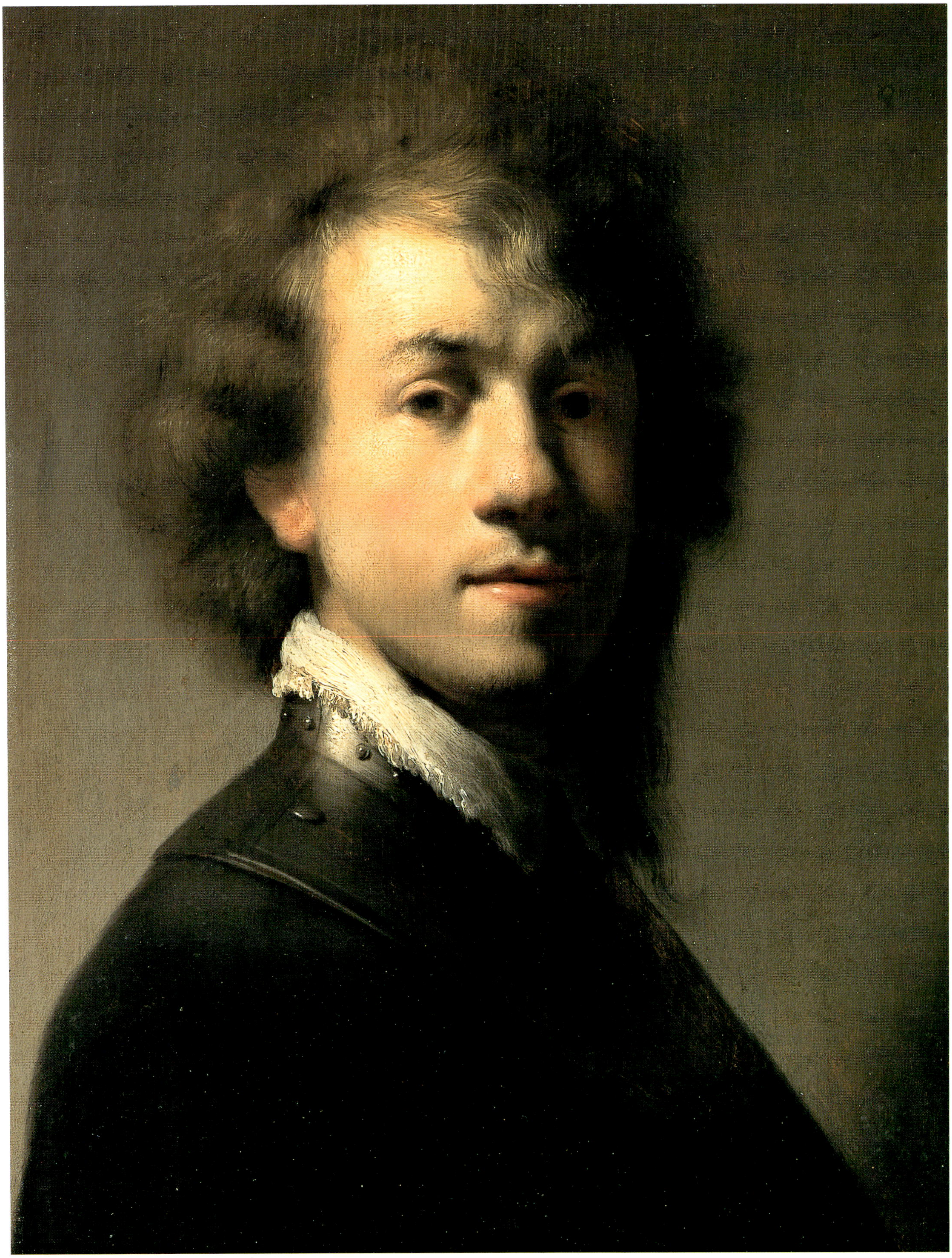

sion, Rembrandt seems to have run a comb through his hair. Indeed, the portrait from The Hague is not a close copy of the Nuremberg self-portrait, although they are very close in size, but instead is an imaginative variation on it. The head is positioned differently in relation to the torso, and the figure has a more elegant, almost aristocratic bearing. The two paintings project overall effects that are quite different.

In the Nuremberg painting, Rembrandt used his repertory of props and devices to present himself as a refined, aristocratic figure. His tousled hair is enhanced with an extended lock—a sign of noble lineage also seen in Rembrandt's self-portrait etching of 1629 (cat. 1). He wears a gorget (an armored collar). This studio prop, or a similar one, is also seen in Rembrandt's figure of an old man (cat. 17) and Lievens' portrait of Rembrandt (cat. 7). Therefore, it is a mistake to interpret the costume too specifically as a militaristic or patriotic gesture.[8] The attire is even less likely to have been a vanitas symbol of the transitory nature of youth.[9]

The Mauritshuis has suggested that Dou might be the author of the exhibited portrait since there are similarities in the underdrawing and Dou worked in a careful, highly finished manner (see for example fig. 4a). As such, it would represent a previously unknown, youthful style. This theory has not gained complete acceptance; the organizers of the Dou exhibition in 2000, Arthur Wheelock and Ronni Baer, do not consider the portrait to be by Dou.[10] There is also little concrete evidence to support Grimm's attribution of the painting to Isack Jouderville, another early pupil of Rembrandt. Grimm suggested Jouderville on the basis of a group of Rembrandtesque works that Ernst van de Wetering assigned to Jouderville, but these attributions remain uncertain.[11] The smooth technique and sharp shadows of the Mauritshuis painting are not dissimilar to portraits from Rembrandt's circle attributed to Jouderville (Cleveland, Royal Collection, University of North Carolina; Corpus A 23, C 54, C 58). Van de Wetering stated that "Jouderville must, for instance, have been greatly impressed by Rembrandt's *Self-portrait* of c. 1629 in the Mauritshuis."[12] It may be dangerous to advocate an attribution to any artist whose early work produced in Rembrandt's workshop cannot yet be identified with assurance.

Some scholars, including Arthur Wheelock (see essay in this volume) and Simon Schama,[13] remain convinced that the portrait in the Mauritshuis was painted by Rembrandt himself. Eric Jan Sluijter argues that Rembrandt deliberately painted two similar portraits in very different manners, one loose and rough, the other smooth and elegant.[14] The unique purpose of this exercise could explain the careful tracing of the Nuremberg portrait's design onto another panel, a practice otherwise unknown in Rembrandt's work. Sluijter also quite rightly suggests that the supposed "mistakes" in the Mauritshuis picture are subject to interpretation and are not in themselves arguments against Rembrandt's authorship.[15] Could the Mauritshuis painting be an exercise in a more elegant, fashionable style marked by slick surfaces and smooth brushwork?

While the issue remains open for discussion, certain factors weigh against an attribution to Rembrandt. The even brushwork and opaque layering of paint in the Mauritshuis portrait are not simply different from the version in Nuremberg, they are unprecedented in Rembrandt's paintings from 1628–30. Rembrandt's attempts at an elegant, socially refined style—seen for example in the self-portraits in the Gardner Museum (cat. 5) and in Liverpool (fig. 5a)—are entirely at odds with the character of the exhibited work. A beautiful painting does not need to have been painted by Rembrandt.

AC

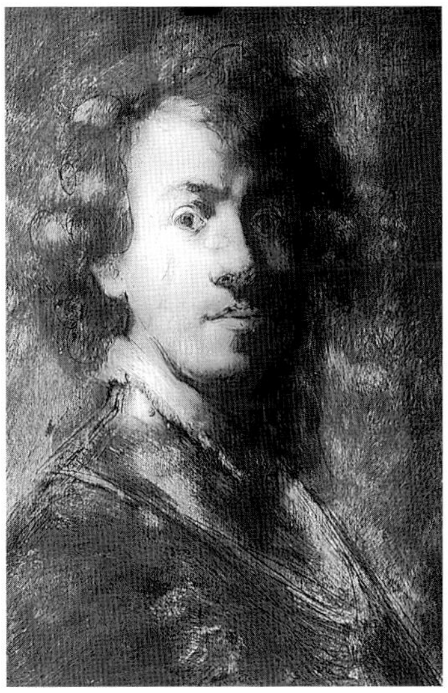

fig. 6b Infrared reflectogram of cat. 6.

1 Corpus 1982, p. 225 (no. A 21).
2 See Catalogue Documentation for references. In 1876 Bode published both paintings as by Rembrandt, but in 1897 (Bode 1897, no. 16) he assigned the Mauritshuis painting the prime entry and wrote that the Nuremberg painting was "perhaps also genuine."
3 Grimm 1991, pp. 21–26.
4 Alan Chong, in a paper delivered at the Rembrandt symposium at the National Gallery, London, in May 1992, agreed with Grimm's theory. Ernst van de Wetering saw the Nuremberg painting in 1993 and was convinced of its authenticity; in 1997 he labeled the Mauritshuis painting "Attr. to Rembrandt" (van de Wetering 1997, p. 160).
5 The technical study of the two paintings is discussed thoroughly by Edwin Buijsen in London 1999, no. 14, and by Buvelot, Wadum 1999.
6 London 1999, p. 116, fig. 14j. Buvelot, Wadum 1999, p. 42, state that two portraits by Dou of ca. 1630–31 in Kassel (inv. GK 258, GK 259) also exhibit similar underdrawing.
7 Edwin Buijsen (London 1999, p. 113) compares the painting to Rembrandt's self-portraits in Amsterdam and Munich (ibid, nos. 5, 7). The Nuremberg painting is not especially similar; the two other works are much smaller and have extensive areas scratched into wet paint.
8 Chapman 1990, p. 39.
9 Corpus, vol. 2, p. 838; the argument rests on the fact that armor sometimes appears in vanitas still lifes by J. D. de Heem. See also P. van Thiel in Berlin 1991, p. 134.
10 *Gerrit Dou, 1613–1675: Master Painter in the Age of Rembrandt* (exh. cat. National Gallery of Art, Washington, 2000).
11 Van de Wetering 1986, pp. 76–88. These attributions to Jouderville rest on comparison with a portrait in the National Gallery of Ireland, Dublin, which is very different in style.
12 Van de Wetering 1986, p. 84.
13 Schama 1999, p. 703: "But inconsistency, of itself, doesn't make for inadmissibility."
14 Paper presented at a symposium at the Mauritshuis, The Hague, December 1999.
15 The "mistakes" noted by van de Wetering include the reflection on the lower lip and the painting of the iris; see London 1999, p. 116.

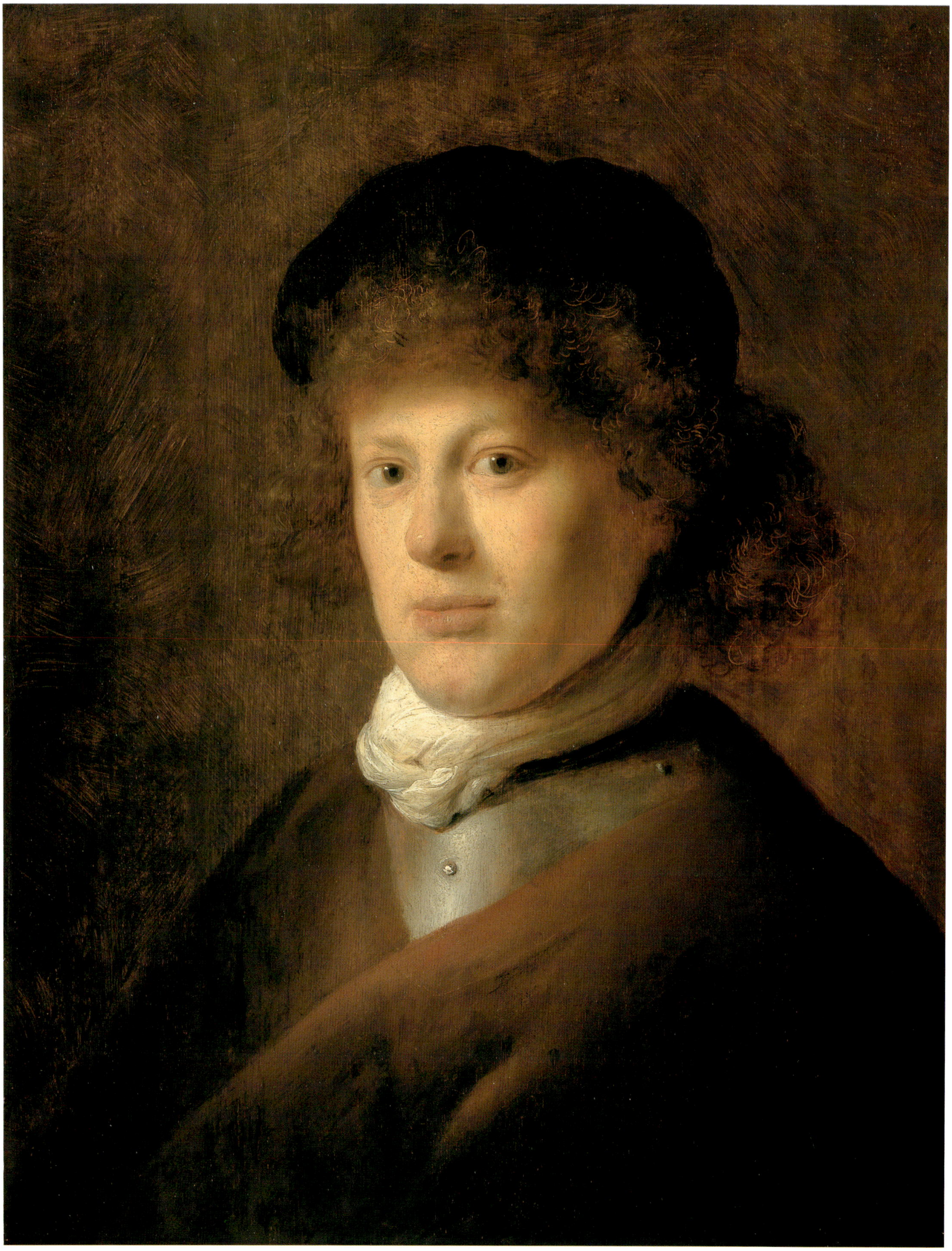

7
Jan Lievens
Portrait of Rembrandt ca. 1629

oil on wood, 57 × 44.7 cm
signed lower left: IL [monogram]
Cevat Collection, on loan to the Rijksmuseum, Amsterdam

This portrait of Rembrandt was painted by his colleague Jan Lievens when they were sharing a studio (see cat. 4), and at about the time they received a visit from the courtier Constantijn Huygens, secretary to the stadhouder. It was made in the same year as Rembrandt's own self-portrait in the Isabella Stewart Gardner Museum (cat. 5). One can easily imagine the scene in the artists' joint studio, with Rembrandt serving as willing model, looking directly at his friend.

The idealized, youthful likeness resembles other portraits and *tronies* by Lievens, most notably the *Portrait of a Young Man Richly Attired* of about 1630–31 (fig. 7a); areas of high finish alternate with patches of open, loose, and quite fluid brushstrokes typical of Lievens. In addition, interesting comparisons can be made with works by Rembrandt and his pupils, especially the portraits in Nuremberg and The Hague (fig. 6a and cat. 6). Notably, Lievens has highlighted Rembrandt's hair in a technique identical to that of his colleague. The face is somewhat softened and more rounded, although it is also blemished and unidealized, as befits its status as a study or *tronie*. The abstract background, jaunty cap, and loose robe make for picturesque contrast with the military gorget.

When the painting was cleaned in 1964, Lievens' monogram was revealed.[1] In 1967 Kurt Bauch dated the work to around 1630, but he did not think the sitter was Rembrandt because in reproductions the eyes appeared to be blue. After he saw the actual work in 1968 and noted that the eyes were grey-brown, he withdrew his objections. Identification of the subject as Rembrandt has since been universally accepted.[2] Rüdiger Klessmann dated the work to around 1629 based on stylistic similarities with Lievens' *Portrait of Constantijn Huygens*, dated that year (fig. 61).[3]

During the eighteenth and nineteenth centuries, this work was identified as a portrait by Lievens of the young Admiral Tromp, that is, Maerten Tromp (1597–1653), whom Lievens did indeed later portray. This was a misunderstanding of a 1736 inventory of the possessions of the 10th Earl of Derby (1689–1776), where the painting is listed as, "A head of one of the Earls of Derby, by Lievens," with the annotation "Van Trump." The annotation might mean that the picture had been bought from someone named van Trump.

HG

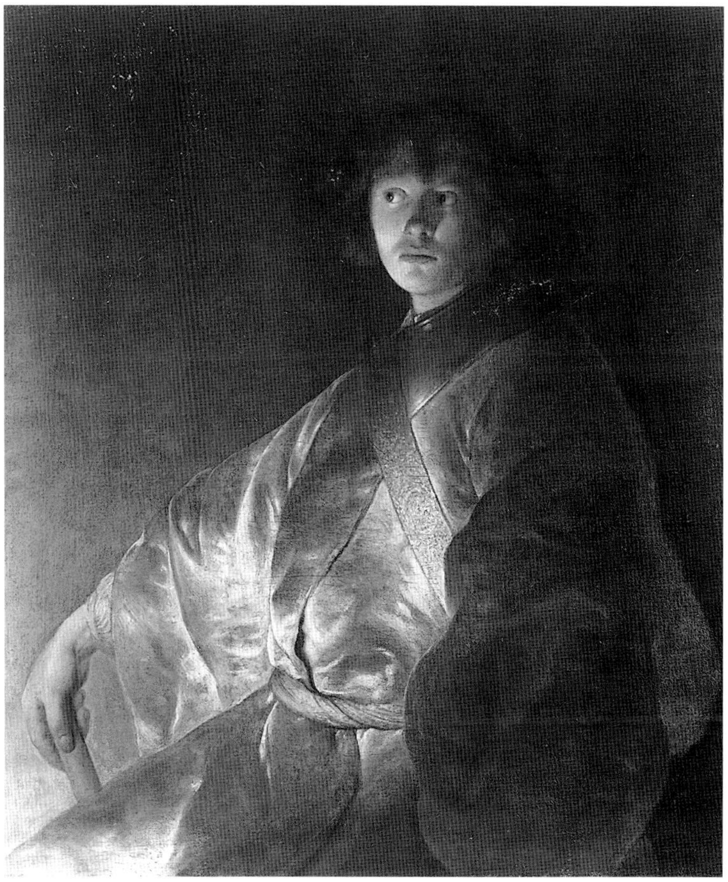

fig. 7a Jan Lievens, *Portrait of a Young Man Richly Attired*, ca. 1630–31. Oil on canvas, 112 × 97 cm. National Gallery of Scotland, Edinburgh.

1 Hans Schneider, in 1932, thought that the painting was probably not by Lievens (Schneider 1932, no. 264b). All other sources consider it autograph.
2 Bauch 1967, p. 263 [as not a portrait of Rembrandt]. The identification was accepted by Bob Haak (Haak 1968, p. 42), J.R. Judson (Chicago 1969, no. 77, as ca. 1629–30), R. Ekkart (Schneider, Ekkart 1973, no. 264b), and R. Klessmann (Braunschweig 1979, no. 19).
3 Braunschweig 1979, no. 19.

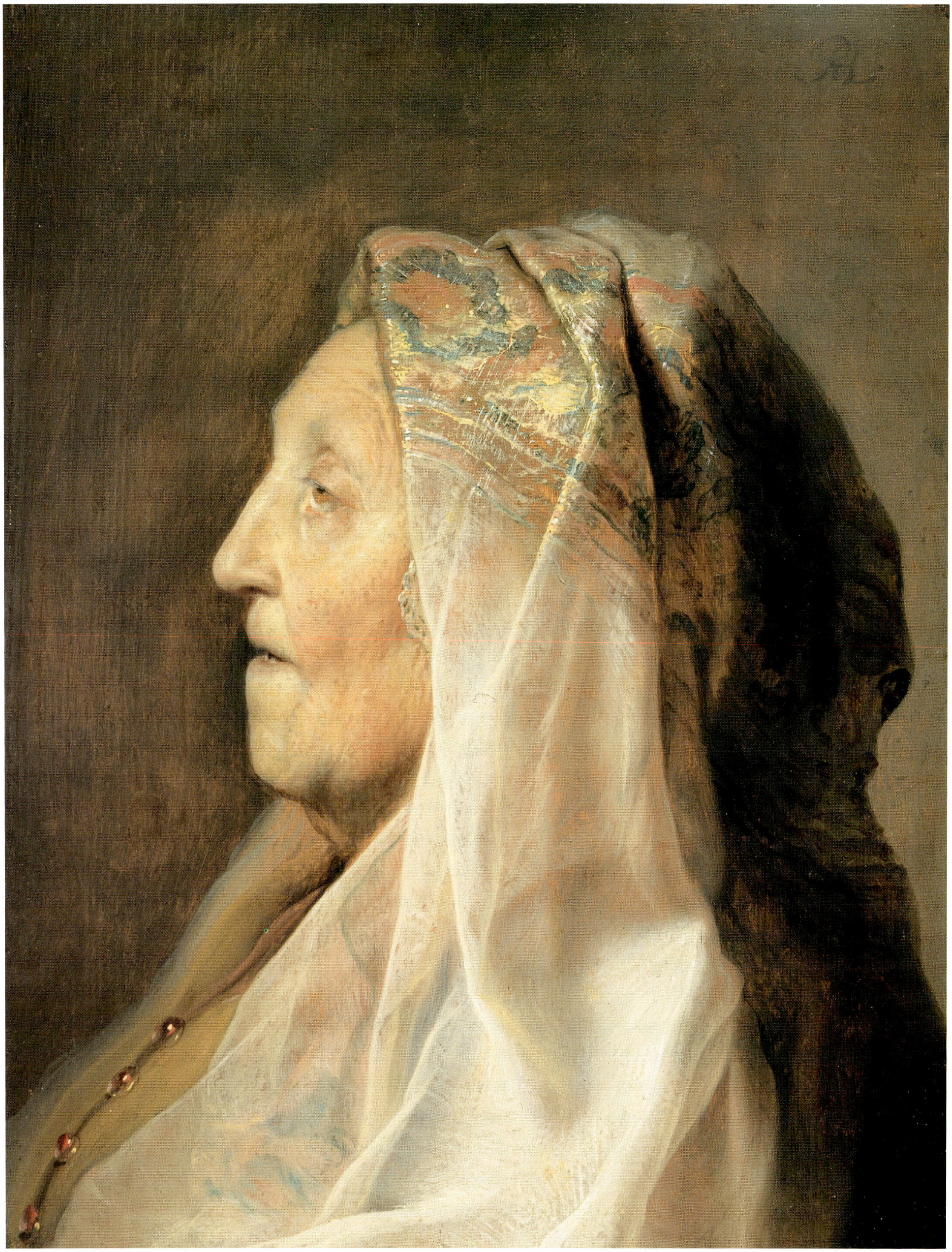

8

Jan Lievens

An Old Woman (called Rembrandt's Mother) ca. 1629

oil on wood, 43.5 × 35 cm
inscribed upper right (falsely): RHL. [monogram]
Isabel and Alfred Bader

This exotically attired old woman, her translucent headscarf shimmering with highlights of vibrant color, seems to have been depicted not just as a character study, but as some historical or biblical figure.[1] The model, who was used by Rembrandt (fig. 8a) as well as Lievens, has traditionally been referred to as Rembrandt's mother. However, although a drawing by Rembrandt survives that is inscribed with his father's name (fig. 16a), we have no secure image of Neeltgen Willemsdr van Zuytbrouck. Neeltgen married Rembrandt's father in 1589 and died in Leiden in 1640; she would have been about 61 years old in 1629. The identification has at least some documentary support, since the 1679 inventory of Rembrandt's friend and client Clement de Jonghe lists an etching plate titled "Rembrandt's mother."[2]

Whoever the woman was, like an old man used by Rembrandt (cats. 14, 16, 17, 18), she served frequently as a model for the two artists. The composition of this painting closely corresponds, in reverse, to the upper two-thirds of Rembrandt's etching *Seated Woman in an Oriental Headdress* (fig. 8b), called "Een oude persiaansche vrou" (an old Persian woman) in de Jonghe's 1679 inventory.[3] This connection illustrates the mutual borrowing between the artists during this period. Furthermore, the woman appears frequently in Rembrandt's etchings between 1628 and 1633,[4] as well as in a wide range of Biblical subjects painted by Rembrandt in this period (figs. 8c, 48, Corpus A 12, A 27, A 32). She was employed again by Lievens in his *Job in Misery* dated 1631 (National Gallery of Canada, Ottawa), as a figure with a long-fringed shawl wrapped about her head, evocative of a prophetess, and in *Prophetess Reading*.[5]

Because of characteristic elements such as the brightly lit head placed against a darker ground, Rüdiger Klessmann associates this painting with other works by Lievens from the late 1620s, such as *Mark the Evangelist* (Kunsthalle, Hamburg) and *Samson and Delilah* (Rijksmuseum, Amsterdam) where the profiled Delilah is similar.[6] Distinguishing this painting from the artist's monochromatic works of the mid-1620s, Klessmann convincingly suggests that it was made around 1629, approximately the same time as Lievens's portrait of Rembrandt (cat. 7).

HG

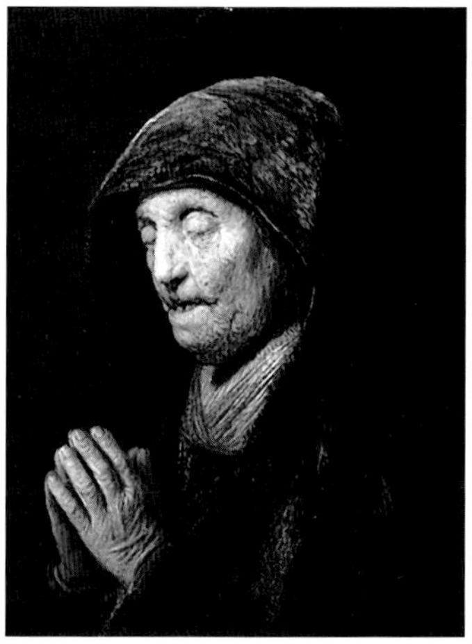

fig. 8a Rembrandt, *Old Woman Praying*, ca. 1629–30. Oil on copper, 15.5 × 12.2 cm. Residenzgalerie, Salzburg.

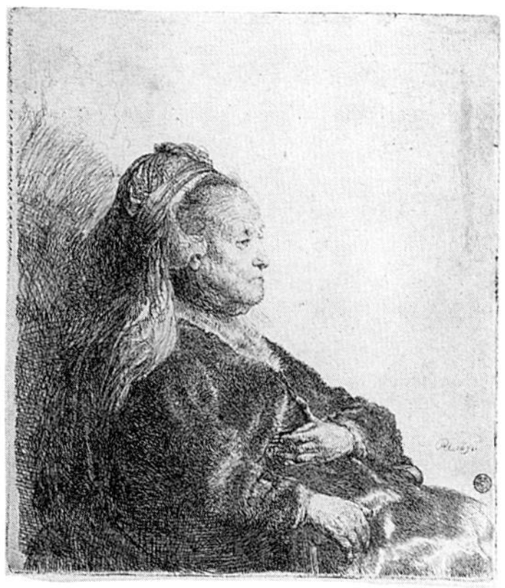

fig. 8b Rembrandt, *Seated Woman in an Oriental Headdress*, 1631. Etching, 14.6 × 12.7 cm. Bartsch 348.

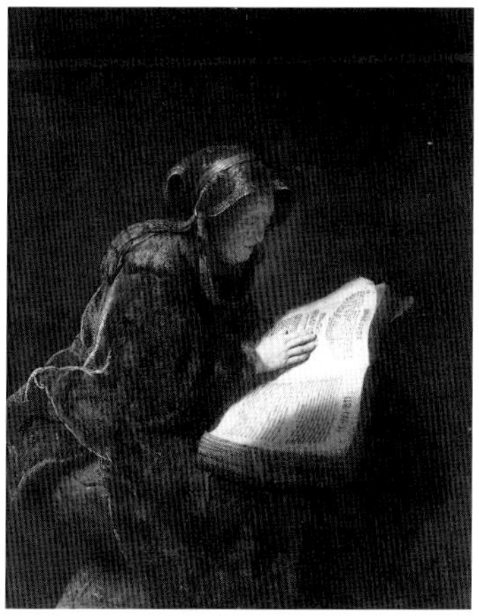

fig. 8c Rembrandt, *An Old Woman Reading (Prophetess Anna)*, 1631. Oil on wood, 59.8 × 47.7 cm. Rijksmuseum. Amsterdam.

1 Peter Sutton, in Melbourne 1997, no. 36. Sutton proposes a rough dating of 1625–29.
2 De Hoop, Scheffer 1971, pp. 6, 14, no. 10: "Rembrandts moeder." This can be identified as Bartsch 343.
3 De Hoop, Scheffer 1971, no. 20.
4 For example, Bartsch nos. 343, 348, 349, 351, 352, 354.
5 See respectively, Braunschweig 1979, no. 25; Schneider, Ekkart 1973, no. S358. There is also another version of the exhibited painting (Sumowski 1973, no. 1262).
6 Braunschweig 1979, p. 70 no. 18. The paintings in Hamburg and Amsterdam are discussed in ibid., nos. 11, 16.

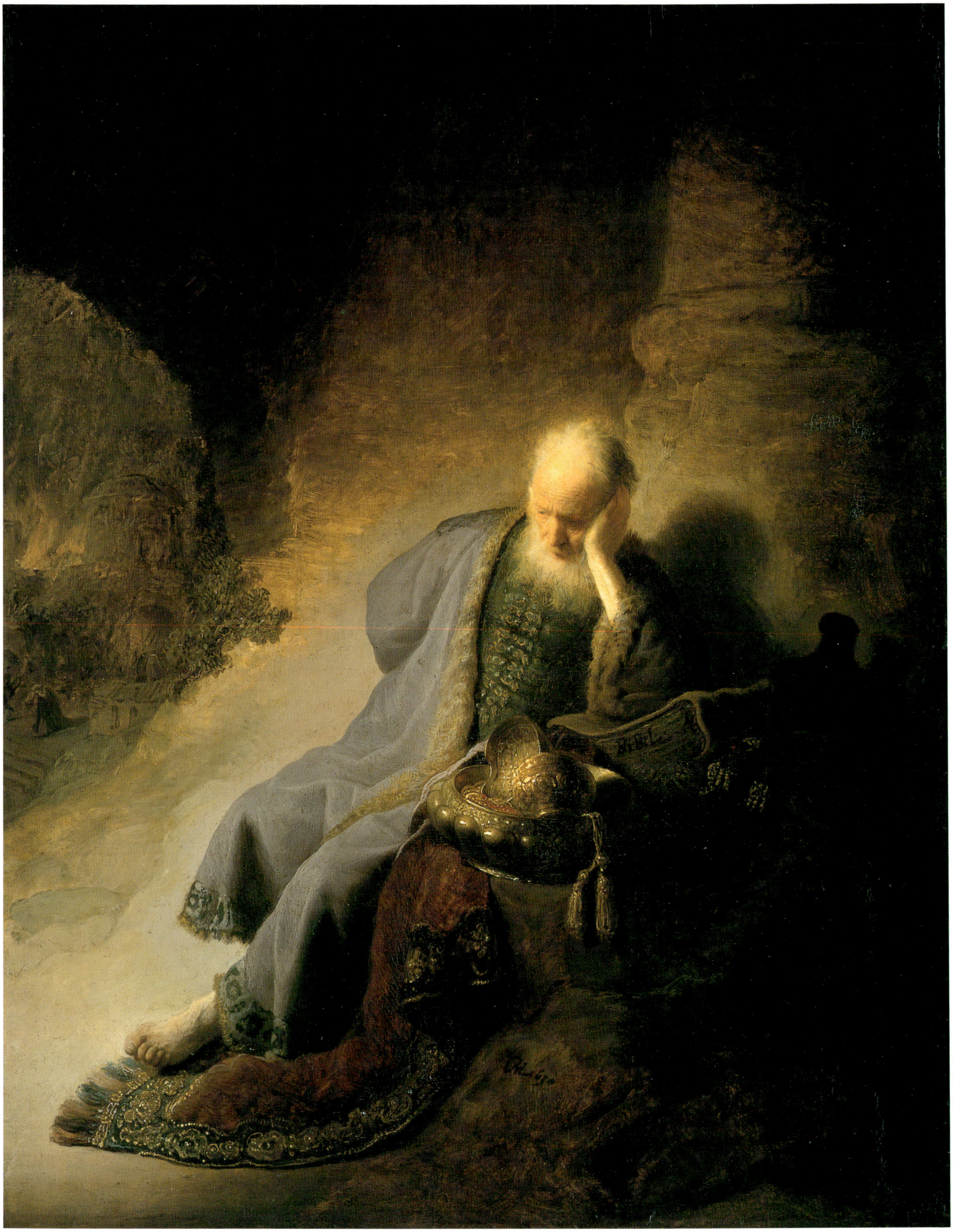

14
Rembrandt
Jeremiah Lamenting the Destruction of Jerusalem 1630

oil on wood, 58.3 × 46.6 cm
signed in center on stone ledge: RHL [monogram 1630]
Rijksmuseum, Amsterdam

This painting belongs to a discrete group of works depicting old, deeply introspective prophets, saints, and apostles that Rembrandt and Jan Lievens produced during their years of partnership and rivalry in Leiden. Rembrandt's *Apostle Paul at His Writing Desk* (fig. 14a), painted shortly before *Jeremiah Lamenting the Destruction of Jerusalem*, shows the same figure similarly absorbed in silent contemplation. The elderly, bearded model, in the past identified as the artist's father, also posed for a series of figure studies in red chalk, as well as for both etched and painted character heads, or *tronies*, of old men (fig. 14b). *Jeremiah Lamenting the Destruction of Jerusalem*, dating from the end of Rembrandt's Leiden period, represents the high point of the group in its evocation of complex psychological mood, allusive imagery, and pictorial refinement.

The aged prophet, in the traditional pose of melancholy or sorrow, leans his head heavily on his left hand to suggest the weightiness of his thoughts. He sits at the base of an immense pillar, which forms part of a cavernous, possibly ruined architectural space. On a stone ledge at his side rest a large book (the inscription "BiBel" was probably added later),[1] ornate metal vessels, an oriental carpet or cloth, a shawl, a simple jug, and a traveler's satchel. Through the archway at the left is a distant view of a city ablaze and under attack.

Early on, the painting had been variously interpreted as representing Lot and the Burning of Sodom, Virgil's Anchises at Troy's destruction, an anonymous philosopher, and a figure in a vanitas image.[2] In 1897, however, Wilhelm Bode and Cornelis Hofstede de Groot recognized the brooding old man as Jeremiah, an identification that has been generally accepted.[3] The various motifs in the painting relate to Jerusalem's destruction and the start of the Babylonian exile in 586 BC—events described in 2 Kings (25.2), 2 Chronicles (36), Jeremiah (32–33, 39, 52), and Lamentations. The Book of Jeremiah records the prophet's warnings to the people of Judah that their faithlessness would be punished, while Lamentations describes Jeremiah's mourning over the tragic fulfillment of his prophecies. How the different elements in Rembrandt's painting cohere as a unified image, however, has been subject to debate. Some observers have even suggested that Rembrandt intentionally created a pictorial puzzle that refuses to yield its meaning in a straightforward manner.[4]

While Rembrandt portrays Jeremiah outside Jerusalem during the Babylonian assault, Jeremiah 32.2 and 33.1 report that the prophet was imprisoned in the court of the guard at that time, and was not freed until after the city's fall. A pictorial tradition of medieval

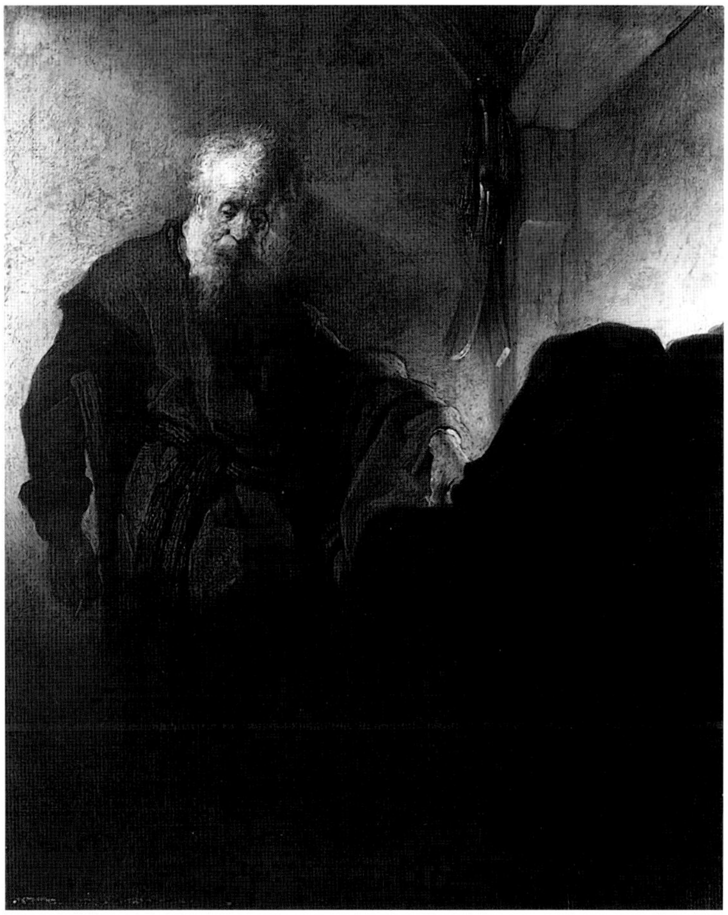

fig. 14a Rembrandt, *The Apostle Paul at His Writing Desk*, ca. 1629–30. Oil on wood, 47.2 × 38.6 cm. Germanisches Nationalmuseum, Nuremberg.

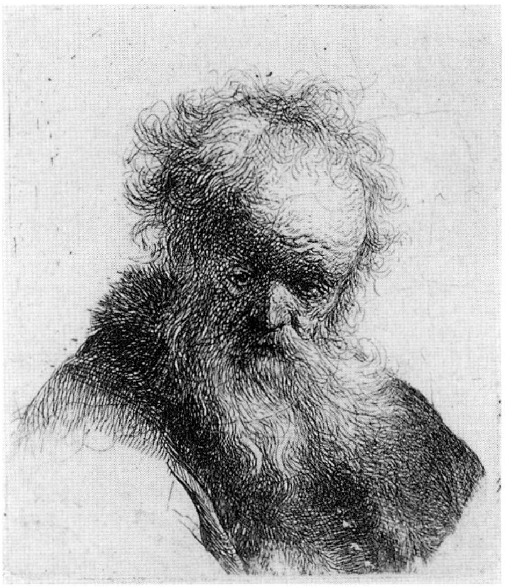

fig. 14b Rembrandt, *Old Man*, ca. 1631. Etching, 7.1 × 6.4 cm. Bartsch 291.

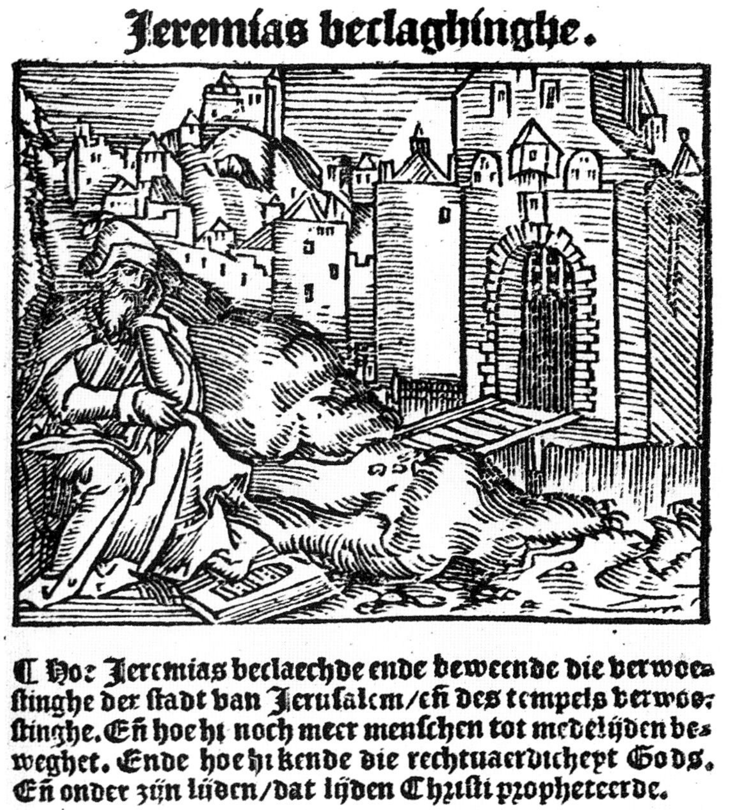

fig. 14c *Jeremiah's Lamentation*, 1532. Frontispiece to Jeremiah in Willem Vorsterman's Bible (Antwerp, 1532).

origin that Rembrandt would have known from sixteenth-century Bible illustrations—such as the woodcut introduction to the Book of Lamentations in Willem Vorsterman's Bible of 1532 (fig. 14c)—shows Jeremiah seated in a similarly melancholic pose outside the city; the book in which he inscribed his sorrows lies at his feet. Such a print may well have served as Rembrandt's starting point.[5] But, significantly, in this visual tradition Jerusalem is seen before the siege. In identifying the vessels at Jeremiah's side as Temple treasures that were subsequently carried off to Babylon, Franz Landsberger argued in 1946 that Rembrandt consulted the apocryphal Book of Maccabees, which relates that the prophet hid the treasures in a cave.[6] More recently, Christian Tümpel has proposed a less obscure source, Flavius Josephus's *Jewish Antiquities*, an illustrated copy of which was recorded among Rembrandt's possessions in the inventory drawn up in connection with his bankruptcy in 1656.[7] Josephus 10.9 recounts that after Jerusalem's defeat Jeremiah was released from prison and offered gifts and provisions by Nebuzaradan, the Babylonian commander, but that he chose to remain in his ruined country. As Shelley Perlove rightly observes, though, the same episode is also recorded in the Bible (Jer. 40.5–6).[8] Furthermore, the precious vessels prominently displayed in the foreground are (as Landsberger suggested) more likely the ritual ladles and bowls that the Babylonians looted from the Temple (Jer. 52.19). Rather than illustrating a specific biblical episode, Rembrandt seems to have gathered a number of iconographic motifs associated with the destruction of Jerusalem. Breaking with the unities of time and place, he has encompassed in a single image the fullness of Jeremiah's tales of woe: his prophecies as the harbinger of God's wrath and his nostalgic ruminations on the desecration of the Holy City and the exile of the Jews.

The assembled motifs form a chain of allusions revolving around the mourning prophet, signaling the tragic events over which he broods. The distant view of Jerusalem's fall includes tiny soldiers storming the gates of the city, scaling its walls, and setting fire to the Temple (the monumental domed structure) and all other important buildings. A figure runs from the conflagration with his hands covering his eyes. He has generally been identified as King Zedekiah of Judah, who was captured and blinded by the Babylonian king, Nebuchadnezzar.[9] Zedekiah, however, had escaped from Jerusalem the night before the final assault; the blinding occurred when he was captured after the city's defeat. Perhaps the figure alludes to a passage in the Book of Lamentations in which Jeremiah likens his ravaged, exiled people to blind men: "Now they grope through the streets like men who are blind" (Lam. 4.14). A curious winged creature with a burning torch, for which no convincing reference has yet been proposed, hovers over the city. This fiery angel may have been intended to give visual form to the multiple references in Lamentations to God's wrath descending upon Jerusalem like a fire from above.[10] Rembrandt probably also intended the large book on which Jeremiah rests his elbow as the chronicle of his prophecies and sorrows. In the meticulously painted still life below Jeremiah's elbow, Rembrandt brings together the ritual objects stolen from the Temple with a sumptuous carpet and a shawl, as well as a simple traveler's bag and bottle.[11] The poignant combination of rich and simple things evokes the Hebrews' past glories in contrast to their present misfortunes and exile. The painting can thus be seen to enfold the scope of Jeremiah's nostalgia and despair as described in Lamentations 1.7: "In the days of her affliction and wandering Jerusalem remembers all the treasures that were hers in days of old." Jeremiah's lonely ruminations on the Hebrews' lost grandeur, furthermore, recall the prophet's resolute hope for restoration to the Holy Land: "it is good to wait quietly for the salvation of the Lord. Let him sit alone in silence, for the Lord has laid it on him.... For men are not cast off by the Lord forever" (Lam. 3.26–28 and 3.31).

Jeremiah Lamenting the Destruction of Jerusalem is a richly allusive image of the prophet reflecting on the catastrophic events he predicted and witnessed. That Rembrandt's contemporaries would have projected onto the thoughts of this isolated figure the larger context of the scriptural narratives is confirmed by Constantijn Huygens' *ekphrasis* of Rembrandt's *Judas Returning the Pieces of Silver* of 1629 (fig. 24). In that case the painting illustrates a specific biblical episode, but Huygens fixes tightly on the single figure of Judas in his moment of despair. Huygens praises "the crazed Judas —wailing, begging for forgiveness, and at the same time completely without hope... the whole body wracked by some horrific misery," and notes that "these things did not occur to Protogenes, or to Apelles, or to Parrhasios... [but] a Dutchman, a miller, a beardless boy, has brought them together in a single figure and depicted them completely." The monumental effect of this relatively small panel exemplifies Rembrandt's extraordinary ability, as Huygens also remarked, to convey the emotional range and grandeur which one "would seek in vain even in the largest paintings of others."

Rembrandt's pose for the reclining Jeremiah, as J. van Rijckevorsel and J. Bruyn have shown, echoes Italian prototypes, notably a figure of Peter in Guido Reni's *Apostles Peter and Paul*.[12] It is unclear, however, how Rembrandt would have known Reni's composition, as no early print after the painting has been identified. In any event, Rembrandt's characteristically varied and lively handling of paint is fully evident in the exceptionally well-preserved painting. Wielding his brush with great confidence, Rembrandt differentiated his movements to delineate the textures and surfaces of the prophet's worried brow, the fine hairs of his beard, and the fur trim of his robe. Dabs and strokes of quite thick paint heighten the illusionistic effect and suggest the fleeting effects of light reflecting on the ritual objects, the tassels, the richly embroidered border of the carpet, and the flames engulfing Jerusalem. Moreover, Rembrandt achieved a translucent atmosphere through thin, sketchy passages of brushwork that expose the light-yellow ground underneath the paint layer; he even drew directly into the wet paint with the end of the brush to create the vibrant highlights in the shrubbery and Jeremiah's braided doublet. No one area of descriptive brushwork distracts, however, from the rich interplay of light and dark that unifies the scene in a heavy atmosphere and suggests a deeply somber mood.

1 The inscription, which is atypical for Rembrandt, does not appear in Georg Friedrich Schmidt's 1768 etching of the painting. See Corpus 1982, pp. 280, 283.

2 For various interpretations of the subject, see Corpus 1982, p. 282.

3 Bode 1897, pp. 52–53. The identification was questioned by J.G. van Gelder (1963) and Gerson (1968, p. 489, no. 24).

4 Albert Blankert, in Melbourne 1997, no. 22.

5 Corpus 1982, p. 282.

6 Franz Landsberger, *Rembrandt, the Jews and the Bible* (Philadelphia, 1946), p. 109.

7 Tümpel 1984, p. 185. Rembrandt's inventory is translated (with some errors) in Strauss, van der Meulen 1979, doc. 1656/12.

8 Perlove 1995, p. 163. No evidence, however, supports Perlove's effort to relate Rembrandt's painting to contemporary debates between orthodox Dutch Calvinists and their Remonstrant opponents.

9 See Corpus 1982, p. 282; and Pieter van Thiel, in Berlin 1991, no. 8. Budick 1988, p. 261, associates the figure with the false prophet Pashur, son of the priest Immer (Jer. 20.1–6), or Rachel weeping for her children (Jer. 31.15), or perhaps Jeremiah himself.

10 Lam. 1.13 and 4.11. Louis Réau, *Iconographie de l'art chrétienne*, vol. 2 (Paris, 1956), p. 371 identified the figure as a demon setting fire to the city. Budick 1988, p. 264, and Perlove 1995, p. 162, interpret it as an angel. The Rembrandt Research Project (Corpus 1982, p. 282) notes that although God's fury is repeatedly likened to fire in Lamentations, the figure "is nonetheless unusual."

11 Budick 1988, pp. 260–64, referring to Jer. 19 and Jer. 13.1–11, attempts to relate the jug and shawl to a broken potter's jug and a ruined girdle.

12 J. van Rijckevorsel, *Rembrandt en de traditie* (Rotterdam, 1932), p. 80; J. Bruyn "Rembrandt and the Italian Baroque," *Simiolus* 4 (1970), pp. 28–48, esp. pp. 32–34.

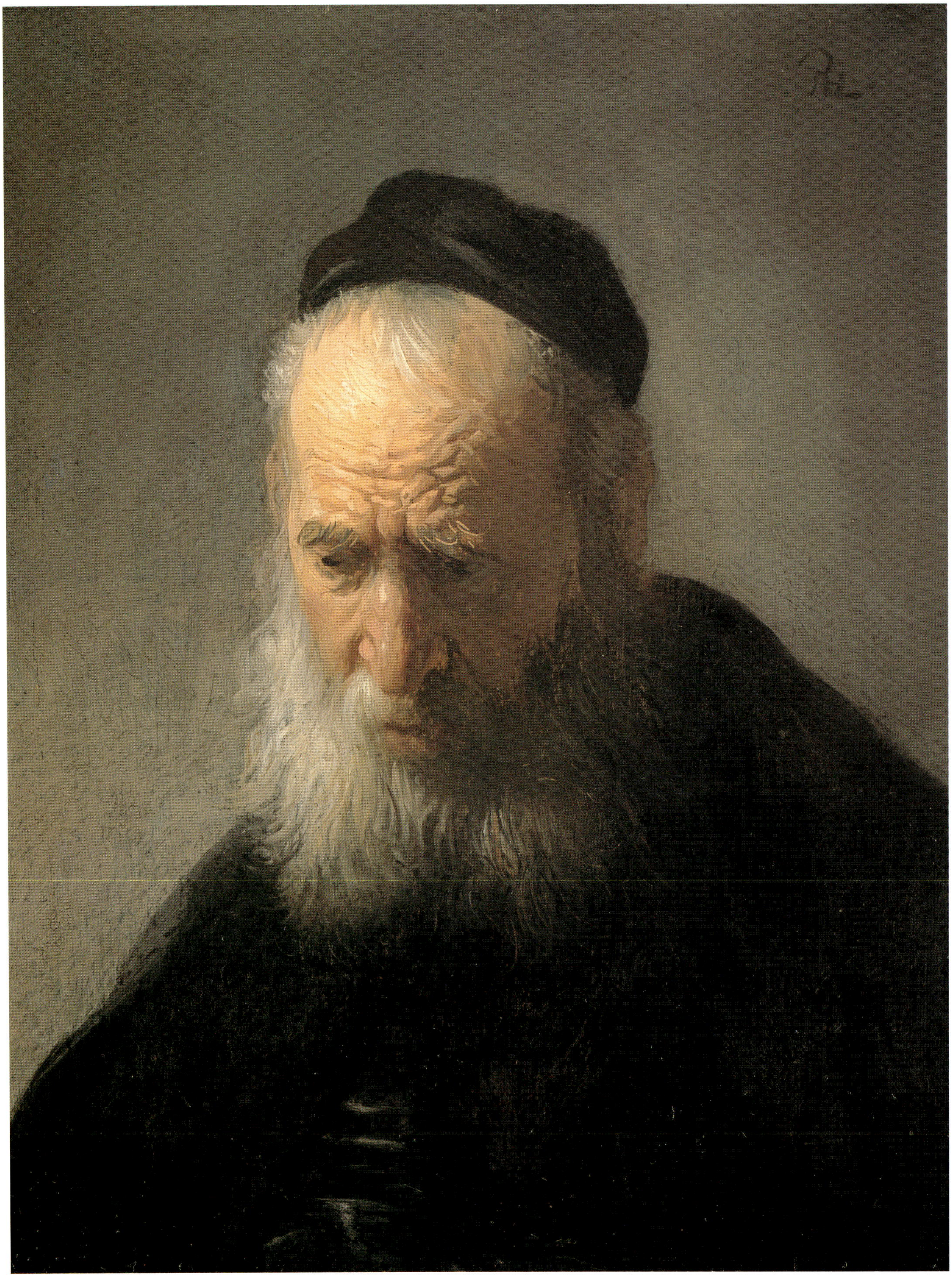

Rembrandt's small paintings on copper are also more broadly handled. *The Laughing Soldier* dated 1630 (Mauritshuis, The Hague) provides a good comparison with the exhibited work.[5] A few years later, Rembrandt painted several monochromatic studies on paper that also show a thick, sketchy technique.[6] Although *Old Man Wearing a Cap* is not painted in precisely the same manner as any of these examples, some of its rich, energetic brushwork has direct parallels in other paintings, especially *Paul at His Writing Desk* (fig. 14a). Moreover the evocative layering and blending of translucent pigments, which often allows the underpaint to show through, is entirely characteristic of Rembrandt. The contrast of the coarse strokes of the head with the smoother background and costume might be due to the quickly sketched nature of a first stage, which was then completed more smoothly.[7] This process accords perfectly with Samuel van Hoogstraten's instructions for creating a painting with a sense of recession. A pupil of Rembrandt in the 1640s, van Hoogstraten wrote in 1678 that objects painted with texture seem to come forward while smoothly brushed objects recede: "Therefore I would like things which should come forward to be painted roughly and lively, and that which is to recede be painted more neatly and more simply the further back it lies."[8]

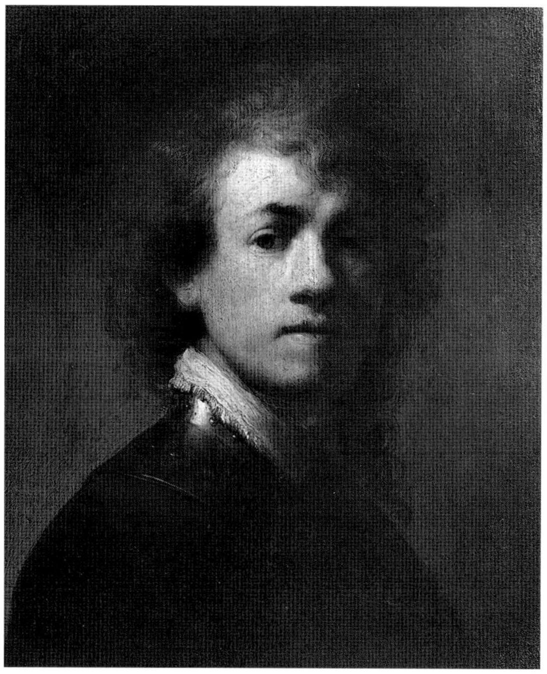

fig. 16c Rembrandt, *Self-Portrait with a Gorget*, ca. 1629. Oil on wood, 38.2 x 31 cm. Germanisches Nationalmuseum, Nuremberg.

A print by J. G. van Vliet in 1634 provides documentary evidence of Rembrandt's authorship. Van Vliet made a number of etchings very closely based on Rembrandt's work. These were almost certainly done in collaboration with Rembrandt himself, an arrangement that seemed to continue past Rembrandt's move to Amsterdam.[9] The print based on this painting (fig. 16d) is almost the same size and is inscribed "RH inventor," indicating that it is a copy of a composition by Rembrandt.[10]

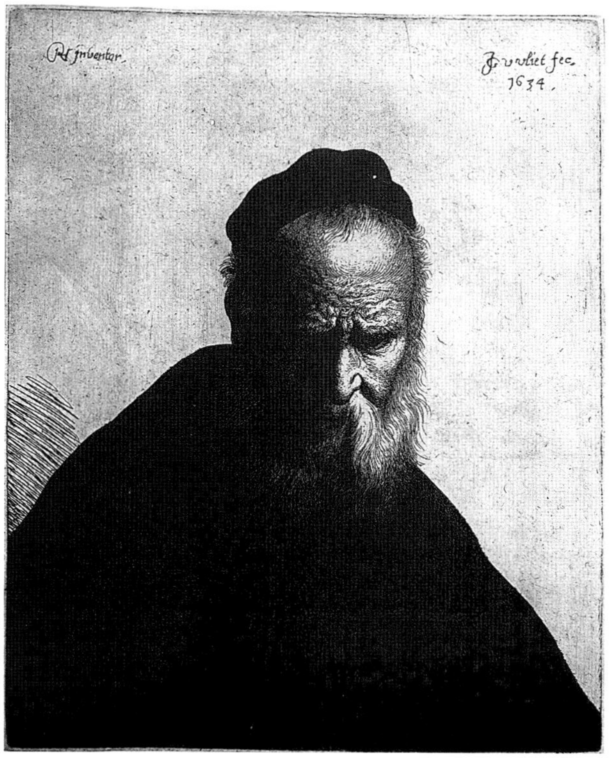

fig. 16d J.G. van Vliet, after Rembrandt, *Old man Wearing a Cap*, 1634. Etching and engraving, 22.4 x 18 cm. Rijksmuseum, Amsterdam. Hollstein 23 (1st state).

Joachim von Sandrart praised Rembrandt's naturalistic paintings of old people: "In the depiction of old people, and their skin and hair, he showed great diligence, patience, and experience, so that they came close to resembling simple life."[11] Academic critics like Roger de Piles and Arnold Houbraken found Rembrandt's interest in old and common folk distasteful, but Lambert ten Kate in 1724, while noting that Rembrandt liked to depict "vile and base" people, conceded that he, "nevertheless, thanks to a skillfully unified light that enhances things, normally gives to his simple people expressive humors and passions, as well as a natural attitude without affectation; although all of this rarely has anything noble."[12]

Even late in his career, Rembrandt continued to paint old men in contemplative poses, the most famous being *Aristotle Contemplating the Bust of Homer* of 1653 (Metropolitan Museum of Art, New York). The *Apostle Bartholomew*, dated 1657 (Timken Museum of Art, San Diego), is a quiet and moving study that focuses on the expressively wrinkled brow. But perhaps nothing surpassed the intensely emotional portrayals of old men and women, redolent with sorrow and repentance, created by Rembrandt as a young man in the years 1629–30.

AC

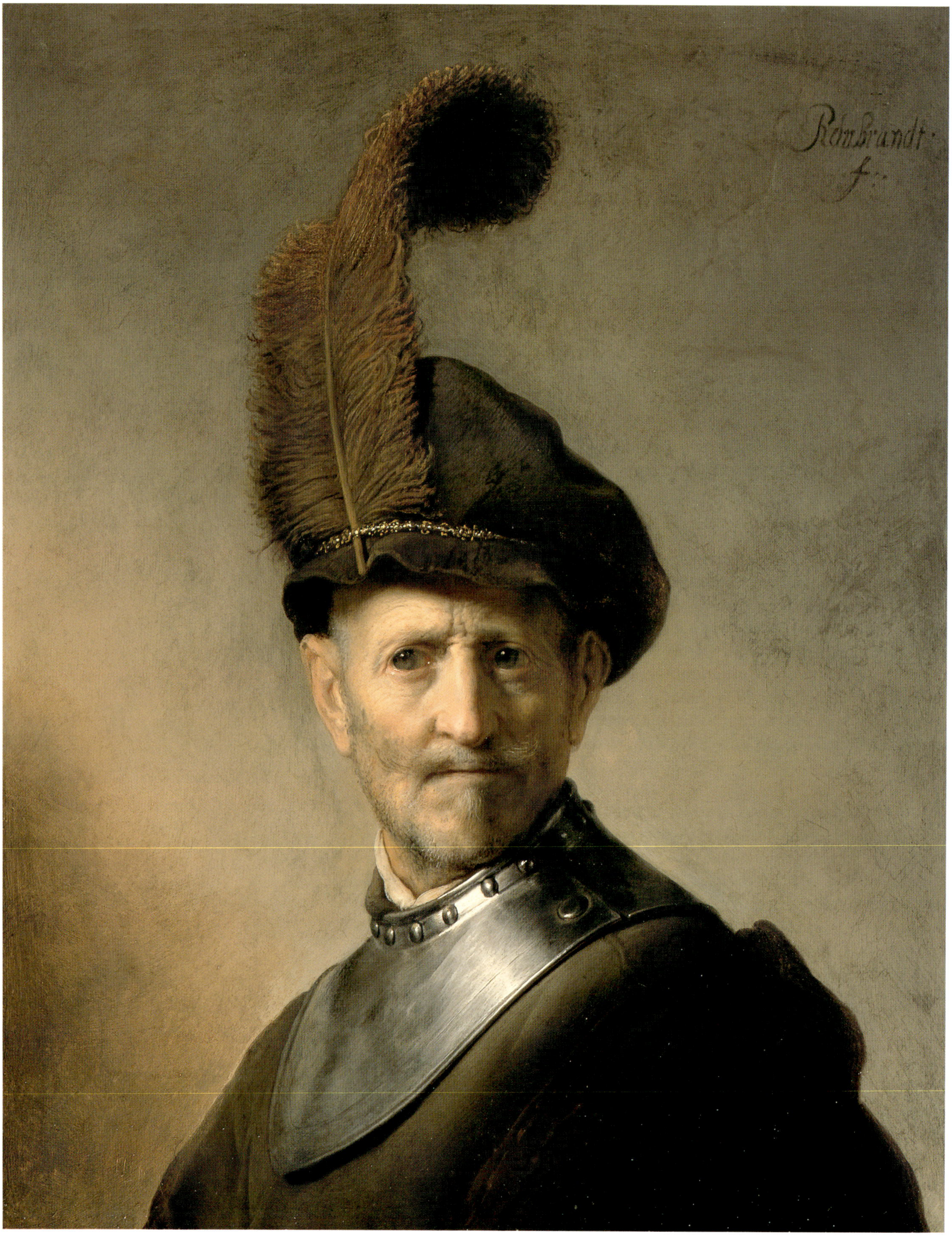
Rembrandt
f.

Several of Rembrandt's early self-portraits and character studies show men wearing a collar of armor and fanciful plumed headgear. It is clear that these are studio props, and it is doubtful that Rembrandt intended that they have any specific meaning. As early as 1627, he painted a rather comical, plump figure dressed in a gorget and an elaborate plumed hat (Corpus A 8), while some self-portraits, including one from 1629 (fig. 6a), show Rembrandt in military costume. An even more extravagant presentation is found in a painting of an old man, *Man in a Gorget and Gold Chain* of about 1631 (fig. 17a), where the figure wears the same gorget, a gold medallion on a chain, and a fabulously elaborate feathered hat. Could such an image be mocking the pretensions of the honorary (and battle-shy) civic guards of the Dutch towns? This painting is ostentatious and considerably larger than the Getty painting, which is an intimate image that focuses much more intently on the inner character of the model. Where the aloof figure in *Man in a Gorget and Gold Chain* stares blankly off into space, his counterpart here looks towards us to reveal a furtive anxiety or melancholy. The careful brushwork used to delineate the eyes and brow evince Rembrandt's struggle to capture a personality.

With this painting, Rembrandt took an important step towards the convincing, psychologically penetrating portraits that he would produce with such commercial success in Amsterdam. It demonstrates a considerable advance on the technique, lighting, and characterization of the self-portrait of 1629 in the Gardner Museum (cat. 5). The turn of the shoulders, rich background illumination, and penetrating gaze are also to be found in the portrait of Nicolaes Ruts (fig. 68) and *Man in Oriental Costume* of 1632 (Metropolitan Museum of Art, New York).

Although the Rembrandt Research Project in 1982 could not come to a definitive conclusion about the attribution of the painting, most scholars have confirmed Rembrandt's authorship.[1] In 1994 it was closely examined together with the Gardner Museum's self-portrait (cat. 5). The results were described by Walter Liedtke, who concluded that the numerous similarities indicated the painting was indeed by Rembrandt.[2]

AC

1 Corpus B 4. Tümpel assigned the painting to Rembrandt's workshop (Tümpel 1986, no. A34), but the painting has been accepted by Schatborn (1986, p. 62), Slatkes (1992, no. 279), Grimm (1991, p. 96), and Liedtke (1995).

2 Liedtke 1995; the article is also a detailed attack on the methods of the Rembrandt Research Project. The self-portrait from the Gardner Museum was conserved at the Getty Museum in 1994, allowing close comparison with the exhibited painting. The Rembrandt Research Project (Corpus 1982, p. 421) had previously pointed to similarities between the two works. X-radiographs reveal that another figure, upside-down in relation to the present one, lies under the painting's surface (Corpus 1982, p. 417, repr.).

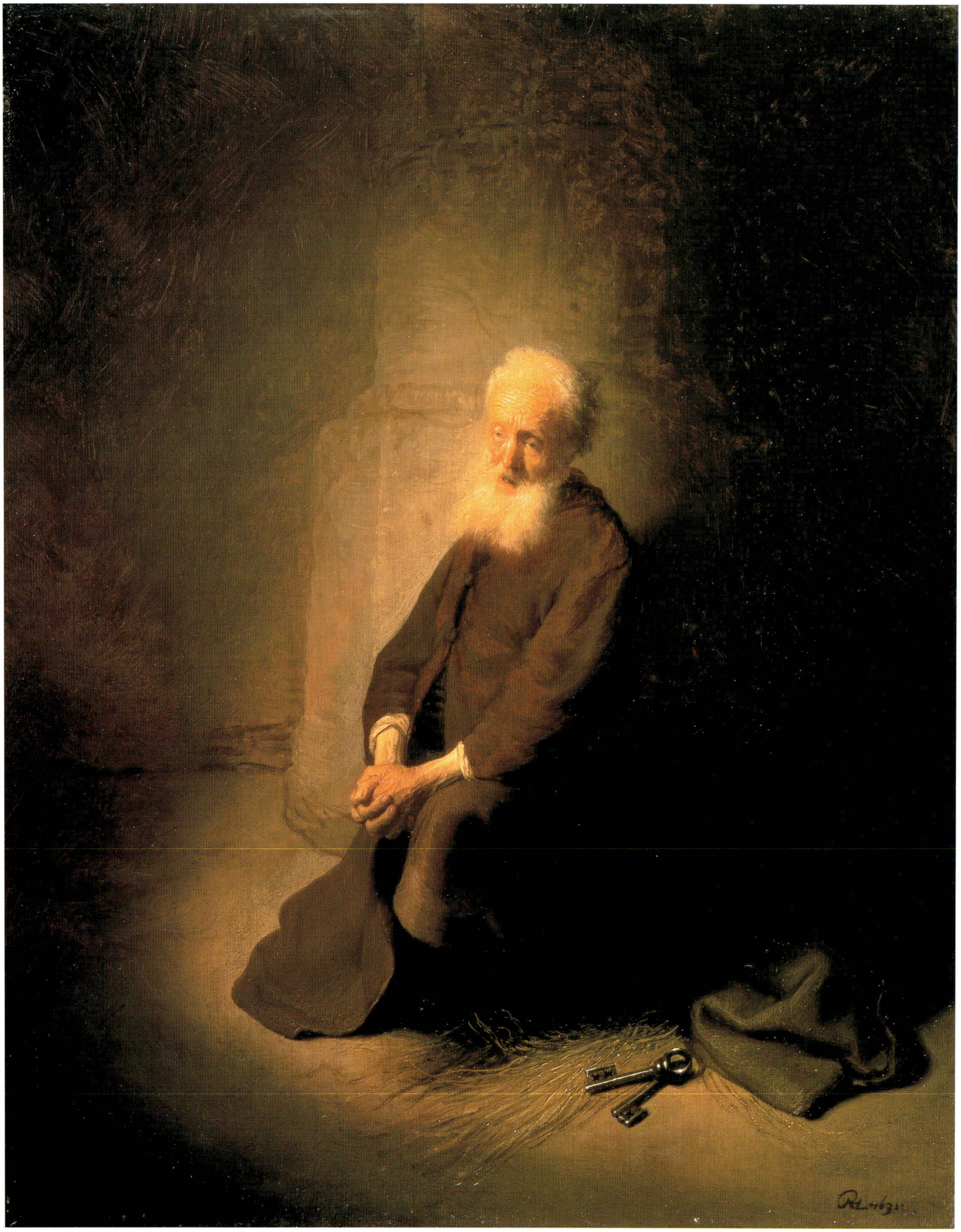

18

Rembrandt

The Apostle Peter Kneeling 1631

oil on wood, 59 × 47.8 cm
signed lower right: RHL. [monogram] / 1631.
private collection

This extraordinarily well-preserved picture is closely related to *Jeremiah Lamenting the Destruction of Jerusalem* (cat. 14) in temperament, composition, and scale. It also relies on the same model. There has been some confusion over the precise subject. Earlier scholars were troubled by the apparently unprecedented iconographic synthesis of Peter in Prison with the Repentant Saint Peter, two events that are separated significantly by time and that employ divergent imagery. In the 1793 Paris sale of the painting it was described as "Saint Pierre représenté à genoux & les mains jointes dans un intérieur de prison..." (Saint Peter kneeling, his hands clasped, in a prison interior). In 1883, Wilhelm Bode identified the subject as Saint Peter in Prison, an appellation that has been adopted by most modern scholars.[1] Recently, however, Egbert Haverkamp Begemann and Albert Blankert have demonstrated that the picture is actually a straightforward depiction of Peter's repentance after his denial of Christ, which was recorded in Matthew 26.69–75, Mark 14.66–72, and Luke 22.54–62.[2]

These narratives place Peter in the courtyard of the house of the High Priest, Caiaphas. Having denied Jesus three times during the night, as Christ had predicted, Peter recalled Christ's words, "Before the rooster crows, you will disown me three times." According to Matthew and Luke, Peter went outside and wept bitterly, while Mark simply says, "And he broke down and wept."

Rembrandt omits details normally associated with the prison episode (Acts 12.3–10), such as jailers, chains, and a liberating angel. In an earlier painting, *Saint Paul in Prison* of 1627 (fig. 18a), the artist did not hesitate to include details of the cell. A 1770 etching by G. F. Schmidt, evidently based on an eighteenth-century copy of the exhibited painting, contains additions of a cock, a serving maid, and soldiers, clearly making the subject Saint Peter Repentant.[3] More recently, it has been pointed out that the authorized Dutch translation of the Bible, the *Statenbijbel* published in 1637, set the scene of repentance "outside in the hall" (Matthew) or "beneath in the hall" (Mark), or "out of the hall" (Luke).[4] Thus, these Dutch texts correspond to Rembrandt's depiction of the scene. Apparently Rembrandt shows the apostle at the portal to the hall, having withdrawn in his grief.

Rembrandt employs powerful chiaroscuro to focus on Peter's poignant expression of repentance and his powerful, workingman's hands. The clasped hands are not without precedent in depictions of the repentant saint. Images readily accessible to Rembrandt include Jusepe de Ribera's 1621 etching (Bartsch 7) as well as a nocturnal, outdoor setting of the composition by Abraham Bloemaert, recorded in an engraving by Willem Swanenburgh.[5] The latter work shows the apostle isolated and in despair, his hands clasped and his keys at his side. X-rays indicate that Rembrandt altered the original contour of the figure's right shoulder and arm, drawing it further in, and extended the lower edge of the drapery to form the fanning of the robe below. He also added the straw and removed the figure's left foot, which originally extended beneath the robe. An early anonymous copy of the painting,[6] evidently executed by an artist with access to the Leiden studio, reflects an intermediate stage, with the left contour as it ultimately appeared, but including the foot and leaving out the straw. All of these changes work together to focus the viewer on the narrative's salient details: the isolation and repentance of the apostle, his identifying keys, and the shimmering stalks of straw. The pose and facial type, the effective use of dramatic, isolating lighting, the apostle's central placement in the composition, and the meditative nature of the subject all recall the Jeremiah of the preceding year (cat. 14).

The remarkable condition of the painting permits a full appreciation of the range of brushstrokes. Rembrandt articulated the folds and wrinkles of the skin with short, thick touches of opaque painting and delicate highlights of red, pink, grey, and white. The hair, keys, and straw are delineated with thin, fine strokes. The artist executed the background with loose, thinly applied, and virtually transparent grey-brown strokes. He apparently even used the butt of the brush to remove the saint's foot.

Rembrandt would return to the subject of Peter's denial and repentance on two other occasions, a print of 1645 (Bartsch 96) and the celebrated 1660 painting, *The Apostle Peter Denying Christ* (Rijksmuseum, Amsterdam), each of which explore a distinct psychological moment of the drama.

HG

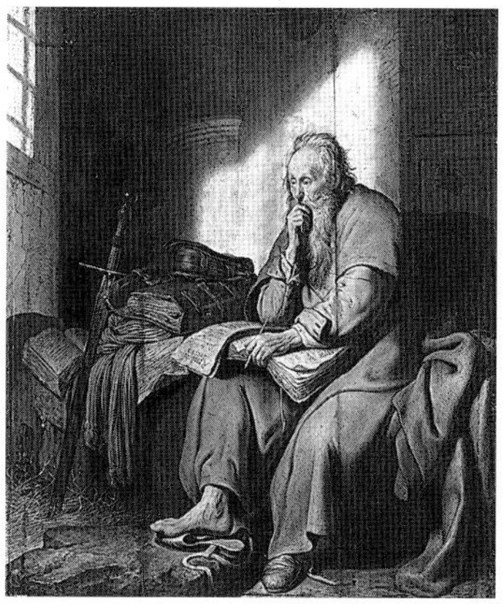

fig. 18a Rembrandt, *Saint Paul in Prison*, 1627. Oil on wood, 72.8 × 60.2 cm. Staatsgalerie, Stuttgart.

1 Bode 1883, p. 385.
2 Haverkamp Begemann 1990; Melbourne 1997, no. 6.
3 See Corpus 1982, p. 349, fig. 4.
4 Albert Blankert, Marleen Blokhuis, in Melbourne 1997, p. 102 and note 8.
5 Corpus 1982, p. 348, fig. 3; Hollstein 549.
6 Corpus 1982, p. 349 (copy 1); Haverkamp Begemann 1990.

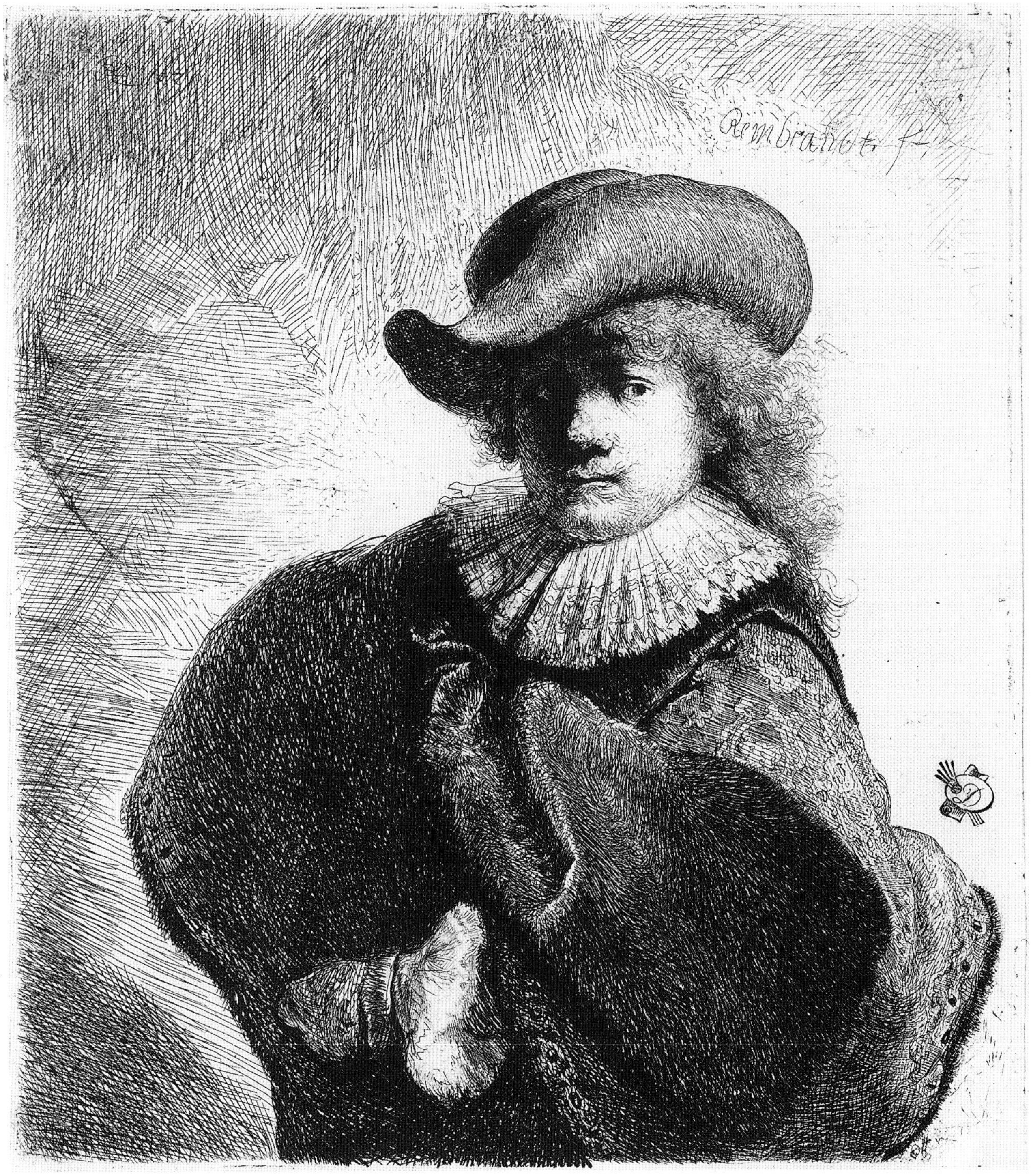
Rembrandt f.

19

Rembrandt

Self-Portrait in a Soft Hat and Cloak 1631–33

Bartsch 7 (10th state of 11)
etching, 14.8 × 13 cm
signed upper left: RHL [monogram] 1631; upper right: Rembrandt f
The Pierpont Morgan Library, New York

This very fine, richly inked impression of a self-portrait was of considerable importance to Rembrandt. Undoubtedly executed with a view to his new, more cosmopolitan clientele in Amsterdam, it differs from earlier etched self-portraits in that Rembrandt has presented himself as an elegant man of fashion. In June of 1631, Rembrandt entered into an agreement with the Amsterdam art dealer Hendrick van Uylenburch, presaging his move to the city later in the year.

The portrait only gradually emerged in its final form seen here. In the first four states Rembrandt worked solely on the head, the hat, and a suggestion of his right shoulder; he also carefully worked out the highlights while subtly adjusting his features (fig. 19a). In the fifth state he added the torso, which is wrapped in a rich mantle; his covered right hand rests on his hip and the left hand on the back of a chair. The image now clearly emulates Rubens' self-portrait of 1630 (Windsor Castle), which Rembrandt would have known through an engraving by Paulus Pontius.[1] Rembrandt also added his monogram and the date 1631 to the fifth state. In subsequent changes he developed the complex shadows, the emergence and shading of a wall, the enrichment of the cloak, and the detailing of the hat, chair, and ruff.

In the tenth state, an impression of which is exhibited here, Rembrandt documents the print's complicated chronology with the addition of a new signature, having already obscured the earlier monogram and date with cross-hatching. Rembrandt began signing his first name in full only in 1633. Previously, he had used his monogram, which suggests that later states of the print date from after 1631, despite the date that actually appears. This is confirmed by an impression of the second state (fig. 19a). Using black chalk, he drew in the torso, lace collar, and rich jacket (simpler than the cloak that appears in later states). Furthermore, he set the figure within an arched frame and signed the sheet, "Rembrandt / AET 27"—the age he was in 1633 or 1634. Rembrandt similarly drew upon an impression of the fourth state (Bibliothèque Nationale, Paris), where he turned the figure to a more frontal stance, but he had still not adopted the mantle found in Rubens' self-portrait. This sheet is also signed "Rembrandt / AET 27." In both sheets, Rembrandt altered the "27" to "24," his age in 1631.

From the fifth state on, the print closely resembles Rembrandt's *Self-Portrait with Wide-Brimmed Hat*, dated 1632 (fig. 19b).[2] That painting seems to have influenced the composition of the print, rather than deriving from it. Therefore, over an extended period, Rembrandt developed his etching in a complex process. At first inspired by Rubens' self-portrait, he then experimented with various poses by drawing over the print, and later echoed his own painted self-portrait. All of this suggests that Rembrandt retained the date of 1631 on the print because that was when, at the age of twenty-four, he produced the original image of himself wearing a floppy, round hat. His borrowing from Rubens seems to indicate his desire to compete with the renowned Flemish master. After he moved to Amsterdam, Rembrandt further elaborated the print in order to present himself in the elegant contemporary fashions of his adopted city.

HG

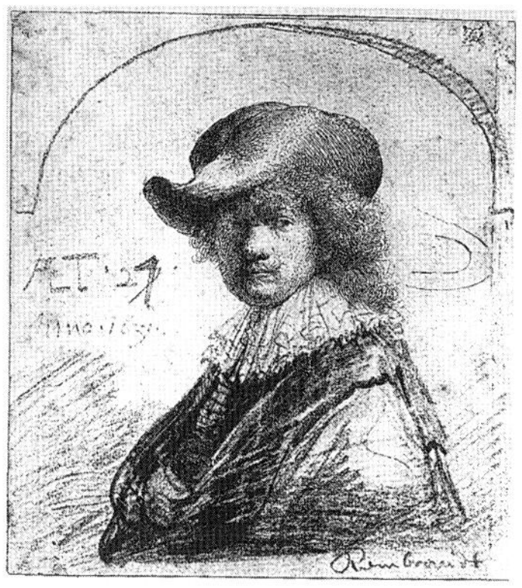

fig. 19a Rembrandt, *Self-Portrait in a Soft Hat and Cloak*, 1631. British Museum, London. Bartsch 7 (2nd state), Benesch 57.

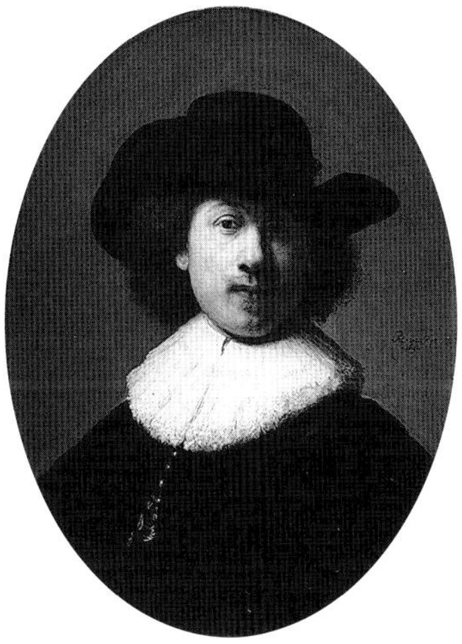

fig. 19b Rembrandt, *Self-Portrait with Wide-Brimmed Hat*, 1632. Oil on wood, 64.4 × 47.6 cm. The Burrell Collection, Glasgow.

1 See Peter Schatborn, in London 1999, no. 32.
2 See Corpus A 58 and Peter Schatborn, in London 1999, no. 32.

Catalogue Documentation

In the references and exhibitions cited, attributions are to Rembrandt unless otherwise noted.

1

Rembrandt

Self-Portrait, Bareheaded 1629

Bartsch 338 (only state)

etching, 17.4 × 15.5 cm

signed upper left in reverse: RHL [monogram] 1629

British Museum, London [1848-9-11-19]

PROVENANCE

Purchased by the museum in 1848 from the dealer John Smith, London.

REFERENCES

Yver 1756, no. 133. Bartsch 1797, no. 338 ["Jeune homme en buste"]. Hind 1923, no. 4. Münz 1952, no. 3. Slive 1963, p. 148 [made with a broken etching needle]. White 1964, p. 17. White, Boon 1969, no. 338. Chapman 1990, pp. 11, 22. White 1999, pp. 115–17.

EXHIBITION

London 1999, no. 11.

2

Rembrandt

Peter and John at the Gate of the Temple ca. 1629

Bartsch 95 (only state)

etching, 22.1 × 16.9 cm

Bibliothèque nationale de France, Paris [Cb 13a réserve, boîte 8]

PROVENANCE

This print was part of a large collection of prints by Rembrandt belonging to Jacques-Louis, marquis de Beringhen (1651–1723), premier écuyer to Louis XIV. The collection was inherited by his son, the bishop of Le Puy, who sold it in 1731 to the Bibliothèque du Roi, later the Bibliothèque Nationale, Paris [See Joseph Guibert, *Le cabinet des estampes de la Bibliothèque Nationale: Histoire des collections* (Paris, 1926), pp. 61–65.]

REFERENCES

Gersaint 1751, p. 84 [under no. 94, describing the Beringhen example]. Bartsch 1797, no. 95. Blanc 1859, no. 65 [perhaps by Lievens]. Vosmaer 1868, p. 481 [as 1640–50]. Middleton 1878, no. 249 [as 1655]. Hind 1923, no. 5. Münz 1952, no. 188 [perhaps influenced by Merian's biblical illustrations]. Gerson 1968, p. 178. White, Boon 1969, no. 95. White 1999, pp. 23–25.

EXHIBITION

Paris 1908, no. 95.

3

Rembrandt

Lion Hunt 1629

Bartsch 116 (only state)

etching, 15.7 × 11.8 cm

Museum of Fine Arts, Boston. Helen and Alice Colburn Fund, 1954 [54.571]

PROVENANCE

An inscription on the back reports that the print was in the Baring collection, and sold in 1847. [The 1954 auction catalogue states that J. H. Hawkins sold this work at Sotheby's, 29 April 1850, but this print was not in that sale.] The print dealer W.B. Tiffin, London, reportedly sold the print for 5 guineas to August Straeter (1810–1897), Aachen [marked with Lugt 787]; it was auctioned by his estate at Gutekunst, Stuttgart, 10 May 1898 (lot 748) 35 marks to Meder. Werner Weisbach, Berlin [marked with Lugt 2659a; acquired soon after the Straeter sale]; auctioned by his estate at Gutekunst, Bern, 11 March 1954 (lot 226), sold for 450 marks to P. & D. Colnaghi, London, who sold the print to the museum in May 1954.

REFERENCES

Gersaint 1751, no. 113 (no. 3). Bartsch 1797, no. 116. Blanc 1859, no. 88 ["dans le goût de Rubens"]. Middleton 1878, no. 275 [as 1641]. C. Hofstede de Groot, "Entlehnungen Rembrandts," *Jahrbuch der königlich preussischen Kunstsammlungen* 15 (1894), p. 175 note 2 [as 1629–30]. N. Beets, "Herscheppingen" in *Feest-Bundel Dr. Abraham Bredius* (Amsterdam, 1915), pp. 1–3 [Tempesta as a source]. Hind 1923, no. 6. Münz 1952, no. 251 [related to Tempesta's print, Bartsch 1123]. White, Boon 1969, no. 116. Ash, Fletcher 1998, p. 234 [foolscap watermark]. White 1999, p. 171.

4

Rembrandt

The Artist in His Studio 1629

oil on wood, 25.1 × 31.9 cm

Museum of Fine Arts, Boston. Zoë Oliver Sherman Collection, Given in Memory of Lillie Oliver Poor [38.1838]

PROVENANCE

The painting is first recorded at the La Roque auction, Paris (Gersaint), April 1745 (lot 65, together with another painting attributed to Rembrandt). It was auctioned again with paintings owned by the dealers Favre and J.B.P. Lebrun, Paris (Basan), 11 January 1773 (lot 25). It was auctioned by the estate of the Countess of Morton (wife of the 18th earl) at Christie's, London, 27 April 1850 (lot 70), sold for £6.6s. to Sir John Buller, created Baron Churston, Lupton, Devon; by descent to his grandson 3rd Baron Churston, who auctioned the work at Christie's, London, 26 June 1925 (lot 14), sold for £1417.10s. to F. Zink for the dealer R. Langton Douglas, London; sold to Mrs. Zoë Oliver Sherman, Boston (by 1935), who presented it to the museum in 1938.

REMBRANDT CATALOGUES

Bredius 1935, no. 419. Gerson 1968, no. 20 [perhaps not a self-portrait]. Bredius, Gerson 1969, no. 419. Corpus 1982, no. A 18. Tümpel 1986, pp. 66/69, no. 157 ["not entirely confident" in the attribution; 1993 edition: "authentic"]. Slatkes 1992, no. 104.

OTHER REFERENCES

C. Hofstede de Groot, in *Burlington Magazine* 47 (1925), p. 265. C.H. Collins Baker, in *Burlington Magazine* 48 (1926), p. 42 [possibly by Dou]. Valentiner 1926, p. 118. Bauch 1933, p. 63. Van Gelder 1953a, p. 37 note 9 [depicting Dou]. Bauch 1960, p. 140. Slive 1964. Van de Wetering 1976, pp. 26–28. Schwartz 1985, p. 55. E. van de Wetering, in Leiden 1991, pp. 43–44. Chapman 1990, pp. 84–85, 97–99. Bal 1991, pp. 247–85. Couprie 1994. Schama 1999, pp. 12–23. De Winkel 1999, p. 66.

EXHIBITIONS

Delft 1964, no. 94. Tokyo 1968, no. 43. Chicago 1969, no. 2. Berlin 1991, no. 3. London 1999, no. 17 [by E. Buijsen].

5

Rembrandt

Self-Portrait 1629

oil on wood, 89.7 × 73.9 cm

signed lower right: RHL [monogram] ...9

Isabella Stewart Gardner Museum, Boston [P21n6]

PROVENANCE

The painting is first recorded in 1788 in the collection of the Marquess of Buckingham at Stowe; it was inherited by the 2nd Duke of Buckingham, who auctioned the entire collection; Christie's at Stowe, 15 September 1848 (lot 421), sold for £54.12s. to Wyatt; sold to 11th Baron Ward, London (by 1854; created Earl of Dudley in 1860; also at Dudley Castle). Lt. Col. Edward Sawyer (Crewherne, Somerset, and London, by 1890) auctioned the painting at Christie's, London, 13 July 1895 (lot 81), sold for £1155 to the dealer Tooth, London; with the dealer P. & D. Colnaghi, London, who sold the painting via Bernard Berenson for £3000 (plus £150 commission; equivalent to $15,379) to Isabella Stewart Gardner, Boston, in February 1896.

REMBRANDT CATALOGUES

Smith 1836, nos. 422, 445 [describing a mezzotint by Richard Cooper]. Bode 1897, pp. 10–11, no. 18 [monogrammed and dated 1629]. Hofstede de Groot 1915, no. 529. Bredius 1935, no. 8. Gerson 1968, no. 38. Bredius, Gerson 1969, no. 8. Corpus 1982, no. A 20. Tümpel 1986, no. 156. Slatkes 1992, no. 238.

OTHER REFERENCES

Stowe: A Description of the House and Gardens of the Most Noble and Puissant Prince, George Grenville Nugent Temple, Marquis of Buckingham (Buckingham, 1788), p. 49 [in the State Drawing Room: "*Rembrandt's* Head, when young"]. Waagen 1854, vol. 2, p. 237 ["clear in colouring and very carefully carried out"]. Thoré 1857, p. 247. Bauch 1933, p. 159, fig. 173. Slive 1963, p. 148. Philip Hendy, *European and American Paintings in the Isabella Stewart Gardner Museum* (Boston, 1974), p. 199. Hadley 1987, pp. 47–49. Corpus 1982, vol. 2, p. 838. Chapman 1990, pp. 46–48. Bal 1991, p. 309. Grimm 1991, p. 28, fig. 43 [as circle of Rembrandt]. Liedtke 1995. Claus Grimm, in *Weltkunst* (October 1, 1999), p. 1884 [as workshop of Rembrandt].

EXHIBITIONS

Manchester 1857, no. 677 ["A Male Portrait. From the Stowe Collection." Lent by Lord Ward]. London 1999, p. 61, no. 10.

6

Circle of Rembrandt

Portrait of Rembrandt with a Gorget ca. 1630

oil on wood, 37.9 × 28.9 cm

Mauritshuis, The Hague [148]

PROVENANCE

The painting was in the collection of Govert van Slingelandt, the receiver-general of taxes for Holland, The Hague, by 1752 when Hoet catalogued it; van Slingelandt died in 1767 and the work was placed at auction in The Hague, 18 May 1768 (lot 11), but the stadhouder Willem V bought the entire collection of 41 paintings for 50,000 guilders. Willem V's collection was removed to Paris in 1795; it was returned to Willem I in Holland and in 1822 incorporated into the Mauritshuis, The Hague.

REMBRANDT CATALOGUES

Smith 1836, no. 243. Blanc 1859, p. 381 [perhaps ca. 1648–49]. Vosmaer 1868, p. 419 [as 1630]. Bode 1897, p. 10, no. 16 [the Nuremberg painting perhaps also genuine]. Hofstede de Groot 1915, no. 544. Bredius 1935, no. 6. Gerson 1968, no. 39. Bredius, Gerson 1969, no. 6. Corpus 1982, p. 838, no. A 21. Tümpel 1986, pp. 65–66, no. 155. Slatkes 1992, no. 239.

OTHER REFERENCES

Hoet 1752, vol. 2, p. 404 [Govert van Slingelandt collection]; vol. 3, p. 709. Filhol, Lavallée 1804, vol. 1, pl. 29 [engraving by Alexis Chataigner, as H. van Vliet]. *Notitie der schilderijen van het Koninklijk Kabinet te 'sGravenhage* (The Hague, 1822), no. 113 ["Portrait van een Jongeling"]. Thoré 1858, vol. 1, p. 210 [as early and perhaps a self-portrait]. Alfred von Wurzbach, in *Zeitschrift für bildenden Künste* 10 (1875), pp. 381–83 [as not by Rembrandt]. Wilhelm Bode, in *Zeitschrift für bildenden Künste* 11 (1876), pp. 125–26 [as Rembrandt]. Bauch 1933, p. 152, fig. 167. Boyer 1970, p. 156 [1796 inventory, no. 149: "Tête, dite Rembrandt" by Van Vliet]. Drossaers, Lunsingh Scheurleer 1974, vol. 3, p. 228 [an inventory up to 1793, no. 132]. De Vries et al. 1978, no. 1. Chapman 1990, pp. 36–40. Grimm 1991, pp. 21–26, fig. 33 [as "Isaac de Jouderville (?), copy after Rembrandt's self-portrait in Nuremberg"]. *Mauritshuis: Illustrated General Catalogue* (Amsterdam, 1993), p. 124. Gutbrod 1996, pp. 198–201, fig. 31. Buvelot, Wadum 1999 [as possibly by Dou].

EXHIBITIONS

Rembrandt (National Museum, Stockholm, 1956), no. 4. Amsterdam 1956, no. 6. Berlin 1991, no. 4. London 1999, no. 14b [anonymous artist after Rembrandt].

The same image appears in a mezzotint by Valentine Green dated 1775, published in London, and is stated to be a portrait of Prince Rupert belonging to Edward Orme (perhaps a reproduction of a copy).

7

Jan Lievens

Portrait of Rembrandt ca. 1629

oil on wood, 57 × 44.7 cm

signed lower left: IL [monogram]

Cevat Collection, on loan to the Rijksmuseum, Amsterdam [SK-C-1598] adolescens, Batavus, molitor, imberbis uno in homine collegit singula et universa expressit. Macte vero, mi Rembranti, non Ilium in Italiam tanti, non omnem Asiam portasse fuit, quanti Graeciae et Italiae summam laudem in Batavos pertractam ab homine Batavo, urbis patriae vix adhuc pomoeria egresso.

that these things did not occur to Protogenes, or to Apelles, or to Parrhasios, and if even these men were to return today, they would not be able to conceive these same things—I am astounded again—which a young man, a Dutchman, a miller, a beardless boy, has brought together in a single figure and depicted completely. Glory to you my Rembrandt. Carrying all those people of Troy and all of Asia to Italy was not so great as carrying the highest praises of Greece and Italy to the Dutch, praises for a Dutchman, one who has hardly journeyed beyond the borders of his town.

◆◆◆

Tam praeclaris adolescentibus, quorum a mentione vix me avello, unum illud vitio rursum nequeo non vertere, quod, ut Livio iam exprobrabam, se secure contenti hactenus Italiam tanti non putant, cui lustrandae paucos menses opus habeant impendere. Est haec scilicet quaedam in tam magnis ingeniis mixtura dementiae, quam qui animis iuvenibus eruat, nae, quod ad artis perfectionem his unice deest, abunde contulerit. O si cum Urbinatibus ac Bonarocciis initâ, quam velim, familiaritate devorare tot oculis ingentium animarum monumenta satagant, quam brevi et exsuperare istaec omnia et arcessere in Hollandiam suam Italos valeant, homines ad consummationem artis, si se norint, nati! Sed ne praetextum quoque sileam, quo se velare solent, et, quantum hoc est desidiae, excusare, aiunt florentibus annis, quorum inprimis ratio habenda sit, non satis otii esse, quod peregrinatione perdant; tum, quae regum hodie ac principum Cisalpinorum picturae avida dilectio est ac delectus, potissimas Italiae tabulas extra Italiam visi, quaeque sparsim ibi magnâ cum molestiâ indages, cumulatim hic ad satietatem offerri. Quam sese sic opportune purgent, non libet expendere. Testari cogor non vidisse me parem diligentiam aut assiduitatem ullo in hominum genere, studio vel aetate. Revera enim ἐξαγοραζόμευοι τὸυ [margin: Ad Ephes.], hoc agunt unice nec, quo ad miraculum nihil desit, adolescentiae vel innoxiis oblectamentis, quia temporis dispendiis, afficiuntur magis, quam si annorum saturos senes videas et haec futilia quaeque praeexpertos. Quam improbi laboris indefessam pertinaciam utcumque magnos subito profectus spondeat, moderari egregios adolescentes saepenenumero optavi et corpusculorum, quibus a sedentaria vitâ iam nunc parum firmis aut robustis utuntur, suam quoque rationem habere.

◆◆◆

I can hardly tear myself away from these remarkable youths, but I do censure one fault for which I have already reproached Lievens: they are self-satisfied, and up to now have not thought it important to spend a few months traveling in Italy. In such talented natures, there is a certain mixture of madness which will destroy young spirits; this alone is lacking in the perfection of their art. Oh, if they were only acquainted with Raphael and Michelangelo, they would visually devour the creations of these magnificent spirits. They would quickly surpass them all, as men born to perfect art (if they only knew it), and would cause Italians to come to Holland. I cannot be silent about the pretext which they give to hide their apathy and make excuses. They say that in the bloom of youth, they must prove themselves, and there is no time to waste on distant travel. In addition, since today there is a great demand for paintings from kings and princes north of the Alps, they can see the best Italian paintings outside of Italy where paintings are inconveniently scattered about, while here they are displayed all together and one can be sated. I do not want to judge the validity of their excuses. I must confess that I have not seen equal diligence and industry in any kind of person, whatever the occupation or age. They are truly "redeeming the time" [margin note: from Ephesians]; this is the only thing that counts for them. And lest something be omitted from this miraculous tale, they are not even affected by the innocent delights of youth, to avoid wasting time. It is as if you were looking at old men of many years, who were already tired of frivolous diversions. This tireless diligence in hard labor may guarantee rapid progress, but I have often hoped that these outstanding youths would moderate and take into account their bodies, which because of their sedentary life, are already less robust and strong.

Bibliography

Alpers 1988
Svetlana Alpers. *Rembrandt's Enterprise: The Studio and the Market.* Chicago, 1988.

Amsterdam 1898
Rembrandt: Schilderijen bijeengebracht ter gelegenheid van de inhuldiging van Hare Majesteit Koningin Wilhelmina. Exh. cat. Stedelijk Museum, Amsterdam. 1898.

Amsterdam 1932
Rembrandt tentoonstelling. Exh. cat. Rijksmuseum, Amsterdam. 1932.

Amsterdam 1956
Rembrandt tentoonstelling. Exh. cat. Rijksmuseum, Amsterdam; Museum Boymans, Rotterdam. 1956.

Amsterdam 1991
Pieter Lastman, leermeester van Rembrandt / the man who taught Rembrandt. Exh. cat. Rembrandthuis, Amsterdam. 1991. By Astrid Tümpel, Peter Schatborn, et al.

Amsterdam 1996
A Collaboration on Copper: Rembrandt and Van Vliet. Exh. cat. Museum het Rembrandthuis, Amsterdam. 1996. By Christiaan Schuckman, Martin Royalton-Kisch, Erik Hinterding.

Amsterdam cat. 1976
All the Paintings of the Rijksmuseum in Amsterdam: A Completely Illustrated Catalogue. Amsterdam, 1976.

Amsterdam cat. 1992
All the Paintings of the Rijksmuseum in Amsterdam: A Completely Illustrated Catalogue. First Supplement: 1976–91. Amsterdam, 1992.

Ash, Fletcher 1998
Nancy Ash, Shelley Fletcher. *Watermarks in Rembrandt's Prints.* Washington, 1998.

Bal 1991
Mieke Bal. *Reading "Rembrandt": Beyond the Word-Image Opposition.* Cambridge, 1991.

Baldinucci 1686
Filippo Baldinucci. *Cominciamento, e progresso dell'arte dell'intagliare in rame, colle vite di molto de' più eccelenti maestri della stessa professione.* Firenze, 1686.

Bartsch *or* Bartsch 1797
Adam Bartsch. *Catalogue raisonné de toutes les estampes qui forment l'oeuvre de Rembrandt, et ceux de ses principaux imitateurs.* 2 vols. Vienna, 1797.

Bartsch 1803
— *Le peintre graveur.* 21 vols. Vienna, 1803–21. [also see: *The Illustrated Bartsch,* vols. 1– (New York, 1978–).]

Bauch 1933
Kurt Bauch. *Die Kunst des jungen Rembrandt.* Heidelberg, 1933.

Bauch 1960
— *Der frühe Rembrandt und seine Zeit: Studien zur geschichtlichen Bedeutung seines Frühstils.* Berlin, 1960.

Bauch 1966
— *Rembrandt Gemälde.* Berlin, 1966.

Benesch *or* Benesch 1973
Otto Benesch. *The Drawings of Rembrandt.* 6 vols. 2nd edition. London, 1973. Revised by E. Benesch. [1st edition: London, 1954–57.]

Berlin 1991
Rembrandt: The Master and His Workshop: Paintings. Exh. cat. Altes Museum, Berlin; Rijksmuseum, Amsterdam; National Gallery, London. 1991–92. By Christopher Brown, Jan Kelch, Pieter van Thiel, et al.

Berlin 1991a
Rembrandt: The Master & His Workshop: Drawings & Etchings. Exh. cat. Altes Museum, Berlin; Rijksmuseum, Amsterdam; National Gallery, London. 1991–92. By Holm Bevers, Peter Schatborn, Barbara Welzel.

Blanc 1859
Charles Blanc. *L'oeuvre complet de Rembrandt, décrit et commenté.* 2 vols. Paris, 1859–61.

Bode 1881
Wilhelm Bode. "Rembrandt's früheste Thätigkeit: Der Künstler in seiner Vaterstadt Leiden." *Die graphischen Künste* 3 (1881), pp. 49–72.

Bode 1883
— *Studien zur Geschichte der holländischen Malerei.* Braunschweig, 1883.

Bode 1897
Wilhelm Bode, assisted by Cornelis Hofstede de Groot. *The Complete Work of Rembrandt.* 8 vols. Paris, 1897–1906. [Also a German edition.]

Boomgaard 1995
Jeroen Boomgaard. *De verloren zoon: Rembrandt en de Nederlandse kunstgeschiedschrijving.* Amsterdam, 1995.

Boston 1980
Printmaking in the Age of Rembrandt. Exh. cat. Museum of Fine Arts, Boston; Saint Louis Museum of Art. 1980–81. By Clifford S. Ackley.

Boyer 1970
Ferdinand Boyer. "Une conquête artistique de a convention: les tableaux du stathouder (1795)." *Bulletin de la Société de l'Histoire de l'Art français* (1970), pp. 149–57.

Braunschweig 1979
Jan Lievens: Ein Maler im Schatten Rembrandts. Exh. cat. Herzog Anton Ulrich-Museum, Braunschweig. 1979.

Bredius 1935
Abraham Bredius. *Rembrandt schilderijen: 630 Afbeeldingen.* Utrecht, 1935. [Also an English edition: London, 1936.]

Bredius 1937
— *The Paintings of Rembrandt.* London, 1937.

Bredius, Gerson 1969
Abraham Bredius; revised by Horst Gerson. *Rembrandt: The Complete Edition of the Paintings.* London, 1969.

Budick 1988
Sanford Budick. "Rembrandt's Jeremiah." *Journal of the Warburg and Courtauld Institutes* 51 (1988), pp. 260–64.

Buvelot, Wadum 1999
Quentin Buvelot, Jørgen Wadum. "Rembrandt's early self portrait unmasked." *Mauritshuis in Focus* 12, no. 3 (Nov. 1999), pp. 32–42.

Chapman 1990
H. Perry Chapman. *Rembrandt's Self-Portraits: A Study in Seventeenth-Century Identity.* Princeton, 1990.

Chicago 1969
Rembrandt After Three Hundred Years: An Exhibition of Rembrandt and His Followers. Exh. cat. Art Institute of Chicago, Minneapolis Institute of Arts, Detroit Institute of Arts. 1969–70.

Chicago 1973
Art Institute of Chicago. *Rembrandt After Three Hundred Years: A Symposium — Rembrandt and His Followers, October 22–24, 1969.* Chicago, 1973.

Cornelis, Filedt Kok 1996
Bart Cornelis, Jan Piet Filedt Kok. "The taste for Lucas van Leyden prints." *Simiolus* 26 (1996), pp. 18–86.

Corpus
A Corpus of Rembrandt Paintings. 3 vols. The Hague, 1982–89. By Josua Bruyn, Bob Haak, Simon Levie, Pieter van Thiel, Ernst van de Wetering.

Corpus 1982
A Corpus of Rembrandt Paintings. Vol. 1: 1625–1631. The Hague, 1982. By Josua Bruyn, Bob Haak, Simon Levie, Pieter van Thiel, Ernst van de Wetering.

Couprie 1994
L. D. Couprie. "De jonge Rembrandt in zijn atelier." *Leids Jaarboekje* 86 (1994), pp. 69–96.

Delft 1964
De schilder in zijn wereld: Van Jan van Eyck tot Van Gogh en Ensor. Exh. cat. Stedelijk Museum Het Prinsenhof, Delft; Koninklijk Museum voor Schone Kunsten, Antwerp. 1964–65.

Drossaers, Lunsingh Scheurleer 1974
S.W.A. Drossaers, Th.H. Lunsingh Scheurleer. *Inventarissen van de inboedels in de verblijven van de Oranjes.* 3 vols. The Hague, 1974–76.

Du Camp 1857
Maxime Du Camp. "En Hollande." *Revue de Paris,* October 1, 1857, pp. 341–90.

Dutuit 1883
Eugène Dutuit. *L'oeuvre complet de Rembrandt.* Paris, 1883.

Ekkart 1991
Rudolf E.O. Ekkart. "Rembrandt, Lievens en Constantijn Huygens" in *Rembrandt en Lievens in Leiden* (Leiden 1991), pp. 48–59.

Emmens 1968
J.A. Emmens. *Rembrandt en de regels van de kunst.* Utrecht, 1968.

Filhol, Lavallée 1804
A.M. Filhol, Joseph Lavallée. *Galerie du Musée Napoléon.* 10 vols. Paris, 1804–15.

Fuseli 1831
Henry Fuseli. *The Life and Writings of Henry Fuseli.* Edited by John Knowles. 3 vols. London, 1831.

van Gelder 1953
J.G. van Gelder. "Rembrandt's vroegste ontwikkeling." *Mededelingen der Koninklijke Nederlandse Akademie van Wetenschappen, afd. Letterkunde* 16, no. 5 (1953), pp. 273–300.

van Gelder 1953a
— "Rembrandt and his circle," *Burlington Magazine* 95 (1953), pp. 34–39.

van Gelder 1963
— "Rembrandt: Jeremia, treurende over de Verwoesting van Jeruzalem." *Openbaar Kunstbezit* 7: no. 15 (1963).

van Gelder, Jost 1985
J.G. van Gelder, Ingrid Jost. *Jan de Bisschop and His Icones & Paradigmata: Classical Antiquities and Italian Drawings for Artistic Instruction in Seventeenth Century Holland.* Edited by Keith Andrews. 2 vols. Amsterdam, 1985.

Gersaint 1751
Edmé-François Gersaint. *Catalogue raisonné de toutes les pièces qui forment l'oeuvre de Rembrandt.* Paris, 1751.

Gerson 1968
Horst Gerson. *Rembrandt Paintings.* Amsterdam, 1968.

Grimm 1991
Claus Grimm. *Rembrandt selbst: Eine Neubewertung seiner Porträtkunst.* Stuttgart, 1991.

Gutbrod 1996
Helga Gutbrod. *Lievens en Rembrandt: Studien zum Verhältnis ihrer Kunst.* Frankfurt, 1996.

Haak 1968
Bob Haak. *Rembrandt, zijn leven, zijn werk, zijn tijd.* Amsterdam, 1968. [Also an English edition: 1969.]

Hadley 1987
Rollin Van N. Hadley, ed. *The Letters of Bernard Berenson and Isabella Stewart Gardner, 1887–1924, with Correspondence by Mary Berenson.* Boston, 1987.

The Hague 1990
Great Dutch Paintings from America. Exh. cat. Mauritshuis, The Hague; Fine Arts Museums of San Francisco. 1990–91. Entries by B. Broos. [Also a Dutch edition.]

The Hague 1997
Princely Patrons: The Collection of Frederick Henry of Orange and Amalia of Solms in The Hague. Exh. cat. Mauritshuis, The Hague. 1997–98. By Peter van der Ploeg, Carola Vermeeren, et al. [Also a Dutch edition.]

Haverkamp Begemann 1990
Egbert Haverkamp Begemann. *An Important Painting by Rembrandt* (sale: Christie's New York, 31 May 1990).

Hazlitt 1821
William Hazlitt. "On genius and common sense" in *Table-Talk; or, Original Essays* (London, 1821), pp. 67–111.

Heckscher 1981
William S. Heckscher. "Egogenesis: Introductory remarks" in *Ars Auro Prior: Studia Ioanni Białostocki Sexagenario Dicata* (Warsaw 1981), pp. 11–19.

Hind 1923
Arthur M. Hind. *A Catalogue of Rembrandt's Etchings.* 2 vols. 2nd edition. London, 1923. [1st edition: *Rembrandt's Etchings* (London, 1912).]

Hinterding 1993
Erik Hinterding. "The history of Rembrandt's copperplates with a catalogue of those that survive." *Simiolus* 22 (1993–94).

Hoet 1752
Gerard Hoet. *Catalogus of naamlyst van schilderyen met derzelver pryzen.* 2 vols. The Hague, 1752. Vol. 3 by Pieter Terwesten: The Hague, 1770. Reprint: The Hague, 1976.

Hofstede de Groot 1906
Cornelis Hofstede de Groot. *Die Urkunden über Rembrandt (1575–1721).* The Hague, 1906.

Hofstede de Groot 1915
— *Beschreibendes und kritisches Verzeichnis der Werke der hervorragendsten holländischen Maler des XVII. Jahrhunderts.* Vol. 6 (Rembrandt). Esslingen, 1915. [Translated as *A Catalogue Raisonné of the Works of the Most Eminent Dutch Painters of the Seventeenth Century,* vol. 6 (London, 1916; reprint: Cambridge, 1976).]

Hollstein
F.W.H. Hollstein, et al. *Dutch and Flemish Etchings, Engravings, and Woodcuts, ca. 1450–1700.* Vol. 1–. Amsterdam, 1949–.

Hoogewerff, van Regteren Altena 1928
G.J. Hoogewerff, I.Q. van Regteren Altena. *Arnold Buchelius "Res Pictoriae": Aanteekeningen over kunstenaars en kunstwerken, 1583–1639.* The Hague, 1928.

van Hoogstraten 1678
Samuel van Hoogstraten. *Inleyding tot de hooge schoole der schilderkonst: anders de zichtbaere werelt.* Rotterdam, 1678. Reprint: Soest, 1969.

de Hoop Scheffer, Boon 1971
D. de Hoop Scheffer, Karel Boon. "De inventaris-lijst van Clement de Jonghe en Rembrandts etsplaten." *Kroniek van het Rembrandthuis,* 1971, pp. 1–17.

Houbraken 1718
Arnold Houbraken. *De groote schouburgh der nederlantsche konstschilders en schilderessen.* 3 vols. The Hague, 1753. [Minor corrections of the 1st edition: The Hague, 1718–21]. Reprint: Amsterdam, 1976.

Huygens 1897
Constantijn Huygens, edited by J.A. Worp. "Fragment eener autobiographie van Constantijn Huygens." *Bijdragen en Mededeelingen van het Historisch Genootschap* 18 (1897), pp. 1–121. [Latin manuscript written ca. 1629–31.]

Huygens 1987
Constantijn Huygens, translated by C.L. Heesakkers. *Constantijn Huygens: Mijn jeugd.* Amsterdam, 1987. [Translation of Huygens 1897.]

Immerzeel 1841
Johannes Immerzeel. *Lofrede op Rembrandt.* Amsterdam, 1841. [1st published in 1840.]

Israel 1997
Jonathan Israel. "Adjusting to hard times: Dutch art during its period of crisis and restructuring (c. 1621–c. 1645)." *Art History* 20 (1997), pp. 449–76.

Kingston 1984
Pictures from the Age of Rembrandt: Selections from the Personal Collection of Dr & Mrs Alfred Bader. Exh. cat. Agnes Etherington Art Centre, Kingston. 1984. By David McTavish.

Kolloff 1854
Eduard Kolloff. *Rembrandt's Leben und Werke, nach neuen Actenstücken und Gesichtspunkten geschildert.* Leipzig, 1854. Reprint: Hamburg, 1971.

Lairesse 1740
Gerard de Lairesse. *Groot schilderboek.* 2 vols. 2nd edition. Haarlem, 1740. Reprint: Doornspijk, 1969. [Minor corrections of the 1st edition: *Het groot schilderboek,* 2 vols. (Amsterdam, 1707).]

Lampsonius 1572
Dominicus Lampsonius, engravings by Hieronymus Cock. *Pictorum aliquot celebrium Germaniae Inferioris effigies.* Antwerp, 1572.

Lebrun 1792
Jean-Baptiste Pierre Lebrun. *Galerie des peintres hollandois, flamands et allemands.* 2 vols. Paris, 1792–96.

Leiden 1976
Geschildert tot Leyden anno 1626. Exh. cat. Stedelijk Museum de Lakenhal, Leiden. 1976–77.

Leiden 1991
Rembrandt & Lievens in Leiden: "een jong en edel schildersduo" / "a pair of young and noble painters." Exh. cat. Stedelijk Museum de Lakenhal, Leiden. 1991–92.

Liedtke 1995
Walter Liedtke. "Rembrandt's 'Man in a gorget and plumed cap' in the J. Paul Getty Museum." *Burlington Magazine* 137 (1995), pp. 458–62.

London 1929
Exhibition of Dutch Art, 1450–1900. Exh. cat. Royal Academy of Arts, London. 1929.

London 1952
Dutch Pictures, 1450–1750. Exh. cat. Royal Academy of Arts, London. 1952–53.

London 1988
Art in the Making: Rembrandt. Exh. cat. National Gallery, London. 1988–89. By David Bomford, Christopher Brown, Ashok Roy.

London 1999
Rembrandt by Himself. Exh. cat. National Gallery, London; Royal Cabinet of Paintings Mauritshuis, The Hague. 1999–2000.

Los Angeles 1991
Masterpieces in Focus: The Raising of Lazarus by Rembrandt. Exh. cat. Los Angeles County Museum of Art. 1991. By Richard Rand with Joseph Fronek.

Lugt
Frits Lugt. *Les marques de collections de dessins et d'estampes.* Amsterdam, 1921. [Supplement: The Hague, 1956.]

Manchester 1857
Catalogue of the Art Treasures of the United Kingdom. Collected at Manchester in 1857. [Provisional.] Exh. cat. Manchester. 1857.

van Mander 1604
Karel van Mander. *Het Schilder-Boeck waer in voor eerst de leerlustighe Jeught den grondt der edel vry schilderconst in verscheyden deelen wort voorghedraghen.* Haarlem, 1604. Reprint: Utrecht, 1969. [For reprint and commentary of the *Grondt,* see Miedema 1973; for reprint and English translation of the *Lives,* see van Mander 1994.]

van Mander 1994
Karel van Mander: The Lives of the Illustrious Netherlandish and German Painters, from the First Edition of the Schilder-boeck *(1603–1604).* Vol. 1: *The Text.* Doornspijk, 1994. Edited by Hessel Miedema.

Melbourne 1997
Rembrandt, a Genius and His Impact. Exh. cat. National Gallery of Victoria,

Melbourne; National Gallery of Australia, Canberra. 1997–98. By Albert Blankert, et al.
Michel 1894
Emile Michel. *Rembrandt, His Life, His Work, and His Time.* 2 vols. London, 1894. [Translation of 1st edition, Paris, 1893.]
Middleton 1878
C.H. Middleton. *Descriptive Catalogue of the Etched Work of Rembrandt van Rhyn.* London, 1878.
Miedema 1973
Hessel Miedema. *Karel van Mander: Den grondt der edel vry schilderkonst.* 2 vols. Utrecht, 1973.
Miedema 1981
— *Kunst, Kunstenaar en Kunstwerk bij Karel van Mander: Een analyse van zijn levensbeschrijvingen.* Alphen aan den Rijn, 1981.
Millar 1960
Oliver Millar, ed. "Abraham van der Doort's catalogue of the collections of Charles I." *Walpole Society* 37 (1958–60).
Millar 1970
— "The inventories and valuations of the king's goods, 1649–1651." *Walpole Society* 43 (1970–72).
Münz 1952
Ludwig Münz. *Rembrandt's Etchings: Reproductions of the Whole Original Etched Work.* 2 vols. London, 1952.
Münz 1953
— "Rembrandts Bild von Mutter und Vater." *Jahrbuch der Kunsthistorischen Sammlungen in Wien* 50 (1953), pp. 163–74.
New York 1995
Rembrandt / Not Rembrandt in the Metropolitan Museum of Art: Aspects of Connoisseurship. Exh. cat. Metropolitan Museum of Art, New York. 1995. 2 vols. By Hubert von Sonnenburg, Walter Liedtke, et al.
Orlers 1641
Jan Jansz Orlers. *Beschrijvinge der stadt Leyden.* 2nd edition. Leiden, 1641.
Paris 1908
Exposition d'oeuvres de Rembrandt: Dessins et gravures. Exh. cat. Bibliothèque Nationale, Paris. 1908.
Paris 1986
De Rembrandt à Vermeer: Les peintres hollandais au Mauritshuis de La Haye. Exh. cat. Galeries nationales du Grand Palais, Paris. 1986. Entries by B. Broos.
Pels 1681
Andries Pels. *Gebruik en misbruik des tooneels.* Amsterdam, 1681.
Perlove 1995
Shelley Perlove. "*Templum Christianum*: Rembrandt's *Jeremiah Lamenting the Destruction of Jerusalem* (1630)." *Gazette des Beaux Arts* (1995), pp. 159–70.
de Piles 1699
Roger de Piles. *Abrégé de la vie des peintres, avec des reflexions sur leurs ouvrages, et un traité du peintre parfait, de la connoissance des desseins, & de l'utilité des estampes.* Paris, 1699.
Preston 1991
Frances Preston. "Rembrandt's paintings: The development of an oeuvre." Dissertation, Columbia University, 1991.
Richardson 1728
Jonathan Richardson the Elder. *Traité de la peinture, et de la sculpture.* 3 vols. Amsterdam, 1728.
Rogers 1778
Charles Rogers. *A Collection of Prints in Imitation of Drawings, to which are Annexed Lives of Their Authors with Explanatory and Critical Notes.* 2 vols. London, 1778.
Rosenberg 1948
Jacob Rosenberg. *Rembrandt.* 2 vols. Cambridge (Mass.), 1948.
San Francisco 1920
Catalogue of the Loan Exhibition of Drawings and Etchings by Rembrandt from the J. Pierpont Morgan Collection. Exh. cat. Palace of Fine Arts, San Francisco. 1920.
Sandrart 1675
Joachim von Sandrart. *L'academia todesca della architectura, scultura & pittura: Oder Teutsche Academie der edlen Bau- Bild- und Mahlerey-Künste.* 2 vols. Nuremberg, 1675–79.
Schama 1999
Simon Schama. *Rembrandt's Eyes.* New York, 1999.
Schatborn 1985
Peter Schatborn. *Catalogus van de nederlandse tekeningen in het Rijksprentenkabinet, Rijksmuseum, Amsterdam: Tekeningen van Rembrandt, zijn onbekende leerlingen en navolgers.* The Hague, 1985.
Schatborn 1986
— Review of Corpus 1982. *Oud Holland* 100 (1986), pp. 55–63.
Schatborn 1989
— "Notes on early Rembrandt drawings." *Master Drawings* 27 (1989), pp. 118–27.
Scheller 1961
R.W. Scheller. "Rembrandt's reputatie van Houbraken tot Scheltema." *Nederlands Kunsthistorisch Jaarboek* 12 (1961), pp. 81–118.
Schneider 1932
Hans Schneider. *Jan Lievens, sein Leben und seine Werke.* Haarlem, 1932.
Schneider, Ekkart 1973
Hans Schneider, revised by R.E.O. Ekkart. *Jan Lievens, sein Leben und seine Werke.* 2nd edition. Amsterdam, 1973.
Schuckman 1992
Christian Schuckman. *Hollstein's Dutch and Flemish Etchings, Engravings, and Woodcuts, ca. 1450–1700.* Vol. 61. Roosendaal, 1992. [Catalogue of J.G. van Vliet.]
Schwartz 1985
Gary Schwartz. *Rembrandt, His Life, His Paintings.* Harmondsworth, 1985. [Also a Dutch edition: Maarssen, 1984.]
Seidlitz 1895
Woldemar von Seidlitz. *Kritisches Verzeichnis der Radierungen Rembrandts zugleich eine Anleitung zu deren Studium.* Leipzig, 1895. [Revised edition: Leipzig, 1922.]
Slatkes 1989
Leonard J. Slatkes. Review of Corpus 1982. *Art Bulletin* 71 (1989), pp. 141–44.
Slatkes 1992
— *Rembrandt: Catalogo completo dei dipinti.* Florence, 1992.
Slive 1953
Seymour Slive. *Rembrandt and His Critics, 1630–1730.* The Hague, 1953.
Slive 1963
— "The young Rembrandt," *Allen Memorial Art Museum Bulletin* 20 (1963), pp. 120–49.
Slive 1964
— "Rembrandt's 'Self-portrait in a studio.'" *Burlington Magazine* 106 (1964), pp. 483–86.
Sluijter 1988
E. J. Sluijter. "Schilders van 'cleyne, subtile ende curieuse dingen': Leidse 'fijnschilders' in contemporaine bronnen" in *Leidse fijnschilders: Van Gerrit Dou tot Frans van Mieris de Jonge 1630–1760* (exh. cat. Stedelijk Museum De Lakenhal, Leiden, 1988), pp. 15–55.
Smith 1836
John Smith. *A Catalogue Raisonné of the Works of the Most Eminent Dutch, Flemish, and French Painters.* Vol. 7 (Rembrandt). London, 1836.
Stockholm 1992
Rembrandt och hans tid / Rembrandt and his Age. Exh. cat. Nationalmuseum, Stockholm. 1992–93.
Strauss, van der Meulen 1979
Walter L. Strauss, Marjon van der Meulen, with the assistance of S.A.C. Dudok van Heel, P.J.M. de Baar. *The Rembrandt Documents.* New York, 1979.
Stroganoff cat. 1807
Collection des estampes d'après quelques tableaux de la galerie de Son Exc. Mr. le Comte A. Stroganoff. Saint Petersburg, 1807.
Sumowski 1983
Werner Sumowski. *Gemälde der Rembrandt-Schüler.* 6 vols. Landau, 1983–94.
Thoré 1857
Théophile Thoré [pseudonym W. Bürger]. *Trésors d'art exposés à Manchester en 1857.* Paris, 1857.
Thoré 1858
— *Musées de la Hollande.* 2 vols. Paris, 1858–60.
Tokyo 1968
Masterpieces of Rembrandt. Exh. cat. Tokyo National Museum; Kyoto National Museum. 1968.
Tokyo 1992
Rembrandt, His Teachers and His Pupils. Exh. cat. Bunkamura Museum of Art, Tokyo; Kawamura Memorial Museum of Art, Chiba; Yamaguchi Prefectural Museum of Art. 1992.
Tümpel 1984
Christian Tümpel. "Die Rezeption der jüdischen Altertümer des Flavius Josephus in den holländischen Historiendarstellungen des 16. und 17. Jahrhunderts" in *Wort und Bild in der niederländischen Kunst und Literatur des 16. und 17. Jahrhunderts*, edited by H. Vekeman and J. Müller Hofstede (Erftstadt, 1984), pp. 173–204.
Tümpel 1986
— *Rembrandt: All Paintings in Colour.* Antwerp, 1986.
Valentiner 1909
W.R. Valentiner, ed. *Rembrandt, des Meisters Gemälde in 643 Abbildungen.* Stuttgart, 1909. [*Klassiker der Kunst.*]
Valentiner 1926
— "Two early self-portraits by Rembrandt." *Art in America* 14 (1926), pp. 118–19.
Van Dyke 1923
John C. Van Dyke. *Rembrandt and His School: A Critical Study of the Master and His Pupils with a New Assignment of their Pictures.* New York, 1923.
Vosmaer 1868
Carel Vosmaer. *Rembrandt Harmens van Rijn, sa vie et ses oeuvres.* The Hague, 1868. [Revised edition: The Hague, 1877.]
de Vries et al. 1978
A.B. de Vries, M. Tóth-Ubbens, W. Froentjes. *Rembrandt in the Mauritshuis.* The Hague, 1978.

Waagen 1854
Gustav Waagen. *Treasures of Art in Great Britain.* 3 vols. London, 1854. [Supplement, London, 1857. Reprint: London, 1970.]

Waagen 1860
— *Handbook of Painting: The German, Flemish, and Dutch Schools.* 2 vols. London, 1860.

Waagen 1864
— *Die Gemäldesammlung in der Kaiserlichen Ermitage zu St. Petersburg.* Munich, 1864.

Westermann 1999
Mariët Westermann. "*Fray en leelijck:* Adriaen van de Venne's invention of the ironic grisaille." *Nederlands Kunsthistorisch Jaarboek* 50 (1999), pp. 215–51.

van de Wetering 1976
Ernst van de Wetering. "Leidse schilders achter de ezels" in *Geschildert tot Leyden anno 1626* (exh. cat. Stedelijk Museum de Lakenhal, Leiden, 1976–77), pp. 21–31.

van de Wetering 1986
— "Problems of apprenticeship and studio collaboration" in A Corpus of Rembrandt Paintings, vol. 2 (Dordrecht, 1986), pp. 45–90.

van de Wetering 1997
— *Rembrandt, The Painter at Work.* Amsterdam, 1997.

van de Wetering 1997a
— "The miracle of our age: Rembrandt through the eyes of his contemporaries" in *Rembrandt, a Genius and His Impact* (exh. cat. National Gallery of Victoria, Melbourne; National Gallery of Australia, Canberra, 1997–98), pp. 58–68.

Wheelock 1983
Arthur K. Wheelock Jr. "The influence of Lucas van Leyden on Rembrandt's narrative etchings" in *Essays in Northern European Art presented to Egbert Haverkamp-Begemann on his Sixtieth Birthday* (Doornspijk, 1983), pp. 291–96.

White 1964
Christopher White. *Rembrandt and His World.* London, 1964.

White 1983
— "Rembrandt: Reputation and Collecting" in *Rembrandt in Eighteenth Century England* (exh. cat. Yale Center for British Art, New Haven, 1983), pp. 1–16.

White 1999
— *Rembrandt as an Etcher: A Study of the Artist at Work.* 2nd edition. New Haven, 1999. [1st edition: London, 1969.]

White, Boon 1969
Christopher White, Karel G. Boon. *Hollstein's Dutch and Flemish Etchings, Engravings and Woodcuts.* Vols. 18, 19: *Rembrandt van Rijn.* Amsterdam, 1969.

de Winkel 1999
Marieke de Winkel. "Costume in Rembrandt's self-portraits" in *Rembrandt by Himself* (exh. cat. National Gallery, London; Mauritshuis, The Hague, 1999–2000), pp. 60–74.

Wright 1982
Christopher Wright. *Rembrandt: Self-Portraits.* London, 1982.

Yver 1756
Pierre Yver. *Supplément au catalogue raisonné de MM. Gersaint, Helle et Glomy.* Amsterdam, 1756.

Index of Works by Rembrandt

Index